D1458235

The Wonderful
Weekend Book

The Wonderful Weekend Book

Reclaim life's Simple Pleasures

Elspeth Thompson

JOHN MURRAY

First published in Great Britain in 2008 by John Murray (Publishers)
An Hachette Livre UK company

2

© Elspeth Thompson 2008

A CIP catalogue record for this title is available from the British Library

ISBN 978-1-84854-046-0

Book design by Janette Revill
Printed and bound by Clays Ltd, St Ives plc

John Murray policy is to use papers that are natural, renewable
and recyclable products and made from wood grown in sustainable
forests. The logging and manufacturing processes are expected to
conform to the environmental regulations of the country of origin.

John Murray (Publishers)
338 Euston Road
London NW1 3BH

www.johnmurray.co.uk

For Frank and Mary
Who make every weekend wonderful

Contents

Contents

Contents

Introduction

'Where did the weekend go?' How often have you asked yourself this question on a Sunday evening, in the realization that, rather than a relaxing contrast to the rest of the working week, the previous two days have gone by in a dizzy whirl of duties, DIY, shopping, hassle, stress and expense – not to mention the exhaustion of carting children hither and thither to their various activities.

But we might also ask ourselves what has happened to the weekend in general. Not so long ago, the British weekend was sacrosanct. Most shops were not only closed on Sundays but shut their doors from lunchtime on Saturdays, too. The majority of the population spent Sunday mornings at church, and many religions disapproved of any kind of work on the Sabbath, even if it meant leaving the laundry. The weekend (known as 'Saturday-to-Monday' in certain social circles) was a time for relaxation, sport, hobbies, family and friends. Indeed, the Great British Weekend was the envy of our European neighbours, whose adoption of the term '*le weekend*' bears testimony to the fact that we 'invented' it (or, rather, our trades unions fought for it) just over a hundred years ago. The European working week remained at six days until much more recently, and under the French Revolutionary Calendar just one in ten days was allowed for leisure. Yet, ironically, these days, you'd be far more likely to find French or Italians sitting down to a long extended family lunch after church, while more and more British are to be found wheeling trolleys soullessly up and down supermarket aisles or worshipping at the altar of the great God of Home Improvement. A survey conducted by Dulux in spring 2008 found that an average of six hours of each weekend day is taken up by food shopping, house and garden maintenance and other mundane tasks – almost as much time as is spent at work on weekdays.

How have we let this happen? How has the odd simple chore – putting up a shelf, filling the fridge, mowing the lawn, keeping our bodies in some sort of shape – mutated into a long list of duties that dominate the weekend? Since when has our favourite pastime been trailing round the shops? When did almost every weekend activity – from sports to children's birthday parties – start to entail parting with ridiculous wads of cash? Most importantly, where has all the fun gone?

Part of the blame must lie with the fact that our working week itself has become more strenuous. Office culture seems to demand longer and longer working hours, making the idea of keeping up with household chores and other duties during weekdays much more difficult. Many of us tip out of bed and into the car or train, delivering children to breakfast clubs or other forms of 'wraparound care' along the way, returning home at the end of the day with enough energy only to read a quick story, pop a ready-meal into the microwave and turn on the telly. Our homes are reduced to dormitories bristling with unused designer goods, though the pressure to keep them pristine and stylish has never been so high. Women, especially, are struggling to combine a role as breadwinner with the images of domestic goddess, earth mother or 'yummy mummy' they see on television or in magazines. We need the weekend just to catch up with ourselves, we say – until we turn into the sort of person who passes on a party, or a barbecue at the beach, because we've got to 'get the garden under control' or, sadder still, 'catch up on work'. Where's the fun and relaxation in that?

Maybe the increase in home-ownership is also to blame – a factor which is, again, less prevalent on the Continent. I remember all too well the heady days before children and mortgages, when the weekend meant lolling about in bed, often to see off a hangover, a little light shopping and the rest of the time spent sitting around eating and drinking to excess with friends. Perhaps for some twenty-somethings this enviable state of affairs does still hold true. But with social and financial pressures of the kind I never had twenty years ago, not to mention student loans to pay off and a growing trend to settle down earlier, I'd warrant that the weekend, even for this last bastion of post-studenthood, is fast becoming little more than a block of time in which to fit all the things they didn't find time to do during the week. Seventy-five per cent of people of all ages interviewed for the Dulux survey said the weekend was no longer a time for putting their feet up and letting their hair down. Even children, it seems, have weekend appointments to keep for ballet lessons, football coaching or Kumon maths. If kids are feeling the pressure, God only help the rest of us . . .

Yet another, more insidious change has crept in. Until

recently, even if Saturday sometimes seemed more duty-bound than might be deemed preferable, you were still pretty much guaranteed a restful change of pace by Sunday. A bit of a lie-in listening to the church bells, a leisurely breakfast leafing through the papers, then maybe a walk, or a drive to the sea, and back home in time for *Mastermind* on TV. Traffic on the roads was confined to what was mockingly referred to as the 'Sunday Driver' – a short and apparently neckless creature doing 20 mph behind the wheel of an ancient brown Morris Minor – making getting out into the countryside relatively easy as long as you were confident overtaking. Venture into town and the streets were surreally empty because all the shops and offices were closed. (It's increasingly hard to remember or imagine this now.) One piece of legislation was to change all that: and ironically, it was the very man who sang the praises of the old-fashioned British weekend, with warm beer and cricket on the village green and so on, who did more than anything else to destroy it. John Major's Sunday Trading Act of 1994 was what finally broke the back of the British weekend. Since then, shops see Sunday as one of their peak opportunities to sell us anything from sofas to fridges to garden furniture, and shopping has replaced church – and even gardening and sport – as the principal Sunday pastime.

'Do not let Sunday be taken from you,' said the Nobel Peace Prizewinner, Dr Albert Schweitzer. 'If your soul has no Sunday it is an orphan.' And I'm inclined to agree. This doesn't mean frogmarching people back into our churches, though setting aside some time on a Sunday for more contemplative pursuits might help restore the weekend's comforting rhythms. What it does mean is rescuing our precious free time from the stranglehold of supermarkets, fast food and flat-pack furniture and getting back to whatever it is we deem most important in our lives, be it family, friends, creativity, contact with nature or finding out more about the world in which we live.

Our jobs and the increased affluence they bring have not, on the whole, made us happy, as books such as Alain de Botton's *Status Anxiety* and Oliver James's *Affluenza* make all too clear. On the contrary, recent research on the nature of happiness suggests that what most people need in order to feel content is not big cars nor fancy clothes but the straightforward stuff: a good walk, watching the sunset, time with family and friends and some wholesome, home-made food. In an over-complicated world, where the headlines are dominated by wars, climate change and economic crises, we are looking for comfort and security – small but positive activities and gestures that both evoke the uncomplicated memories of childhood and help inspire a way of life that makes more sense, emotionally, environmentally, ethically and the rest. We need to return to the simple pleasures.

It's here that I should perhaps step in with a personal confession. My own weekend is not confined to the usual Friday night to Sunday evening routine, and hasn't been for some time. But this is only because, many years ago, when on the full-time staff of a magazine, it struck me that, much though I loved my work, I did not want to do it five whole days a week. The balance between work time and free time seemed out of kilter, and I vowed there and then that as soon as I could, I would create a work pattern that was spread over fewer days and done in my own time. Fifteen years later, happily self-employed (or, as I describe it, 'unemployable'), I would far rather spend the odd late night in front of the computer to make up for a sunny afternoon when my daughter and I took off for the sea or I spent the time sowing seeds or reading in the garden. This way of part-time working allows me to earn a decent living while still indulging the inner Doris Day who likes bustling about in a pinny, putting flowers on the table and home-baked cakes in the tin. For, in spite of a university education and a feminist mother who taught my sisters and me that 'a man is not a meal ticket', there is still a Fifties Housewife inside me struggling to get out and carve a place for herself in my busy life. The success of Nigella Lawson's *How to Be a Domestic Goddess* and Jane Brocket's *The Gentle Art of Domesticity* are proof that I'm not alone in striving for a better work/life balance. And the sense of freedom my lifestyle brings may be contagious: within a year of us getting together my husband had thrown in his full-time office job for a freelance radio career. He now does a four-day week, enabling us to enjoy a long weekend every week – and we still feel that's too short!

I often think we should all be campaigning for a four-day working week. This used to be Green Party policy, with the assertion that it would create more employment and encourage people to contribute to local life via volunteering in schools, hospitals and so on. Cutting one's working hours voluntarily is not for everyone, and usually entails a drop in income. But many people find that what they do with the freed-up time, and the increased happiness it brings, can actually lead to a corresponding drop in spending. Not only do they save money by taking time to shop more carefully, but they also need less in the way of stress-busting, compensatory 'treats'. In the meantime, however, we all need to bring back fun and relaxation to our weekends as they stand.

The premise of this book is to reclaim the weekend as time in which to recharge our batteries and enjoy our relationships. Most of us spend much of the week doing jobs that use just a fraction of our true potential. The weekend should be a time for restoring the balance in our lives, making room for what we really want to do – and be. This can be tremendously creative. In so-called primitive societies, there was no strict division between 'work', 'art' and 'pastimes'; people would sit around talking while making or decorating pots and other useful items. And we can learn from children, whose simple urge for creativity will see them spontaneously make up a song, slip into role-play or turn an empty cardboard box into a boat. We neglect our creativity at our peril, as many people stuck in routine jobs who develop depression discover to their cost.

When I began researching this book, the environmental consequences of the way in which we live our lives were uppermost in my mind as I sought out straightforward, low-impact ideas and activities to bring fun and inventiveness back into the British weekend. Now, as I finish writing, the credit crunch is biting, too. As many people are tightening their belts for the foreseeable future, there is surely even more reason to eschew the shops for simple, home-based, home-made pleasures. I passionately believe that consuming less does not have to mean a drop in our standard of living. On the contrary, a home filled with flowers from the garden, the smell of baking, and friends and family sitting around the table is surely something to which we all aspire, while home-made cards and presents are losing their *Blue Peter* stigma to become the smart alternative to over-packaged shop-bought stuff. When it comes to travelling, with cheap flights an environmental no-no (and, given oil prices, increasingly unlikely) and exchange rates plummeting, British holidays are hip again. Ostentatious spending is not only increasingly uncommon – it's fast becoming unfashionable.

There's actually great comfort and inspiration to be found in a simpler, more organic way of life. I remember reading, during the miners' strike of the 1980s, that most miners, given the choice of their jobs back or a small plot of land, would have taken the land every time. There's personal dignity, as well as a degree of profitability, in being even slightly self-sufficient – as many more of us are discovering by growing our own fruit and vegetables and keeping chickens for eggs. By loosening our reliance on the shops and our jobs for some of the most basic provisions in life, we are not only doing our bit for the planet, we are also increasing our own resourcefulness and independence. Many of the ideas for pastimes in this book are time-worn, age-old activities that – quite literally – do not cost the earth. Baking bread and cakes, making marmalade, writing proper letters, growing soft fruit or salad leaves, sharing favourite films or photographs with friends, getting involved in community life, going on walks and celebrating the seasons are all pursuits that cost very little but in my experience can enhance life immensely.

Now I'm not saying we should go back to medieval times and spend our weekends gathering nuts and berries, brewing mead and dancing round a fire (though on the odd occasion, this could be rather fun). Our complicated modern-day lives are not just going to dissolve away – and nor, on the whole, would we wish them to. I wouldn't want to live without my laptop, wireless broadband or comedy shows on TV. The key surely lies in finding the elusive balance between work and life, between doing and being: not filling every single free moment, but trying to arrive at a mixture of the indoor and outdoor; the cultural and the sociable; of communal and solitary time. If there are things that 'rule' your weekend (e.g. kids' parties, sports events, DIY, visits to relations) try to concentrate them into one day and leave the other free. Make the chores part of the fun. Think outside the proverbial box.

This book is packed full of ideas for restoring the weekend as the peak of our week, with time to spend on ourselves and with others. From a luxurious Quiet Night In on Friday to ideas for overcoming Sunday Evening Syndrome, there are ideas and activities to take you through the weekend during every season of the year. Of course, everyone is different, and people at different stages of their lives will have varying ideas about what constitutes a simple pleasure, what is an occasional indulgence, what can be taken for granted and what is a boring old fart's activity, to be avoided at all costs. When I was single and lived alone, for instance, staying in bed for a day on a wet winter Sunday, if I had nothing planned, was a wonderful treat which sometimes just used to happen of its own accord; now, with a husband and child in the equation, such an occurrence (and I have to say I do dream of it sometimes) would entail weeks of planning, or possibly faked ill-health, to attain. On the other hand, I know many people in their late twenties and thirties who wish they'd discovered the joys of gardening and home-baking much earlier in their lives, or who are loving the daily walks and connection with nature and the seasons that come with owning a dog. I make no claims to providing a comprehensive or even fairly spread range of weekend pleasures: train-spotting, blood sports, medieval battle re-enactment and matchstick model-making do not feature on the following pages – not that I have anything against them.

Many of the ideas and activities inevitably reflect my own personal passions such as gardening, cooking and outdoor life, but these are the areas on which I can speak with the most authority and enthusiasm. Some have their roots in my own childhood on a farm in Kent, born to a mother who, from necessity as much as inclination, made rather than bought cakes and biscuits and sewed many of our clothes from scratch. Others were instilled during long spells spent in Italy, where the celebration of home-cooked food and its place in family life is long engrained and has recently been revived by the excellent Slow Food Movement, now active in 132 countries and expanded and re-branded to form the Slow Movement. And many are the fruit of the technological advances of recent years that have transformed our ability to communicate, access information and share everything from our favourite music to photographs. Not all the suggestions will be for everyone, though I'd recommend trying at least one that takes you beyond your hitherto 'comfort zone' – you never know when a new hobby is just waiting to 'out' itself . . .

When it comes to weekend chores, however, I reckon just

about everyone will be interested in discovering enjoyable, creative ways around them. Again, some of the ideas you may already have happened upon yourself without, perhaps, realizing their radical potential to free up or transform your spare time. There are plenty of suggestions: choosing a farmers' market or small local shops over the supermarkets; frequenting car boot sales and country antiques markets rather than DIY superstores; even growing your own food, getting a bike instead of going to the gym, and holding clothes swap parties with girlfriends. Better still, set yourself the challenge of a weekend without any shopping at all!

The opening chapters are divided into year-round and seasonal pleasures that reconnect us to the earth, to our friends and families, and to the real meaning of age-old festivals and celebrations from Valentine's Day to Easter, Hallowe'en, Advent and Christmas. These quiet but fun activities, many of which I remember from my own childhood, do not cost much, if anything, to carry out. If the age-old adage holds true that 'The world is divided into people who spend money in order to save time, and others who spend time in order to save money', they would definitely fall into the latter category. But if it is time enjoyably spent, that's surely the whole point? It has to make more sense than spending even more time at work in order to pay others (whether that means gardeners, child-care providers or merely the manufacturers of mass-produced, over-processed food and drink) to make or do stuff for us which we could have fun doing ourselves if only we went about it in the right way? The book ends with a plea to Bring Back Sunday as a day of rest – for quiet contemplation, communing with nature and relaxing with family and friends.

Some of the suggestions are just very simple ways in which to enhance the fabric of our lives. From stargazing in summer to visiting a palm house in winter, from learning the ukulele to feeding the birds, from volunteering and campaigning to starting your own film library or keeping a journal, there are ideas to appeal to all ages, abilities and inclinations. The aim is not to do them all, but to explore the possibilities and get inspired to think up more. In the words of the novelist Susan Ertz, 'Millions long for immortality who do not know what to do with themselves on a rainy Sunday afternoon.' Don't let yourself be one of them!

1.

Things to do: Year Round

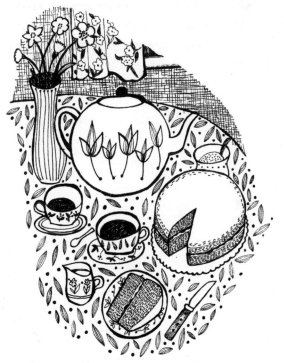

❧ · *Have a Quiet Night In* · ❧

We all need a Quiet Night In from time to time – especially on a Friday at the end of a hard week. And if you're going to stay in, why not do it in style? Plan ahead: get the right sort of food in, something nice to drink, a DVD, a good book, your favourite magazine. If you're a frequent subscriber to the Quiet Night In and its many charms, you'll already have a bathroom cabinet stocked with bath oils and unguents, a wardrobe full of luxurious lounging wear and a bed made up with the softest of pillows, the crispest of sheets, the prettiest and most comfortable covers and cushions. If not, the following suggestions and suppliers will soon have you sorted.

The ideal bath

A bath simply has to form a part of your Quiet Night In, and it's a great luxury to do it in style, with lots of bubble bath, scented candles, a glass of wine on a table alongside and even a book or magazine, if you can see through the fragrant, candlelit fug. To get the best benefit for your body, start off with five minutes' skin brushing, using a soft-bristled brush in gentle but long sweeping strokes, working from the soles of the feet up the legs to the bottom, then from the hands up the arms to the shoulders, and finishing with light circular movements around the tummy and down the chest, always brushing towards the heart. This not only aids the lymph system to eliminate toxins, but also seems to have an almost magical effect on skin texture and muscle tone if done regularly.

At this stage, I would then jump under the shower for a further five minutes, to rinse off all that dead skin. Ever since reading how the Japanese always shower before a bath and regard our way of bathing as wallowing in our own filth, I have veered towards this practice myself, provided I have time. Washing your hair is always best done in the shower, anyway, and if you follow it with a bath, you can bundle your wet hair up in a towel and out of the way – adding leave-in conditioners and other hair treatments should you choose. For those who are looking askance at the water consumption involved in such bathing rituals, I would counter by saying I do this maybe once a week, and make up for it by very brisk showering habits (five to ten minutes of alternating hot and cold water) at other times.

When it comes to products, I now use almost exclusively organic or naturally made skin and bath preparations. Not only is their production process kinder to the environment, I'd just rather not slap a load of unnecessary chemicals on to my skin, which, as any aromatherapist will tell you, has an incredible capacity to absorb whatever it comes into contact with. This concern arose when I began to grow my own organic fruit and vegetables; if I was going to try to avoid eating chemicals, why put them on my body? Pregnancy and caring for a young baby made me even more convinced, and there is growing evidence that many childhood allergies may be linked with skincare and sun protection products.

Lecture over. Using natural products doesn't have to mean less luxury – far from it. Not only do companies such as Neal's Yard Remedies (0845 262 3145/www.nealsyardremedies.com), Dr Hauschka (01386 791022/www.drhauschka.co.uk) and REN (020 7724 2900/www.renskincare.com) tend to spend far less on packaging (not to mention not testing on animals) than their glamour-mag rivals, they are more likely to contain higher percentages of pure essential oils and other fragrant ingredients. Use them for a few months and you'll find the smell of your former favourites gives you a headache. There are also a growing number of smaller UK-based companies making high-quality organic skin and beauty products, of which Essential Care (01638 716593/www.essential-care.co.uk), Figs and Rouge (01244 344321/www.figsandrouge.co.uk), Long Barn (01962 777873/www.long-barn.co.uk) and Tree Harvest (01531 650764/www.tree-harvest.com) are among the best. (Check out Figs and Rouge's splendid retro-style packaging to prove that beauty products can be glamorous as well as natural and ethical.) Add a few drops of an essential oil such as lavender, jasmine, vetiver or ylang ylang to bath water just before you step in to enhance the whole sensual experience of bathtime, and scent your entire home at the same time. Each oil will have a corresponding effect on the mind and spirits, as well as the body; see the Neal's Yard website for books and further information on using essential oils.

Towels

After a bath, good towels are essential. John Lewis (08456 049049/www.johnlewis.com) as usual has a great basic selection, or for a little more luxury try The White Company (0870 900 9555/www.thewhitecompany.com), whose twice-yearly sales are well worth waiting for, Toast (0844 557 5200/ www.toast.co.uk) for its lovely striped and fringed Hammam towels, and Designers Guild (020 7893 7400/ www.designers guild.com) for jewel-bright bath sheets and pretty embroidered hand towels. Greenfibres (0845 330 3440/ www.greenfibres.com) is the eco-option, with lots of soft organic terry towelling, absorbent waffle cotton or even hemp and linen bath, shower and hair towels.

Then it's just a matter of slapping on some body lotion (see previous page) and slipping into some lovely lounging wear (see box, p.23) to enjoy the rest of your evening.

What to eat and drink

For me, luxurious snack food – a sort of upmarket indoor picnic – is ideal Friday night fare, consisting of dishes that don't need much, if anything, in the way of cooking and can just be spread out on a large tray and picked at in random order throughout the course of the evening. I might have some prawns or smoked fish with a garlicky or horseradish mayonnaise, a bowl of good olives, some hummus or guacamole with crisp carrot sticks, or Parma ham with figs or melon. A big bowl of salad is another favourite option – a home-made Niçoise, for instance, with fresh grilled tuna and blanched French beans, or a proper Caesar salad with the crispest cos lettuce, organic grilled chicken breast, marinated anchovies and shaved Parmesan. For pudding – well, need you ask? A Quiet Night In just has to include a tub of good ice cream (eaten, more often than not, with a spoon straight from the tub, but we needn't tell). You can always add an accompaniment of fresh fruit in season – a bag of cherries or raspberries in high summer takes some beating – to make it feel more healthy. When it comes to drinking, some will wind down with a large glass of wine, others will prefer a smoothie or a nice cup of tea. If you are drinking, the idea is to treat yourself and relax – to add a heightened enjoyment to solitude – not get horribly, wildly drunk on one's own and start ringing up ex-boyfriends or worse . . .

What to do

For some people, a long bath and an hour or so in front of the telly is more than enough; but as we all know, there's never anything worth watching on the one night you're in, no matter how many channels you have. If you're clever enough to have started up your own movie collection (see p.200) you'll always have the perfect film for your current state of mind, be it Wim Wenders' *Wings of Desire*, *The Simpsons Movie* or an old Ginger Rogers and Fred Astaire musical. If not, forget rental shops, they are so old-hat. Lovefilm (0844 482 0123/ www.lovefilm. com) will send you DVDs that you can keep for a whole month before sending back (see pp.201–2 for some all-time great movies). Or splash out on a huge boxed set of your favourite TV show – whether it's *Life on Earth*, *Sex and the City* or *Curb Your Enthusiasm* – so you can catch up on all the episodes you missed and see all the good bits again. (Razamataz

0844 557 5316/www.erazamataz.co.uk) is a good source of old TV shows and classic movies if you want to buy online.) If you don't want to watch the small screen – and heaven knows there is absolutely no reason why you should – you may want to relax with some knitting, crocheting, drawing, playing some music or reading a book or magazine. Or, if you are having friends round tomorrow, for lunch, tea or dinner, you can cook. I find this very therapeutic, wafting around the kitchen in a kaftan and a pinny, filling the whole house with delicious smells.

The only problem with the Quiet Night In, as far as I can see, is that people either don't understand and get uppity if you say you can't see them because you're staying in, or else want to join you, which can sometimes be all very well, but is not at all the same thing. Better, perhaps, to be vague and say you have 'other plans', but a close friend won't be fobbed off by that; she'll think you are having a secret affair and may well tell everyone so. A true friend will understand, however. One of the things that makes a night in even nicer for me is the long conversation with a girlfriend in the bath (thank the Lord for cordless technology) or lying on our individual beds, many miles apart but each with the phone up to our ear, with cotton wool between our toes while our new nail varnish dries.

An earlyish night is key – and after all that luxuriating and pampering you'll probably be ready for it. Sleep really is the great healer, whatever the past week may have held. A good night's sleep helps us restore our batteries and wake up full of energy for the rest of the weekend. You owe it to yourself to make sure you get a good one. (For tips on the perfect bed and getting a good night's sleep, see pp.319–20 and 322–5.)

Lounging Wear

Toast (0844 557 5200/www.toast.co.uk) has silk camisoles and shorts and long linen dressing gowns for summer and full-length Moroccan-style djellabas and cosy striped pyjamas for winter, plus lovely throws and blankets for snuggling up in.

Denny Andrews (01793 762476/www.dennyandrews.co.uk) is a small family business that orders and imports simple clothes direct from village projects in India – great for very reasonably priced silk and cotton kaftans in pure white or bright colours.

Plumo (0870 241 3590/www.plumo.com) often has quirky yet glamorous kaftan-type dresses and attractive throws along with all its trademark pretty accessories.

The White Company (0870 900 9555/ www.thewhitecompany.com) is famed for its bed-linen (see p.320) but is also a good source of classic, well-cut nightwear and dressing gowns in crisp cotton or softest terry towelling – for children as well as adults.

The Linen Press (017683 72777/www.thelinenpress.co.uk) does a lovely long linen nightshirt, generously cut with a collarless neck, which can be worn by men and women alike.

Greenfibres (0845 330 3440/www.greenfibres.com) has some delightful designs in soft organic cotton – perfect for those with allergies, as well as the eco-conscious. Gorgeous blankets and cable-knit cashmere throws as well.

Celtic Sheepskin (01637 871605/www.celtic-sheepskin.co.uk) is the absolute best when it comes to slippers, with boot and mule styles beautifully made in sheepskin, left *au naturel* or dyed in almost any colour, in child's sizes too. It even does sheepskin insoles to pop inside your favourite shoes or slippers.

❦ • *Get – or Borrow – a Pet* • ❦

If you have animals – a dog, or chickens, say – a fair part of the weekend may be dominated by their needs. But how lovely. A walk – whether a stroll in the local park or a long hike in the country – is always enhanced by a dog running or plodding alongside, and letting the chickens out for a peck around the garden (cover prize plants first!) is a good way to get rid of unwanted pests. Even on a night in, it's cosy to have a furry creature cuddling up beside you in front of the television. If you are not a pet owner, perhaps planning to become one might become a weekend project?

Here I have to let you in on an irrational prejudice of mine. I find people who do not have pets peculiar. I'm sure that they (or you, if you are one of them) think the exact opposite: that the very idea of sharing one's home with creatures whose personal and hygiene habits often leave much to be desired is downright strange and not to be encouraged. In many ways they are right: pets usually cost a fair amount of money to buy and maintain, and they need care and attention, not to mention awkward and potentially expensive arrangements when you go away. And yet I find a home without some kind of animal presence a sad and sterile place.

I would certainly find it very hard to live without a dog. My lurcher Wilma is not only a loving, fun and loyal companion, she is also, or so I read, an asset to my health. She gets me out of the house every day, come rain, come shine, for a good forty-five minutes' brisk walk (one of the healthiest forms of exercise, according to doctors), and simply sitting stroking her apparently keeps my blood pressure within healthy limits (watching fish in an aquarium does this too). People who own or grow up with animals are far less likely to have allergies, and as for hygiene – well, I have always been of the school of thought that a little bit of dirt never did anyone any harm.

I'd even argue that pets are good for mental health. They are such good role models, for a start. When Wilma lies snoozing on her bed in the sunshine she is not thinking, Should I be a Dalmatian? Or how about a Labrador? or, Am I running fast enough? No, she is simply enjoying the sun on her coat, and is totally content and at ease with doing what she is best at: being a dog. The maverick Dominican scholar Matthew Fox refers to his dog as his 'Spiritual Director' for this very reason: animals live in the present moment. I'm reminded, too, of Mary Oliver's uplifting poem, 'Wild Geese':

> *You do not have to be good.*
> *You do not have to walk on your knees*
> *   for a hundred miles through the desert repenting*
> *You only have to let the soft animal of your body*
> *   love what it loves.*

Animals remind us that we are animals, too, and that we ignore our basic needs and appetites at our peril. They are also an excellent way of introducing children to a variety of important aspects of life: responsibility, reproduction and death, to name but three.

If any of the above has inspired you to go out and get a dog, a cat or even a guinea pig or gold-fish, the rant was not wasted. Owning a pet is a serious commitment, however, and not to be entered

Preferred Weekend Activities of Various Breeds of Dog

Labrador – lolloping about on family walks, wagging tail energetically enough to swipe things off tables, swimming in sea or lakes.

Lurcher – running like the wind on walks, especially on flat beaches or large expanses of grass. At home will lounge for hours in decorous fashion – on furniture if given half a chance.

Weimaraner – owing to astonishing beauty of their smooth pale grey coats, often seen posing with owners in stylish bars and cafés, but would rather be digging holes in your garden.

Pug – bustling about your feet making snorting noises, snoozing making snorting noises, being cuddled, sitting on owner's lap to be photographed for features on People with Pugs.

Jack Russell – hunting for rabbits etc. with lurchers; yapping at heels when time for a walk; playing games involving digging, making tunnels and the like with small children.

Rottweiler – snarling at trespassers and biting faces off babies may be the public perception of this bear-like hound, but most are friendly enough if well trained.

Toy poodle or Chihuahua – being carried about in fashionistas' handbags and fussed over and stroked by well-manicured hands. Some actually forget how to walk.

German shepherd – patrolling your property with its policeman-like presence, but not averse to a good long walk (good at rounding up slackers) and games with well-trained children.

Dalmatian – walking and playing ball games in the park and counting the number of times people say 'Isn't that a Dalmatian?' and 'Where are the other 100?'

Saint Bernard – given general lack of stranded mountaineers to rescue, will lavish heroic attentions on owner and family which, given lion-like bulk and tendency to dribble, needs patience.

into lightly. Dogs, in particular, need someone at home for most of the day (unless you are prepared to shell out for a dog walker), and most animals are happiest with a fair amount of company. Cats come and go as they choose throughout the day, and other smaller animals are happy enough on their own for periods provided they have other animals with them.

Make two lists: one of your/your family's preferences and what you like about the idea of owning a pet, and one of the realities of what you can offer in the way of time, money and care (the two may not immediately match up). Gather information from the library, from the internet, from specialist magazines, pet shops, breeders and other pet owners. Best of all, visit people who own the type of animal you are considering and, if feasible, arrange to borrow or look after it/them for a day or weekend. This will really allow you to understand what is required. It may be that, having borrowed a dog, you decide that occasional care is all you are up for, and this can be a fantastic arrangement for you and the owner – and the dog. (Incidentally, a new 'flexible pet ownership' scheme pioneered in the US, whereby you can regularly borrow (or loan – the fees are pretty high) a pet is on its way to the UK – see www.flexpetz.com (020 3002 0190) for further details.)

Cats, dogs and small rodents are by no means the only options. A tank of fish can be beautiful and calming to contemplate: I remember a scheme on *Grand Designs* where an aquarium formed a see-through dividing wall between the kitchen and sitting room of a house, and you can create stylish or witty effects with photographic backdrops behind the tank and anything from shells and stones to plastic figures arranged inside.

If you live in the country you may like a couple of Muscovy or runner ducks in your garden – they are terrifically comical, and a good natural alternative to slug killer. Or how about a para- keet or pot-bellied pig? Do be cautious with unusual pets, however. A friend of mine has had terrible problems with a handsome Bearded Dragon lizard called James, bought as a present for her son. Not only does James cost a fortune in elec- tricity (he basks in the sun in his native Australia) and his diet of live crickets and locusts has to be collected weekly by car, but he also gets depressed if he cannot hear human voices and is not taken out and cuddled regularly.

So choose carefully. But choose something. Even a goldfish is proof of some sort of acknowledgement of the existence and importance of other forms of life besides the human – which has to be a good thing. And look after it well. A happy, well- trained pet should give you untold joy.

❧ · *Bring Back Teatime* · ❧

Teatime is a great British institution that deserves to be reinstat- ed in style, and I like to make it a part of my weekend. If I haven't gone out for lunch, going out for tea is a great treat, anywhere from the timeless glamour of Fortnum and Mason's or the Ritz to the more homely charms of a café or tearooms – Maison Bertaux and Patisserie Valerie in London, Betty's in Harrogate and Harri- ets in Bury St Edmunds are among my all-time favourites. See *Where to Take Tea* by Susan Cohen for more ideas. Alternatively, I might invite friends and/or family round to my house for tea. This works particularly well with friends with young children, I find, as there is far less pressure to get food down their throats – and, hey, everyone likes cake. I love the ritual of brewing proper leaf tea and setting out a tray with flowers and pretty (if mismatching) teacups and saucers from my collection of junk shop and sale finds. Personally, I also love making cakes – see below for recipes that look and taste impressive but only take a matter of minutes – but if you don't, it's a great excuse to visit a proper patisserie or baker's shop and choose a wonderful selection to be packed up in a box with ribbon. (Let a small child open this and watch their face!) Teatime can be an extremely relaxing way to socialize: the cooking and preparation has all been done beforehand and, as there's less food involved than at a lunch or dinner, more time to chat. It's also relatively short, making it a good opportunity to invite people who you may not know very well yet or who for various reasons (age or health, for instance) might not enjoy mixing with your other friends over a long-drawn-out meal.

Classic teatime recipes

 FLAPJACKS

This is my own recipe. They always turn out slightly different, as the quantities are not precise, but that is part of their charm, and they're always appreciated. When I was pregnant, I started with a traditional flapjack recipe, took out the sugar and added the seeds to make them more healthy. I did experiment with alternatives to golden syrup but there's no way round it, you need it for the chewiness – but using half blackstrap molasses gives a darker colour and a lovely depth of flavour.

'Healthy' flapjacks

> *225g butter*
> *2–3 tablespoons golden syrup (run hot water over the spoon*
> *before use to help it come off easily)*
> *1–2 tablespoons blackstrap molasses*
> *450g organic rolled porridge oats (up to one-third can be*
> *jumbo oats)*
> *a generous handful each of sesame seeds (reserve 2 teaspoons to*
> *decorate), golden linseed, sunflower and pumpkin seeds*

Preheat the oven to 190°C/375°F/gas mark 5. Grease a 20 × 30 cm baking tray or brownie tin. Melt the butter in a large saucepan, stir in the other ingredients (apart from the reserved sesame seeds) and mix well. Tip out into the tin, smooth down and sprinkle with the remaining sesame seeds. Bake for 15–20 minutes, depending on your oven, until the top is just starting to go brown – you don't want to overcook them as they go all crunchy and lose their chewy bite. Cool on a wire rack in their tin and then pop into the fridge. The flapjacks are easier to cut into squares and remove from the tin when very cold.

SCONES

Freshly baked scones are a simple but magical baking spell that it's good to have up your sleeve. Master the technique, memorize the recipe and keep the necessary staples in your kitchen and you'll never again be flummoxed by unexpected visitors. I mix mine by hand, but with a bread-making hook on an electric mixer the process would be even quicker. You can add a handful of sultanas, or even grated cheese to the mix (for the latter, omit all but a dessertspoonful of sugar and sprinkle more grated cheese on the top), but to my mind, it's hard to beat classic plain scones, warm (not hot) from the oven, with home-made jam (see pp.138–41) and thick whipped cream. The cream of tartar in this recipe is not essential, but does seem to ensure the desired fluffiness.

Basic scones

500g plain flour
1 teaspoon salt
2 teaspoons bicarbonate of soda
4½ teaspoons cream of tartar
75g cold unsalted butter or mixture of butter and
    Trex or similar
50g caster sugar
300ml milk
1 egg, beaten
6.5cm round crinkle-edged cutter
baking tray

Preheat the oven to 220°C/425°F/gas mark 7. Sift the first four ingredients together into a large bowl. Rub in the fats with your fingers till the mixture resembles breadcrumbs. Stir in the sugar, make a well in the centre and pour in the milk. Mix briefly, then turn out on to a floured board and knead lightly to form a dough. Roll out to a thickness of 3cm. Dip the cutter in flour and cut out as many circles as you can, re-rolling the dough for the last few. Line up the scones close together on the baking tray so that they bulge together while cooking. Brush the tops with the beaten egg and bake in the oven for 10 minutes until risen and golden brown. Eat warm, with clotted or whipped cream and jam.

CUPCAKES

These are popular with everyone, but a great standby if children are expected. Making and decorating cupcakes with children is also a fun pursuit, but don't expect them to look like the chic little offerings from the Hummingbird Bakery (020 7584 0055/www.hummingbirdbakery.com) and its like if kids are in sole charge of decorating. The amounts – 110g of everything and two eggs – are easy to remember if you want to whizz them up when you are away for the weekend. This basic recipe makes about 12. A box or tin of them also makes a lovely impromptu present.

No-nonsense cupcakes

110g self-raising flour, sifted
110g caster sugar, sifted
110g softened margarine or butter
1 teaspoon baking powder
1 teaspoon pure vanilla extract
2 large free-range eggs

To decorate

200g icing sugar, sifted
juice of 1 lemon or 50ml boiling water
food colouring (optional)
sprinkles, icing paste, candied fruits, etc.

Preheat the oven to 160°C/325°F/gas mark 3. Line a 12-hole muffin tin with paper cake cases. Put all the cake ingredients in a food mixer and mix well – or use a hand-held whisk – until the mixture is light, pale and fluffy.

Decant in heaped teaspoons to the cake cases and bake for 20 minutes until the tops are firm yet springy to touch. Let them cool on a wire rack before preparing the icing.

Sift the icing sugar into a bowl and add lemon juice or water a teaspoonful at a time, stirring till the consistency resembles thick double cream. If using food colouring, add just a drop or two at a time to avoid unintentionally violent shades. Pour a little on top of each cake and add sprinkles, sugar flowers, candied fruit, icing paste shapes or other decorations. Leave for the icing to set.

For further inspiration see Kate Shirazi's heavenly book, *Cupcake Magic: Little Cakes with Attitude.*

❧ · *Write Proper Letters* · ❧

I love writing and receiving letters. In this age of mobile phones and e-mails, it is easy to forget the pleasure of sitting down and writing to a friend or relation, and the excitement of a hand-written envelope arriving through the letterbox. Of course, instant communication has its uses and appeal; I'm not Luddite enough to deny the convenience (and, when done well, wit and charm) of texts and e-mail, but they can't compare with the tactile delights of a 'proper' letter or a pretty card. The weekend is the ideal time for letter-writing, when there is time to spare and thoughts turn to friends and family.

In an ideal world, I'd have an old-fashioned writing bureau just for letter-writing, with a drop-down flap with little compartments for communiqués in and out, different papers and cards, address books, birthday books, stamps and a little set of weights for weighing (far preferable to waiting in line at the post office). This is what I imagine those great letter-writers, the Victorians and Edwardians, always had. In reality, my work desk has to double up, but I do have a separate deep drawer in which all the necessary paraphernalia is housed. In fact, my best and most enjoyable letter-writing is never done at a desk anyway – it will be in bed at night, in the garden with a cup of coffee in the morning, at a café table or lounging on a beach on holiday.

Taking some time over the raw materials gives pleasure to both writer and recipient. You don't have to splash out on personalized stationery from Smythson's (020 7318 1515/ www.Smythson.com for untold pleasures at a price) but thick good quality paper beats thin sheets torn from a cheap pad any day. I get mine from The Green Stationery Company (01225 480556/www.greenstat.co.uk), who do heritage watermarked recycled writing paper and envelopes as well as serviceable everyday stuff in every size. Cards can be lovely, too. I have a stash of different cards for different people and uses: postcards from exhibitions, pretty birthday cards, boxes of note cards I pick up here and there – not forgetting the free ones displayed for the taking in bars and restaurants (there are always a few good ones). I'm also not above cutting (neatly) the fronts off especially attractive birthday or other cards and reusing them, or sticking spare photos on to plain card to send.

Choose a pen that suits your writing and does not scratch, soak into or wrinkle the paper. Personally, I favour a good fountain pen – and in these eco-conscious days that choice rather than a throwaway Biro or Pentel seems less fuddy-duddy. Millions of disposable Biros are bought in the UK every day, and they will all end up in landfill.

Good strong envelopes are essential; buy ones made from recycled paper from The Green Stationery Company who also supply labels for reusing old envelopes and Jiffy bags. The other great advantage of letters over e-mail is that you can always tuck a little extra item into the envelope – anything from a photo or newspaper cutting to a pressed flower, packet of seeds or small bar of chocolate – which makes the whole practice even more of a treat.

When it comes to the writing, it's impossible to be prescriptive, as so much depends on the recipient, the time you have available, the purpose of the letter and your own personal style. A few suggestions, however. Begin in positive mode: express the hope that the recipient is well and thank them for their previous correspondence (ideally have it with you so you can refer to it). Never kick off with an apology – it's such a downer. Even if you should have written sooner, say something like, 'You've been much in my thoughts recently, but there has been so much going on it's been hard to find time to write. For instance . . .' And then you are off. Letters are essentially about exchanging news and shared interests; the best have a light conversational tone that allows you to hear the person's real voice in your head. Funny letters are the best. It's so good to hear someone laughing out loud as they read a letter on the tube. Love letters (or just a note) are *always* welcome, especially when they are least expected. And letters sent at times of hardship or emotional stress – following a bereavement, the loss of a pet or even before a godchild or grandchild starts at 'big school' – can often mean more than you will know. Sometimes it *is* hard to know what to write, but the important thing is to write *something*, even if it is only a few lines in a card or a poem copied out on to a postcard (see p.55). It's the letters never written that we regret, and seldom those sent.

For further inspiration, there are books such as *The Art of Letter Writing* by Lassor A. Blumenthal available on Amazon, a quarterly print publication called the *Letter Exchange* 'that supports and encourages the age-old art of letter-writing', and a few rather fun and eccentric websites (check out www.wendy. com/letterwriting: How to write proper beautiful letters by etiquette expert Ms Demeanor and www.love.ivillage.com). By far the best and most enjoyable option, however, is to immerse yourself in the correspondence of letter-writers of the past, when pen and paper were still the main form of communication. My favourites include:

Dear Friend and Gardener, a year's correspondence, by no means just about gardening, between Beth Chatto and the late Christopher Lloyd; *Gardening Letters to my Daughter* by Anne Scott-James with hilarious replies from non-gardener Clare Hastings; and any of the published correspondence of members of the Bloomsbury set such as *The Letters of Vita Sackville-West to Virginia Woolf* edited by Louise DeSalvo and Mitchell A. Leaska.

Incidentally, if you would like to combine a love of letter-writing with being useful in the world, many charities and campaigning organizations such as Amnesty International and Avaaz (see p.65) would be delighted to have more letter-writers on board. Letter-writing is also a vital factor in sponsoring deprived children abroad through organizations such as Action Aid (01460 238000/www.actionaid.org.uk) or the excellent Tibetan Children's Villages (00 911892221348/www.tibchild.org) in India, which care for and educate young children exiled from Tibet.

☙ · *Learn the Ukulele* · ❧

Learning a new musical instrument as a weekend hobby requires dedication – not to mention tolerance on the part of your family and friends. Though I do know people with no existing musical ability who have taken up the violin and trumpet in later life, this is quite a tall order, and likely to lead to disappointment, if not divorce. Might I suggest the ukulele? With only four strings, it is not difficult to learn, and even in the novice stages is relatively easy on the ear. Ukuleles are cheap – you can buy one for under £20 at any good music shop – and pleasingly portable. Thanks to recent converts such as Tom Hodgkinson of the *Idler* extolling its virtues in the press, they are even becoming fashionable. What more could you ask of an instrument?

Ukulele Shops and Sites

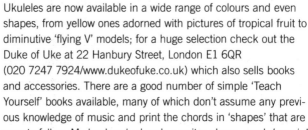

Ukuleles are now available in a wide range of colours and even shapes, from yellow ones adorned with pictures of tropical fruit to diminutive 'flying V' models; for a huge selection check out the Duke of Uke at 22 Hanbury Street, London E1 6QR (020 7247 7924/www.dukeofuke.co.uk) which also sells books and accessories. There are a good number of simple 'Teach Yourself' books available, many of which don't assume any previous knowledge of music and print the chords in 'shapes' that are easy to follow. My husband, already a guitar player, used *Jumpin' Jim's 60s Uke-In* to teach himself the ukulele a few years ago. You can also learn online, and Frank's recommended websites include Jumpin' Jim (Beloff)'s site www.fleamarketmusic.com; www.easyukulele.com; www.sheep-entertainment.nl/ukulele; www.beatlesite.info and www.alligatorboogaloo.com/uke

Then it's just a matter of choosing your tunes. Somehow, the jaunty strains of the ukulele lend themselves to a vast array of musical styles, from George Formby classics and the 'Dambusters March' to Jimi Hendrix and beyond. If you need convincing, go and see a performance by the wonderful Ukulele Orchestra of Great Britain. Formally dressed like classical musicians, and cradling their instruments close to their chins, this cheerful bunch of eccentrics are guaranteed to give you a good night out – not to mention inspiration for new tunes to learn. Check out their website, www.ukuleleorchestra. com (020 7284 1419), for the dates and venues of their next tour.

Once you have mastered the basics, the ukulele is the perfect instrument to sling into a bag to take to weekends away, outdoor festivals or just a picnic in the park. In contrast to arriving with a guitar which, unless you have been asked to bring it, smacks of 'You *shall* have a jolly good singsong, like it or not', a ukulele is unobtrusive, and can easily be played in the background. But pick the right tune for the gathering, and I bet it will only be a while before others start joining in or singing along; 'Hey Jude' and 'Yellow Submarine' are good standards to start with, but because the chords are so simple, it's possible to make even more complicated songs sound very good indeed.

Some songs that sound unexpectedly good on a ukulele include: 'Penny Lane' and 'Something' by the Beatles; 'Surfer Girl' by the Beach Boys and 'Sheena Is a Punk Rocker' and 'Blitzkrieg Bop', both by the Ramones.

Take Up Photography

These days, advances in digital photography mean it's not only getting easier to take good pictures, but it's also a lot cheaper and easier to edit, manipulate and print them yourself for eventual use in any number of ways. Enrol on a course in digital photography if you feel you'd like to learn a lot more, or resolve to spend the weekend reading the instruction manual and experimenting; one of the joys of digital is that the effects of subtle differences in setting can be viewed and experienced straight away, and any mistakes deleted. Invest in a new camera; digital SLRs that enable you to experiment more with depth of field have become much more affordable in recent years, as have very small 'compact' cameras that you can slip into a pocket. Or enhance your skills by

Ten Great Weekend Outings With Children

Any of these (depending on the age/sex/interests of the children involved) will make you hugely popular with your children/ grand-children/godchildren etc., not to mention their parents. And you should have fun yourself, too.

A trip to a castle

Great for boys, but little girls could bring their princess dresses. Bodiam in Kent (arriving by steam train adds to the fun – 0844 800 1895/www.nationaltrust.org.uk); dramatic Dunnottar in Aberdeenshire (01569 762173/www.dunnottarcastle.co.uk); Hurst Castle in Hampshire with its 360-degree views out over the Solent (01590 642344/www.hurstcastle.co.uk) and Castle Howard in North Yorkshire, complete with costumed characters (01653 648444/ www.castlehoward.co.uk) are all superb.

Water sports

Older children would love a day's canoeing or kayaking (try Wye Valley Canoes (01497 847213/www.wyevalleycanoes.co.uk); Port Edgar, Edinburgh (0131 331 3330/www.portedgar.co.uk)) or white-water rafting (The National Whitewater Centre in Snowdownia National Park (01678 521083/www.ukrafting.co.uk) is one of the most beautiful places in which to do it).

A day at the zoo

Longleat Safari Park (01985 844400/www.longleat.co.uk); Chester Zoo (01244 380280/www.chesterzoo.org) and Bristol Zoo (0117 974 7399/www.bristolzoo.org.uk) are among the best and most animal-friendly.

A boat trip down the river

Whether it's a tourist boat down the Thames (020 7740 0400 www.citycruises.com), a punt in Cambridge (01223 301845 www.puntingincambridge.com) (don't forget a picnic to eat in Grantchester Meadows) or a day out on a row boat on your local river, messing about in boats is endless fun for all ages. Don't forget the life-jackets.

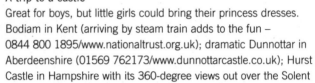
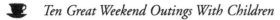

All the fun of the fair

Stock up with pound coins and head for the fairground, if you really want to be popular. Aesthetes may find Carters Steam Fair, which features only steam-powered, immaculately painted traditional machines rather easier on the eye (and ear): 01628 822221/ www.carterssteamfair.co.uk (only in the south-east).

Show-Time

Whether it is classical ballet for the girls (and some boys), an old-fashioned musical or a traditional pantomime around Christmas-time, a trip to the theatre is always a hugely anticipated treat – especially if interval ice creams and other treats are thrown in. Giffords Circus (0845 459 7469/www.giffordscircus.com), a traditional little circus with a pretty tent and stylishly dressed performers, which does an annual tour of Gloucestershire, Wiltshire, Berkshire and Oxfordshire, is also completely enchanting – for adults too!

Pop concerts

These days, many children love the same music as their parents' generation, so taking them to a gig may not be the ordeal it was when Take That and Steps were the only option. For maximum brownie points, take them to a weekend festival such as Glastonbury; the only trouble is, if they are old enough to enjoy it, they may not want old farts like you around. (See www.efestivals.co.uk for the year's events, availability and line-ups.)

Going out to eat

Some children will love the ritz and glitz – not to mention the mountains of delicious cakes – of the tearooms at grand hotels such as the Ritz and Claridge's. Make sure your bank balance is up to it – the payoff is its effect on their manners. Or take older children to a good Chinese or Indian restaurant to help broaden their palate.

A day at the beach

(See pp.133–7) and don't forget the kite and shrimping nets.

Camping

(See pp.247–52) Check the site is child-friendly first.

buying a new lens: a more powerful zoom, for instance, or a macro lens for close-up shots of plants and insects.

Rather than just confining your photography to document-ing the highlights, why not concentrate on a specific project, which could be artistic, social or campaigning in nature? Some unusual or fun ideas include:

- Take one picture of yourself – or your child, or partner – every day, week or month for a year.
- Choose a scene you see every day – a tree in your park, the sea at your local beach, the view from your bedroom window – and document it through the changing seasons, taking care to stand in exactly the same place each time. If it's an area under threat from development or climate change, the collection of pictures might form part of a campaign (see p.44 and pp.64–9).
- Take pictures of your average day – or that of your child. We all have photographs of holidays, weddings, parties and so on, but the everyday minutiae – such as breakfast, feeding the dog, the walk to work or school – go unrecorded. They may not seem like much now, but they'll be of far more interest when you're older, and even to future generations, when daily life may have changed beyond recognition.
- Choose a colour such as red or green and take a series of photo-graphs of objects – both natural and man-made – only of that colour. Make a collage with them when you have enough.
- Choose a theme – games, love or freedom, for example – and look for subjects that illustrate it, however obliquely.
- Take a shape – circles, stars, hearts, for instance – and look out for it in everything from natural phenomena such as stones,

shells and leaves to shop signs, patterns on fabric or the ephemeral forms of clouds, shadows and the gaps between buildings. The pictures could be made into a fantastic collage, calendar or computer photo book.

- Choose to document in detail a specific area of plant life, architecture or whatever and take pictures wherever you find it. It could be doorways or windows; different types and colours of lichen; corrugated-iron buildings, from barns to Methodist churches (an old favourite of mine); cloud patterns; traditional cafés or barber shops. Having this project at the back of your mind will always give you something to look out for on walks or weekends away and, who knows, if you choose the right subject and your photography is half decent, there could be the makings of a book one day.

- Take photographs of your local area. It might be an area of outstanding natural beauty; it might be a sleepy suburb; it might be an inner city with its tower blocks and street markets. Take pictures of it at all times of day and night; of people, of buildings, of local events. The results will not only be a fascinating personal record for yourself and family but they may also be of interest to your local authority, or be good enough to form the basis of an exhibition or campaigning project.

- Take photographs that illustrate the lines of a favourite song. I recently saw the amazing touring exhibition Hard Rain in which the photographer Mark Edwards has illustrated each line of the famous Bob Dylan song with a photograph documenting aspects of the world today, with the emphasis on the consequences of global warming (020 8858 8307/www.hardrainproject.com for further information). The concept was simple; the effect on viewers powerful, moving and motivating.

- Make your photographs part of a campaign project (see pp.64–9). Choose something you really care about which you feel may be under threat: it could be a local park or beauty spot, an ancient apple orchard, a street market or children's play project. Take pictures (asking permission where necessary, of course), being sure to get a good mixture of the emotional aspects as well as the physical and get them printed as postcards, a calendar, or see if it might be possible to mount an exhibition in your library, community centre or church hall to raise awareness. In my experience, it's often easier to galvanize people into action with images of something beautiful, rather than with gloomy horror stories.

- Take unusual portraits of close friends or children. Print an entire contact sheet or its modern equivalent of stacks of shots taken at the same time but showing different moods and expressions. Or choose just three and place them side by side in a long wooden frame with three 'windows'. Or, if you are feeling ambitious, make a large-scale collage for a wall of your house. A friend of mine took pictures of his four children dressed up in two distinctive outfits each on the tube and then had them blown up huge so it looks like eight people – a spy, a ballerina, a football player and so on – sitting next to each other, in very different postures, on a London tube train with a seaside backdrop visible through the windows, which all adds to its surreal appeal. You'll need professional help here with the printing, and I can't promise it will be cheap, but the above is a cracker of a conversation piece and a wonderful record of the family at that age.

Share your photographs

I know I'm not alone in having thousands of photographs stashed away where they are giving pleasure to no one, least of all me. And it's not just the trunks and boxes full of old holiday snaps and records of my garden. When I bought my first digital camera a few years ago, I remember thinking it would put paid to such storage problems, but soon became haunted by the vast library of shots languishing unsorted on my computer. Slowly but surely, I'm getting through them, and the process is surprisingly satisfying, especially when it involves sharing the pictures with others. Here are some ideas for getting the best from your store of photographs:

✻ *Sorting*: Go through the photos with old diaries and calendars, sorting them into sequence of years and events, wherever possible. If you don't already do so, resolve to date and label photos as you get them developed/downloaded – it saves such time and trouble later. My family's enjoyment of a stash of old black and white photographs, some of them more than a hundred years old, has been so much enhanced by my grandfather's admirable habit of dating each photo in fountain pen on the back, and supplying all the names of those present.

✻ *Editing*: Sort into piles – for framing, for keeping, for sending to others – and throw away or delete the rest. One reason why the few albums from my childhood give so much pleasure is that there are relatively few photographs compared to what we keep today: my first teeth and steps are documented, but not seventeen almost identical shots of me asleep in my cot.

✻ *Personal albums*: A good discipline a friend of mine keeps is to compile an album for every year; even now that they have gone digital, she still prints just enough to fill an average-sized album, and devotes the few days between Christmas and New Year to sticking them in. This practice makes the retrospective sorting of old photographs much more manageable. Or devote separate albums to particularly enjoyable or exotic holidays, or to the creation of a new garden or building project, however large or small. Don't feel you've got to do it all at once; just completing one or two albums in the course of an afternoon is hugely satisfying.

✻ *Albums for others*: Making albums for other people is a lovely thing to do which, in my experience, is always greatly appreciated. Get two sets of photos of a holiday, wedding, party, weekend away or other occasion printed and send one, arranged in a nice album, to the friends or family involved; or compile post-dated 'baby albums' for each of your children. One of the nicest gifts I've ever been given is a scrapbook customized by an American friend as a baby book when my daughter was born, with hand-painted pages devoted to 'Early Days', 'First Christmas', 'First Birthday' and so on, which I have so enjoyed keeping up to date. But if you did not have a baby book yourself, or have not kept one for your children, it's now possible, thanks to digital scanning and processing, to create them retrospectively. Get a few of the best photos blown up large, while you are at it, to frame and/or give as presents (see below).

Another lovely idea is to present a personalized album to a friend who is getting married/leaving a job/moving to a new city. I treasure an album given to me on my hen night, when all my closest girlfriends contributed a photograph of a favourite trip or memory, along with a few lines of handwritten text. And a friend who left Bristol after twelve years for a new life in Scotland was presented with a similar album in which photos and other contributions from all her friends were interspersed with shots taken all over Bristol, from the street signs of all the roads where she'd lived, to snaps of her favourite bars, shops and restaurants, her various workplaces and outdoor haunts. If, however, this seems like too much work for you, or you'd rather get it done professionally, Bob Books (020 7243 7404/ www.bobbooks.co.uk) will do it for you in superb style.

* *Framing*: Pick out your favourite shots and get them printed so everyone can enjoy them. How you display them will depend on your own sense of style, as well as budget. Some people will choose just a few shots, blown up large, perhaps in black and white, and arrange them, gallery-like, along their entrance hall. Others will prefer an eccentric mismatch of frames on a shelf or table-top, or simply stick the pictures, unframed, in a Blu-Tacked patchwork on the walls of a downstairs loo, or in a 6 × 4-foot panel by a teenager's bed. I've seen stairwells used as good galleries for family photographs, or the area directly above the parents' bed. And a particularly good or meaningful picture, attractively framed, makes a wonderful present for a birthday or wedding.

✳ *Digital*: Most computer operating systems include a simple way of editing your photographs into albums or slideshows, and it is worth keeping up with this every time you download; or do it one year at a time, instead of or as well as making up a physical album. Again, it takes very little time or skill to compile a customized selection on a CD of a special event for friends. With a little more know-how, it's possible to create a patchwork collage of a holiday or party and get it printed on A3 or larger paper for framing – again, just one per holiday, or even per year (perhaps of each child), or to document the life of a much loved and departed pet. You can buy monitors on which a random selection of one's stored digital photos will appear in an ever-changing display (some can also be programmed to communicate via WiFi with various photo-sharing sites and accept incoming pictures sent by others; see 0844 922 1010/www.firebox.com). And there are digital picture frames that can be loaded up with fifty or so photographs that can be changed at the press of a button or run as a continuous slideshow; these can be a wonderful present for someone going to live abroad, or embarking on a long spell in hospital.

✳ *Photo sharing*: Computer sites such as Flickr (www.flickr.com) allow you to display your photos in collages, exhibitions and slideshows, either on your own website (if you have one) or through sites such as Facebook and MySpace. They are good ways of displaying and sharing photos of a big event such as a wedding, party or school reunion so that everyone present or interested can browse through them at their leisure and download what they want. It's also a great way of storing favourite images from all over the place that you love or find inspiring, filed by category, date, place, person or any other criterion. Once you master the pretty basic technology, it's a doddle and can become a most seductive way in which to while away the hours.

✳ *Send off*: When sorting your existing printed-out photos, there will be endless repetitions, or spare shots that will not make their way into a frame or album. Make it a project to send some, straight away, to people who might appreciate them; tuck them in with a letter, or just stick on to postcards with a few personal lines on the back. Others – such as landscape shots or close-up shots of flowers or plants – can be made into greetings cards by sticking on to white or coloured card. Digital photos can be shared in the same way: print them out when you think of it and send or email them off, or choose particularly pretty generic shots and print on to matt card to be used as postcards or birthday cards.

✳ *Presents*: If a framed photograph seems too old-hat, you can always get favourite photographs collated into calendars or printed on to everything from T-shirts to handbags and mugs. Many high street photo stores now do this, or visit www. photobox.co.uk.

✳

Start a blog: Among all the nerdy and boring stuff, there are a lot of beautiful visual blogs out there. The ones I look at tend to be geared around gardening or crafts (see www.yarn storm.blogs.com and similar). For inspiration visit www.liivian talossa.blogspot.com – unless you speak Finnish you won't understand a word, but the record of this Finnish woman's daily domestic life with her young daughter, interspersed with breathtaking nature shots, is touching and inspiring – and http://3191/visualblogging.com for pairs of photographs taken every morning (2007) and evening (2008) documenting the different lives of two friends who live 3,191 miles apart. I have recently started my own (reached via www.elspeththompson. co.uk) and have enjoyed all the comments from America and beyond (indeed, checking on its progress can become strangely addictive) but find it time-consuming to keep up.

❧ · *Compile a Recipe Book/Box* · ❧

One of the objects I'd rescue from our house if it caught fire is the recipe book I've kept since my teenage years. In it, in the various permutations of my handwriting over the years, are much loved and repeated recipes for everything from my favourite cheese pie (see opposite page) to Auntie Audrey's gingerbread and those for minestrone (pp.209–10) and tiramisu learned as an au pair in Italy. Especially prized (though I did not realize it at the time) are the recipes copied out or photocopied from others in their own hand, including my grandmothers, who died decades ago. In recent years I've made a habit of asking people whose dishes I have particularly enjoyed to write me out their recipes on scraps of paper and have simply stuck them into the pages of my book. If you do not have such a book, it's never too late to begin one. Buy an attractive book or ring binder (it's useful if the book can lie flat while you are working) with alphabetical sections and ask everyone from parents and grandparents to friends and the owner of that little village restaurant on holiday in Greece for contributions. Done carefully, these collections can be as evocative of time and place as any diary, and make wonderful heirlooms to pass on. Boxes of postcards are another alternative (you can even pick up old 1970s ones in junk shops), but I find the cards too small to fit in newspaper cuttings and the like.

You can also incorporate recipes from books that you want or need to get rid of. When we first moved into our London house, twelve years ago, I had some slim shelves built, alongside those that house our glasses, on which to store my collection of recipe books. All those years of Christmas and birthday presents later, it is hard to keep the books within their bounds, in spite of several culls. But before taking unwanted books to the second-hand shop, I always trawl through them and copy out the few recipes I think I might use regularly.

A customized recipe book along the above lines would also make a great gift for a son/daughter/godchild leaving for college or to set up home on their own.

 FAVOURITE CHEESE PIE

A sort of anglicized version of the *spanakopita* served in Greece, this goes down well at parties, picnics, or as a light lunch with salad, and is wolfed down by vegetarians and non-vegetarians alike. It takes about ten minutes to make but no one would know from its professional-looking, puffed and golden appearance and heavenly taste. Keep the ingredients in your freezer/ fridge/ larder so you can make it whenever the need or inclination arises; the amounts don't need to be absolutely precise, and the inner ingredients can be added to. Mushrooms, for instance, make a welcome addition, as do sliced leftover boiled potatoes.

Cheese pie

500g puff pastry (frozen or ready-made is fine)
milk or extra beaten egg for brushing
1 free-range egg (2 if additional fillings are added)
110g strong cheddar cheese, grated
2 handfuls of washed spinach leaves, shredded (fresh is best;
   frozen equivalent will do, if well drained)
pinch of English mustard
ground black pepper
100g feta cheese (optional)

Preheat the oven to 220°C/425°F/gas mark 7. Roll the pastry into 2 oblongs around 24 x 36cm (to fit the base of a greased swiss roll tin, baking tray or similar). Lay one oblong in the base of the tin and brush the edges with beaten egg or milk. Mix the egg and grated cheese in a bowl and stir in the spinach and mustard. Season with black pepper. Spread on to the pastry base and crumble the feta over (if using). Cover with the second oblong, sealing well, turning over the edges and crimping with your fingers. Brush with egg or milk and mark the top lightly in a lattice design. Bake for 15–20 minutes and then, if needed, reduce the temperature to 190°C/375°F/gas mark 5 and cook for a further 10 minutes until the top is puffed up and golden brown. It is best served warm.

◈ · *Make a Movie* · ◈

Many of the ideas mentioned in the photography section (pp.39–50) can be adapted in movie format. Making films used to be a far more fiddly and expensive process than it is now, thanks to small, relatively cheap digital camcorders that can be wired directly into a laptop for editing and showing. This is not something I have managed to do myself yet, but, inspired by a good friend's example, I intend to try. After a handful of lessons in filming and editing (included in the price of her laptop when she bought it from the Apple Shop in Regent Street, London), she has edited down many hours of footage from a family holiday in Cornwall into a wonderfully quirky ten-minute film set to music that perfectly evokes the spirit of a seaside holiday. The opening sequence sees her two daughters write the word 'Cornwall' in pebbles in the sand, and at the end they dismantle it, throwing the stones into the sea. It's a wonderful document, both of the holiday, and of that particular time in the girls' lives – still very much children, but edging into adulthood.

Though photographs are much my preferred method of documenting my life, I do think it's worth taking at least some moving film of family and friends to keep for posterity. We've come a long way from the grainy, jerky, black and white Super8 films of my generation's childhoods, and yet today's offerings are every bit as evocative and conducive to nostalgia. There's nothing like footage of a child's first wobbly steps, or of a now departed member of the family laughing into the camera, to take you straight back to a particular time and place.

❧ • *Reinstate the Nature Table* • ❧

Draped in a white cloth and bearing objects of seasonal inter-est, the nature table figured large in the classrooms of my child-hood. In recent years, due, no doubt, to some EC regulation or another, it has disappeared, though *Country Living* magazine has conducted a spirited campaign to reinstate it. But there is no reason why this simple way of honouring and enjoying the seasons should not become part of our homes as well, whether or not you have children. Since the arrival of my young daugh-ter, I've enjoyed making a place where we can display the finds we pick up on our walks, but I get so much out of it that I wish I'd done it long before she was on the scene.

Don't worry if there's no room for an actual table; we use a large white plate, but a small tray is just as good (and portable), or even the top of the telly. All that's needed is room to display a few feathers or fallen leaves, pretty shells or stones, shiny conkers or dried seedcases and perhaps a small vase in which to put flowers or a sprig or two of blossom. Place it somewhere where you are likely to see and admire it each day – in the hall, for instance, or on the kitchen table. You could even make a seasonal collage or mobile (using fishing wire and twigs or lengths of wood) with the objects you have found. Be mindful of what you take: it's usually against the law to remove more than a few shells and stones from beaches, and to pick wild-flowers or plants growing in parks. But a few fallen or bent sprigs are fine in my book, particularly as they're going to get far more attention and admiration in my house than they would do in the wild. And, come the change in season, returning the objects to where you found them becomes part of the ritual of the changing year. Particularly prized stones or shells, or seed-heads that have dried well can be incorporated into other more permanent displays such as mosaics, mobiles or unusual Christmas or autumnal decorations (see pp.175–6 and 189). And if you meditate (see pp.314–5), they can take pride of place on a home altar.

⟨⟩ • *Start an Anthology* • ⟨⟩

I still have the large hardback notebook, covered in beige flow-ered Laura Ashley fabric, in which I started my own anthology of favourite poems, lyrics and fragments of prose when in the sixth form at school. It makes great reading: from stirring hymns and Bob Dylan ballads to melodramatic ravings from Henry Miller's *Tropic of Cancer*, copied down during a break-up with a boyfriend, my drunken scrawlings smudged with tears. Give or take a few howlers, it's amazing how many of the passages are still among my favourites. In fact, I found leafing through my anthology so enjoyable that I've decided to take it up again, starting at the blank pages rather than compiling a new book. Choose a good big book or ring file, and have an index, or at least a section in which you copy down lines you think might one day be useful at a wedding or funeral, or to comfort a bereaved friend, as there's nothing more frustrating than failing to find a good poem when you need one – although these days practically everything seems to be available on the internet, just by tapping a few key words into Google.

❧ • *Write a Journal* • ❧

All over my house – by the bedside, stacked on shelves and packed away in boxes – are thick hardback notebooks of a certain size, the first quarter to a third of pages filled with writing and the rest empty. These are my (usually) failed attempts to keep a diary. The only one I managed to keep all year and beyond was the one I started when I became pregnant and continued through my daughter's birth and the first year of her life. And perhaps there is something to be learned here. Rather than reviving the general, all-round approach to journal-keeping of our own childhoods ('Got up, got dressed, brushed teeth etc.) why not keep a diary geared to recording in detail a single aspect of your life – from attempts to get fit to the creation of a garden. Or, instead of attempting to record the events of a day in their entirety, restrict yourself to an agreed number of sentences. It could be three: one on the weather, one on your mood and the last on the major event in the day. Or, inspired by the popular blog Three Beautiful Things (www. threebeautifulthings.blogspot.com), it could be a day's-end focus on three things that gave you pleasure, from a child's smile on waking to a compliment from a friend to a conversation overheard in a shop. In her companion site, Once Around the Park (www.oncearoundthepark.blogspot.com) this blogger (known only as Clare from Tunbridge Wells) sums up – or recounts a single aspect of – her daily walk around the park in just thirty words. Not only are these shorter journals more stimulating and fun to write, they are also far more likely to be reread in the future.

There's no doubt that journal-keeping is a real art, and for further inspiration, I turn to my favourite examples of the craft:

- Derek Jarman's *Modern Nature*: In which his struggles with Aids are interspersed with accounts of his no less heroic efforts to coax a garden from the stony beach of Dungeness in Kent, with snippets of poems and plant lore spliced in between.
- May Sarton's *Journal of a Solitude* and *The House by the Sea*: Both document the quiet contemplative life of a poet shot through with a fierce, fiery love for family, friends and the flowers in her garden.
- Brother Roger of Taizé's *Festival*: The founder of the Taizé community in France writes lyrically and with great honesty about the challenges and blessings of community life.

◈ • *'Browse' a Museum or Art Gallery* • ◈

Rather than setting aside a whole day or afternoon to 'do' a big museum or gallery in its entirety, I'm a great fan of 'dipping in' to them to look at only one room or a small collection in depth, take in a couple of favourite paintings or show a child just one extraordinary exhibit. After wasting an entire precious day in Paris getting lost, brain-befuddled and exhausted in the bowels of the Louvre, I swore never again to try to see too much at one time – it's actually counter-productive. A quick 'culture fix' at the weekend can also be a great antidote to shopping and other chores. For a while this practice seemed threatened by compulsory charges, but thankfully most museums are now free again and a fantastic resource. For city dwellers, it's a real privilege to

Games For a Wet Weekend

The following can be enjoyed by people of all ages – just vary the words/names etc. to suit the participants.

In the Manner of the Adverb

The person who is 'it' thinks of an adverb (e.g.: benevolently, sexily, nonchalantly, rudely). The others take it in turns to give them certain tasks – such as scratch their ear, ask the time, take off an item of clothing – which must be done 'in the manner of the adverb'. The person who guesses the adverb is 'it' next. Older children and adults can get completely hysterical and it's better than charades as people cannot complain that they have never heard of the title being enacted.

Names in the Hat

To prepare, everyone taking part has to write down as many names of famous or not-so-famous people (which can include those present) as they can on slips of paper (ideally at least 50 for 5–10 people) which are then put in a hat. A timer is set for one minute, while the first player takes out names from the hat, one by one, and tries to describe the person in question without mentioning their name. If someone is able to name the person from their description, the player picking the names keeps that slip of paper; however, if they are having difficulty or have not heard of the person, they can replace that slip in the hat. They keep on picking names till the time is up, then pass to the next player, until all the slips of paper are used up. You can, at this point, count up each player's slips and announce a winner, but a fun version repeats the method, with the proviso that only three words can be used to describe the person. For a final round, no words at all may be used, and the person must be mimed (as everyone knows the names in the hat by now, this is easier than it sounds and can be very funny).

The Book Game

Great fun for older children and upwards, and can get wildly

competitive if literary types are present. One person chooses a book from the shelves – the less well known the better – and writes down the first sentence in secret. The other players are then given the title of the book, and have to try to make up a feasible first sentence which they write on a slip of paper. The slips of paper are then handed in and read out (numbered anonymously) by the person who chose the book, with the 'real' one inserted somewhere, and the others have to try to spot the real one (writing down the number). A point is awarded for spotting the right excerpt, and two for each time your own version is guessed by someone else. The winner is the one with the most points once everyone has chosen a book. This game is particularly good in rented holiday cottages where no one is familiar with the books on the shelves.

Alphabet City

The players come up with ten or so categories: cities, countries, pop songs, foods, sportsmen and women, items of clothing, diseases and so on. A letter of the alphabet is then chosen, and a timer set for, say, five minutes while everyone tries to write down one word in each category beginning with that letter. When the time is up, everyone reads out their entry for each category in turn, scoring 1 point for every category where they had thought of a word, and 5 points when no one else had picked their choice.

have world-class museums and galleries almost on our own doorstep. I still get a thrill from walking into the imposing main entrance of the Victoria and Albert Museum, the stunning covered courtyard of the British Museum or the cavernous Turbine Room at Tate Modern, with its sloping concrete walkway and beguiling acoustics. And I enjoy making similar short forays on visits to other cities, in the UK and abroad. After a short visit, adults and children alike emerge energized, brimming with ideas and enthusiasm for the next.

Some favourite examples in central London

The Rothko Room at Tate Modern: A gallery to sit and meditate in if ever there was one.

The Cast Courts and Fakes and Forgeries Room at the V&A: Totally fascinating. I spot something new whenever I visit.

William Blake at Tate Britain: His otherworldly genius shines through ever more brightly in the atmospheric gloom.

The Jameel Gallery of Islamic art at the V&A: Some 400 objects of exquisite beauty in one of the most extensive and renowned collections of Islamic art in the world.

Whatever is on at the Royal Academy Sackler Galleries: Just to enjoy the journey up in the modern glass-walled lift.

Many city museums and galleries now do evening openings, which can be a wonderful opportunity to take in an exhibition or share a few favourite pictures or pieces with a friend or partner (allow two or three each) before going out to dinner together. Try dinner at Tate Modern, with the restaurant's stunning views over London, followed by a dip into the galleries for a great Saturday night date.

Favourite smaller regional museums and galleries

The UK excels at these, with gems ranging from state-of-the-art modern edifices to tumbledown temples to obscure or eccentric crafts or trades. A roll-call of the best would include:

✱ *The Sailors' Reading Room, Southwold, Suffolk*: A lovely old room right on the seafront where you can sit and read the papers, look at the local exhibits in the glass-fronted cabinets and peer at portraits of sailors old and young from across the centuries.

✱ *The Fishermen's Museum, Hastings, East Sussex*: In 1956 local people concerned about preserving the town's maritime history took over the old Fishermen's Church, knocked down part of a wall and pulled inside one of the last old luggers (sailing fishing boats), the *Enterprise*, which only just fits. Packed in around it are models, photos, paintings, nets, ropes and other fishing artefacts.

✱ *Kettle's Yard, Cambridge*: One of the most inspiring and beautiful places in the world – the former home of art curator Jim Ede, who took as much trouble in the placement of plants and pebbles as he did in the positioning of invaluable works of art.

✱ *District Museum for the Warner Textile Archive, Braintree, Essex*: A unique record of the manufacture and design of textiles over the past 200 years, housed in the original nineteenth-century mill where most of the textiles were created.

✳ *Kew Palace, Royal Botanic Gardens, Kew, Surrey*: The restoration of King George III's country retreat and Britain's smallest royal palace revealed rooms that had not been seen for 200 years, with a ghostly, atmospheric sound and shadow display.

✳ *De La Warr Pavilion, Bexhill-on-Sea, East Sussex*: One of the world's finest examples of Modernist architecture, now a leading centre for contemporary art, architecture, education and live performance (even if, on my last visit, true to the town's reputation as a retirement zone, one of the exhibitions was on the history of the hearing aid).

✳ *Horniman Museum, London*: Eclectic displays acquired by a Victorian collector and given a recent revamp, including a fantastic new-look aquarium.

✳ *Pallant House, Chichester, West Sussex*: One of the world's best twentieth-century British art collections, housed in a stunning contemporary building space and Queen Anne townhouse.

✳ *Weston Park Museum, Sheffield*: Victorian treasure-house highlighting the best from Sheffield's archaeology, natural and social history, visual and decorative art collections.

All national museums across the country have been free since 2001. To find museums in your local area or check details and opening hours of the above visit www.24hourmuseum.org.uk or ring 01273 623266.

◈ · *Watch the Sunset* · ◈

At the end of the gruelling but beautiful film of Paul Bowles's novel, *The Sheltering Sky*, the narrator (Bowles) remarks:

Because we don't know when we will die, we get to think of life as an inexhaustible well. Yet everything happens only a certain number of times, and a very small number really. How many times will you remember a certain afternoon that's so deeply a part of your being that you can't even conceive of your life without it? Perhaps four or five times, perhaps not even that. How many more times will you watch the full moon rise? Perhaps twenty. And yet it all seems so limitless.

How right he is. For half an hour or so a night, on a fairly regular basis, the sky puts on an amazing free light show of spectacular colours, shafts of light and shifting clouds. The least we can do is take the time to watch. Of course, it's easier in the country, or by the sea where the skies are bigger and the view unimpeded by buildings. But even in the thick of the inner city you can climb a hill, book into a top-floor bar such as the one at London's Hilton, haul yourself up to your roof or simply seek out a friend with a west-facing terrace. If the signs are promising – a good pinkish glow to the west, and fine weather with a few interesting cloud formations – why not plan a little expedition in search of the sunset? Take whatever you think will make the experience more enjoyable – a friend or partner, a pet dog, a blanket for lying on, a camera or notebook, even a bottle of wine (and glasses and corkscrew) with which to toast the last rays. (On a motherly note, don't forget that the temperature often plummets the moment the sun disappears, so make sure you won't freeze on your way home.) When you get there, sit back and contemplate and enjoy. And resolve to do it more often.

⬥ · *Get Involved* · ⬥

Getting involved in your local community, campaigning or volunteering for a charity might seem like yet another chore to work through during your already busy weekend. But sitting at home watching the news and thinking how wrong so many things are in the world is pretty stressful too, as is seeing local shops, parks and other amenities suffer as a result of cuts or unwelcome developments.

Campaigning

Done in the right spirit, campaigning can be fun; indeed it's always going to be easier to convert people to a cause through activities that are enjoyable, and which connect them to what they love about the world, than by mongering doom and gloom. Waiting for politicians to bring about changes is never going to get things done. Just one person's conviction and energy can make a whole lot of difference, as Rebecca Hosking proved when she inspired her home town of Modbury in Devon to become the first plastic bag-free town in the UK. Many other towns and villages are now following suit. Then there's Hugh Fearnley-Whittingstall with his chickens; and the band of 1980s clubbers who founded the splendid Trees for London (now Trees for Cities) as they walked home from raves in the early hours and noticed how much leafier the richer areas of the city were compared to the poorer quarters. There are many other causes that would appreciate your help, from banning more airports to building cycle paths to guerrilla gardening in cities to protesting against the planting of GM crops. You might be inspired to volunteer your time, or it might just be a case of sending the odd letter or e-mail. See the Think Local section (pp.67–9) for more locally based ideas. Here are a few national and international campaigns to get you thinking, or maybe telephoning, or e-mailing . . . It feels better than doing nothing – and may do the world of good.

A few campaigns and charities

✳ *Amnesty International* (020 7413 5500/www.amnesty.org)
Campaigns for human rights worldwide, an end to torture and the release of wrongly held prisoners. Its well-organized site takes you through the steps to join and help out by donating money or writing letters.

✳ *Avaaz* (www.avaaz.org)
'Avaaz' translates as 'voice' in various languages, and this new website, just over a year old, makes the most of new media to drum up effective e-mail petitions protesting about a wide variety of current global issues, from the effects of climate change to the plight of Tibet. It's not just e-activism, however: you can volunteer to help with research, translation or direct action, experiences of which are detailed in the blogs.

✳ *Campaign for the Protection of Rural England* (020 7981 2800/ www.cpre.org.uk)
A strange but wonderful alliance of old-school, right-wing

huntin', shootin' and fishin' types and the rural radical fringe, all of whom are fed up with the current government's mishandling of countryside issues. The current planning white paper, with its potential to exclude the public from participation in the planning process for everything from new homes on flood plains to nuclear power stations, is rightly a target for action.

✳ *Mast Sanity* (08704 322377/www.mastsanity.org)
Mobile phone and Tetra masts are sprouting up around the country, often with no planning consent or consultation, and in the face of scanty research as to their long-term hazards to health. Mast Sanity is a good first port of call if your local area is threatened with an unwanted mast; it has provided information, research, advice and practical tools for fighting against or removing countless installations.

✳ *Compassion in World Farming* (01483 521950/www.ciwf.org.uk)
The life's work of the late Michael Sutcliffe, this campaign currently has four drives to bring about change in farming practice, targeting egg-laying hens, broiler meat, live export and convincing the public to eat less meat. All forms of action are welcome, from signing e-petitions to attending demonstrations – even participating in media stunts.

✳ *Tibetan Children's Villages* (00 91 1892 221348/www.tibchild.org)
Around £200 per year sponsors a refugee child in one of the Tibetan Children's Villages in India, set up by the Dalai Lama's sister to care for exiled children and keep the Tibetan culture alive. You can also exchange letters with your sponsored child

and the women who care for and teach them. A friend who has done this for twenty years since her own children were small has found this tremendously enriching for all her family.

* *Walk to School* (020 7820 1010/www.walktoschool.co.uk)
More than half the children in this country are driven to school, to the detriment of their own health as well as the environment. The campaign provides lots of practical ideas and inspiration from schools that have made it work with 'walking buses', walking to a central school bus pick-up point and so on.

* *This Is Me Reporting* (www.thisismereporting.com)
Share the news on your own campaigns and community efforts through this grassroots site, started on a computer in a hallway and now with 50,000 visitors per month, all by word of mouth.

Think local

More and more these days, people are banding together to protect their local environment and provide facilities, from community child care and car-pooling to communal food production. Clubbing together with other people in your community of like mind is a good way to get things done, lessen the load and responsibility on individuals, and make some new friends into the bargain.

* *The Transition Towns movement* (www.transitiontowns.org) can provide an organizational model for those who seek to fight the twin challenges of peak oil and climate change with local food and energy production and endeavouring to cut the community's

carbon footprint. The website is a source of inspiration and information from all the communities, from Totnes in Devon to Brixton, south London, that are in the process of adopting it.

✳ *Common Ground* (01747 850820/www.commonground.org.uk) is an arts and environmental charity that helps people celebrate and preserve their everyday surroundings by offering information and ideas on everything from saving land under threat to making or commissioning artwork to celebrate a particular place to planting a community orchard.

✳ *Taking on an allotment* (see pp.280–5) is a great way to meet local people of all ages – or how about a spot of guerrilla gardening? Inspired by Liz Christie, who threw 'seed bombs' of soil and flower seed into derelict lots and sowed sunflowers along the central traffic reservations in New York City in the 1970s, Richard Reynolds, a young Londoner, has transformed neglected land around London bus stops and roundabouts, and the blog on his site, www.guerrillagardening.org, has inspired many others to do the same. Look around you for potential guerrilla sites: a litter-strewn turf verge, a weed-ridden roundabout, a large planter whose contents the council have allowed to die. A few packets of sunflower or nasturtium seeds, some leftover plants or seedlings, a clear night and a trusty assistant or two are all you need to make a real difference. I'm not saying this is legal – and I wouldn't like to encourage anyone to break the law – but the world is definitely a brighter place for such acts of horticultural heroism.

Or you might want to start a car-share scheme (Carshare

08700 780225/www.carshare.com has details of groups all over the UK), or campaign to save your local park or prevent yet another new supermarket being built. Talk to local friends and neighbours, tack up a poster in a health food shop or post office window, or visit www.myneighbourhoods.co.uk to be put in touch with local events and other like-minded people in your area. Or why not join your local residents' association? This might seem to smack of middle-aged Middle England, but a bit of new blood might be just what it needs. If nothing else, you could help organize a jolly good street party.

Volunteering

Volunteering is another great way of helping a good cause while also meeting new people and getting involved in your local community. There are loads of opportunities, from tree planting and conservation work to visiting people in hospitals or hospices (even taking a dog or pet with you: see www.petplanet.co.uk for further details). Your local museum or stately home may need volunteers to help collect money or show round visitors; or you could learn at the same time by working in the garden (many large gardens in the UK, including those owned by the National Trust, have excellent volunteer programmes – see p.70). Or perhaps you could help out at your local stables or dog kennels; take inner-city or disadvantaged children on country outings; clean up beaches or beauty spots. It's a matter of fitting your personality and skills to the opportunities available. A few years ago, I spent a spell helping look after the plants and gardens at a London hospice. Without the excuse of looking after their bedside plants, I might have found it difficult to strike up conversations with the people there, but that simple shared subject gave us somewhere to start, and I found the experience tremendously enriching. We even did some bedside planting of bulbs and sowing seeds; people seemed to like the hope and optimism involved, even if they knew they themselves would probably not be there to see the flowers grow.

Make a list of the sort of work you feel you can do, or would like to learn how to do. And visit websites such as www.volunteering.org.uk (0845 305 6979); www.justgive.org (for a useful list of various categories of different volunteer work); www.do-it.org.uk (type in your postcode for local opportunities); www.timebank. org.uk and www.nationaltrust. org.uk for more ideas and inspiration. If you are stuck in a spell of despond or depression, helping people less fortunate than yourself can be a great way of putting a new perspective on things and beginning to dig a way out. A friend of mine was marooned in a serious, clinically diagnosed depression which only lifted when she dragged herself out and began helping in a homeless hostel. It might seem like just another job to factor into a busy weekend, so don't take on more than you can manage. But altruism can be invigorating – and sometimes a change really can be as good as a rest.

❧ · *Gratitude* · ❧

In his extraordinary book *The Hidden Messages in Water*, Japanese Professor Masaru Emoto establishes a link between our emotional and physical states and declares that the best state of mind for all-round well-being is one of 'two parts gratitude, one part love'. I'm inclined to agree with him. My mother, a great fan of the book *Pollyanna*, in which a young girl goes through life trying to find the good in every situation, held no truck with my inevitable episodes of feeling fed up as a child. 'Think of all the good things you have,' she would trill, 'nice family, nice friends, a nice face . . .' and so on. Though I rebelled against it in my teenage years, of course, I have now very much returned to her way of thinking, convinced it's not only cheaper but heaps more effective than years of one-on-one therapy in a dreary darkened room – and much more fun to boot. 'Gratitude keeps the door wide open,' as the old saying goes; and I try to make it my practice, if I feel my heart beginning to close through anger, anxiety or irritation, to concentrate on gratitude in order to heave its portals open again. After years of trying, provided I get there in good time, by focusing on gratitude I usually find I can turn my mood around in a matter of minutes. Being grateful anchors you in the here and now – our only opportunity in which to be happy, not when we're finally rich/thin/in love with the right person or living in a different house. Psychologists such as the American author Denis Waitley believe that being grateful is a significant step in the path towards achieving that holy grail called happiness. 'Happiness cannot be travelled to, owned, earned, worn or consumed,' he says. 'Happiness is the spiritual experience of living every minute with love, grace and gratitude.'

Other ideas for nurturing a sense of gratitude include keeping a 'gratitude journal' – an idea spread by Oprah Winfrey which has had surprisingly far-reaching and positive effects on people suffering from depression, alcohol and drug addiction and the like. It's basically a little notebook you keep by your bed and in which you write, each night before you go to sleep, five things for which you are grateful. These might be qualities or relationships, as on my mother's list from my childhood, that you've had for some time, or they might be large or small events that have happened to you, or that you have witnessed, in the course of the day. No matter how bad the day might have seemed, there will always be something. (If you are desperate, this quote from Buddha might help: 'Let us rise up and be thankful, for if we didn't learn a lot today, at least we learned a little, and if we didn't learn a little, at least we didn't get sick, and if we got sick, at least we didn't die; so, let us all be thankful.')

Going through this process with children is a good way to help them remember the best from their day as they slip into bed; sharing the process with a partner can be helpful, even healing, especially in troubled times. My mother was right all those years ago: this really, really works. This quote from self-help author Melodie Beattie seems to say it all:

Gratitude unlocks the fullness of life. It turns what we have into enough, and more. It turns denial into acceptance, chaos to order, confusion to clarity. It can turn a meal into a feast, a house into a home, a stranger into a friend. It turns problems into gifts, failures into success, the unexpected into perfect timing, and mistakes into important events. Gratitude makes sense of our past, brings peace for today, and creates a vision for tomorrow.

◈ • *Have Sex* • ◈

Well, a book on life's simple pleasures has got to come round to this one sooner or later. Far be it from me to tell you how to conduct your love life, but just in case yours could do with spicing up, read *The Modern Kama Sutra* by Kamini and Kirk Thomas, leave *She Comes First: The Thinking Man's Guide to Pleasuring a Woman* by sex therapist Ian Kerner lying around, or visit Coco de Mer (www.coco-de-mer.com) and the Women's Erotic Emporium (www.sh-womenstore.com) for sensual suggestions that won't scare the horses. Some people even set aside a couple of days for the proverbial Dirty Weekend; dependent on budget, energy and inclination this could involve ideas from Stay In Bed All Day (pp.316–21) or Going Away (p.232).

2.

Seasonal Pleasures: Spring

'Oh, to be in England, now that April's there!' Robert Browning's poem, shot through with yearning for his native land, was one of my favourites during the year I spent as an au pair in Italy many years ago. Like him, I'd enjoyed the mild Mediterranean winter and welcomed the blue skies and clear air. But, come April, cooped up in a city with too many people and far too few trees, I too was nostalgic for home. In fact, I don't think there is any place I would rather be than in England in springtime, when even the city streets are billowing improbably with cherry blossom in every shade from white to deepest crimson, and the country lanes are frothing with cow parsley. The hedgerows are full of primroses and wild garlic, with sheets of bluebells still to come, and the young leaves opening are the lightest, brightest shades of lime green and chartreuse. Birds are singing, lambs are gambolling, the sun is (sometimes) shining and all is well with the world – no matter what the economists and environmentalists might be saying. Small wonder spring festivals are celebrations of fresh life and renewal: you can almost feel your body waking up in the sunshine, just like the leaves and the flowers. Time to sow seeds, watch buds open, hear the dawn chorus, make a Simnel cake, plan an Easter egg hunt and celebrate Valentine's Day, Easter and Mothering Sunday; and how about a detox, to spring-clean your body as well as your home?

❖❖❖   *Celebrate Valentine's Day*   ❖❖❖

On 14 February garage forecourts up and down the country will be doing a brisk trade in tired daffs and jet-lagged lilies sent halfway around the world and marked up to double the price for the day. But it's not hard to come up with something far more original and romantic. All it takes is a little time and inge-nuity. The weekend before Valentine's Day falls is the perfect time to make an extra-special fuss of your loved one, or to plan a treat for the day itself.

Many years ago, in the early days of our courtship, I gained secret access to my husband's *Young Ones*'-type flat via his housemate and installed troughs of daffodils along his window ledges. I knew he would not be observant enough to spot them from outside when he came in (the flat was on the second floor), but when he drew open the curtains on Valentine's morning, there they all were, just bursting into bloom. I've even heard of people writing 'I LOVE YOU' or 'MARRY ME' in bulbs or bedding plants on the lawn, but this would involve either dig-ging up the lawn (which could well backfire) or planning and planting it up the previous autumn, thus displaying a distinct-ly unromantic lack of spontaneity – not to mention running the risk that passions might have cooled in the interim.

No, smaller gestures are every bit as welcome. One of the most romantic, to me, is the heart made from her partner's and children's shoes laid out on the floor that greeted a friend of mine when she came downstairs in the morning. Okay, it helped that the shoes and the floor were all beautiful and the light falling on them just right, but it was the resourcefulness and creativity behind it that she most valued. Even if (as she suspects was the truth), her man had only remembered at the last minute, there was no nipping out to the service station for him. She still treasures the Polaroid photo she took of it.

If you are set on flowers, how about giving a living plant instead of a bunch of blooms? If it simply has to be red roses – and they are the traditional 'I love you' flower, after all – a live bush is a lot more suggestive of lasting passions than a bunch of roses almost guaranteed to droop when still in bud (the remedy here, by the way, is to cut an inch off the base of the stems and sear them in boiling water for twenty seconds). Look through Peter Beales's (01953 454707/www.classicroses.co.uk) and David Austin's (01902 376300/www.davidaustinroses.com) catalogues for some really gorgeous reds, from the deep velvety hues of Empereur du Maroc and the neat modern climber Guinee to the scarlet, single-flowered species *Rosa moyesii* or sweet, spicy-scented Souvenir du Docteur Jamain beloved of Vita Sackville-West. Some have names as beautiful and romantic as their flowers: check out fiery, floriferous Intrigue or, if pink is preferable to red, coral-pink Belle Amour or pink-tinged Cuisse de Nymph. The only problem with giving a rose bush at this time of year, little patio roses forced into bloom aside, is that they are likely to resemble a bundle of thorny twigs

The Language of Flowers

Anemone – 'I expect you'

Arum lily – 'Burning love'

Bluebell – 'Our love will last'

Camellia – 'I am longing for you'

Carnation (red) – 'I am carrying a torch for you'

Carnation (striped) – 'Wish I were with you'

Carnation (white) – 'Always remembering'

Carnation (yellow) – 'You have disappointed me'

Daffodil – 'The sun always shines when I am with you'

Dahlia – 'You are indifferent'

Foxglove – 'I cannot trust you'

Heather – 'Good luck'

Honeysuckle – 'Devotion'

Hyacinth – 'Please forgive me'

Lily of the valley – 'You are sweet and pure'

Love-in-a-mist – 'Do you love me?'

Magnolia – 'Have courage'

Marguerite – 'I live in hope'

Narcissus – 'You are selfish'

Orchid – 'You have cast a spell over me'

Pansy – 'I am thinking of you'

Peony – 'Bashfulness'

Pinks – 'You are bold'

Poppy – 'Please wait'

Primrose – 'I might love you'

Rose (pink) – 'Please believe me'

Rose (red) – 'I love you'

Rose (white) – 'You are divine'

Rose (yellow) – 'Please come back soon'

Stock – 'Lasting beauty'

Sweet pea – 'Gratitude'

Violet – 'I am faithful evermore'

Wallflower – 'Constancy'

in a pot. If your Valentine has a sense of humour, you could always tie a few fake plastic or paper flowers on to the bare branches with ribbon, or, to be on the safe side, present a single, stunning, deep black-red Baccarat cut rose alongside.

But roses are not the only flower of romance. According to my old embossed copy of *Flower Lore* (published 1880), many other flowers had associations that were every bit as romantic. Myrtle, for instance, has been a symbol of 'glory and happiness in love' since Ancient Roman times and was used down the ages in wedding rituals. Indeed, fluffy white myrtle flowers figured large in Queen Victoria's own wedding bouquet, and many of the myrtle plants in public and private gardens in southern England are directly descended from a tree in the grounds of Osborne House that her gardener grew from a cutting. A small tree or bush of *Myrtis communis*, prettily wrapped and with a card explaining the symbolism, would make a great gift for male and female Valentines alike. A potted camellia (I am longing for you), winter honeysuckle (Devotion), violas (Let's take a chance on happiness) or orchid (You have cast a spell over me) would also be most suitable, and all can be found in bloom at this somewhat bleak time of year. For more traditional meanings and symbolism behind flowers, see opposite page.

If you do have to fall back on buying or sending cut flowers for Valentine's Day, might I remind you that beautiful scented Paperwhite narcissi, grown in the famously mild climate of the Scilly Isles, are an environmentally sound alternative to exotics flown in from Kenya and Columbia? (see box on p.82 for more on sending flowers). Just don't let on to the recipient that the Victorian meaning for narcissi is 'You are selfish'. If only the

Sending Flowers

Whether for Valentine's Day, Mothering Sunday, as a thank you for a weekend away, a pick-me-up for someone who is ill or down, or just a nice surprise for someone you love, you can't beat a delivery of fresh flowers. Unless, that is, it consists of garish carnations or chrysanthemums, over-packaged in cellophane and tied with a hideous pink bow. To avoid expensive disasters and ensure gasps of gratitude, use the companies below.

Narcissi from the Scilly Isles
From October to Easter a box of fifty stems, picked at dawn, shipped by noon and sent by first-class post, costs well under £20 (incl. p&p) from Scent from the Islands (01720 422169/ www.scillyflowers.co.uk – last orders usually a couple of days before). For around £25 you get a hundred blooms – enough to fill an entire house, which is both wildly romantic and a wonderful bargain. Be warned, though: in the summer months they supply pinks and carnations, which may not be to everyone's taste.

Forever Flowering (020 8392 9929/www.foreverflowering.com) This stylish, London-based company sends out truly beautiful bouquets by post; you can specify what you want but I would trust the charming and skilful staff entirely. Also flowering plants and shrubs for indoors and out, depending on the season, and optional extra gifts of chocolate and champagne.

Wiggly Wigglers (01981 500391/www.wigglywigglers.co.uk), famed for its wormeries and compost-makers, has recently branched into locally grown flowers by post and its enormous informal bouquets cost from £35 incl. p&p.

The Real Flower Company (01730 818300/
www.realflowers.co.uk) supplies traditional, blowsy, scented roses in more than thirty varieties and a wide range of colours that look as if you had just picked them from your own (30-acre) garden. Really beautiful.

message behind the dreaded yellow carnation ('You have disappointed me') were widely enough known to dissuade any desperate beau from snatching a bunch from a garage on Valentine's eve.

Go Wild Food Foraging

Whether it's wild garlic, sea kale or 'salad greens' that gardeners might more often call 'weeds', there is no doubt that 'wild food' is desirable now. But rather than pay top whack for it at fashionable restaurants and farmers' markets, why not spend some time at the weekend foraging for it yourself? It's easy if you know what to look for and where to find it. Good local knowledge is your best bet, but people can be cagey about their sources. Spring is the ideal time to start, with the hedgerows and woodlands dotted with wild garlic and fresh young leaves and shoots. Arm yourself with a good book on the subject: Richard Mabey's *Food for Free* is the classic pocket-sized guide, but *Edible Wild Plants & Herbs* by Pamela Michael is wonderful, if unwieldy, and offers simple recipes and remedies too. I'm also a fan of a great little book called *Cooking Weeds* by Vivien Weise, which includes tables showing wild food to be up to five times richer in proteins and vitamins than vegetables. So, anyone for braised hop shoots, yarrow polenta, wild garlic tzatziki or even nettle and ground elder pizza? As a gardener, I find it far easier to put up with weeds now that I can not only eat them myself but also feed them with impunity to guests. Here are just a few of my favourite foraged foods.

* *Dandelion*: Known in France as *pissenlit* for its diuretic properties, it is a great cleansing herb for spring, when its small, slightly
bitter leaves are a tasty addition to both mixed leaf and new
potato salads. The bright yellow flowers can also be deep-fried
in batter, like elderflowers – good news for gardeners if you pick
them all before they seed.

* *Lemon balm*: Otherwise known as bee balm or *Melissa offici-
nalis*, it grows readily in gardens and is often found as an
escapee. Chopped and crushed, with hot water added, the
lemony leaves make a fragrant and soothing herbal tea, or can
be added to softened butter to serve with fish (shape into a roll,
firm up in the fridge and cut into rounds).

* *Meadowsweet*: This has a creamy, candy-floss foam of flowers in
midsummer, which are imbued with an uncanny aroma and
taste of honey. Use eight flower-heads to sweeten 750g cooking
apples or rhubarb (with just a tablespoon of sugar added) or
four flowering heads to 300ml water to make a fragrant tea.

* *Stinging nettles*: These can be harvested (wearing gloves, of
course) in spring and early summer, when the tiny top leaves
are young and tender. Wash and remove the stringy stalks, then
add boiling water to make a surprisingly tasty detox tea (see
p.112), or simmer with fried onions and potatoes in vegetable
stock for a really good soup (opposite page).

* *Samphire*: Found growing on salt marshes and tidal mud flats,
this can be fun to pick if you are on a coastal walk and armed

Nettle Vichyssoise

Bursting with vitamins and minerals, this is a far cry from the grey-green sludge often served up in the name of nettle soup. (Don't worry – the sting disappears once cooked!) I defy you not to like it. Add a swirl of cream and some flaked almonds at the end if you want to tart it up. This amount serves 4 and can be consumed cold, as with a traditional Vichyssoise, though I prefer it hot.

butter for cooking
2 onions, chopped
500g potatoes, peeled and cut into pieces
1 litre good vegetable stock
a good bunch of young stinging nettles – at least 100g of
    leaves once stalks and leaf-stems removed
salt and ground black pepper
2 teaspoons lemon juice
100ml cream
flaked almonds and more cream (optional)

Melt the butter and fry the onions and potatoes till the onions are translucent. Add the stock, bring to the boil and simmer for 10 minutes. Wash the nettle leaves (wearing gloves) and add to the soup, cooking for a further 10 minutes. Whizz up with a hand-held blender, season and stir in the lemon juice. Just before serving, stir in the cream.

For a luxury topping, roast flaked almonds in a heavy pan with no fat till light brown, swirl a spoonful of cream into the soup and sprinkle the nuts on top.

with a tide book to tell you when the plants will be safely exposed to the air. The salty taste of the sea seems to be distilled into the fleshy, jointed leaves and stems; you can eat them raw but they are delicious steamed for just a few minutes to preserve that all-important crunch, and served with fresh fish.

* *Wild garlic* (otherwise known as ramsons, broad-leaved garlic or more formally *Allium ursinum*): This grows on shady banks and woodland, where its six-point starry white flowers are one of the joys of spring. Use the leaves chopped up to flavour garlic butter, soups or stews. I went to a wedding once where pickled garlic flowers were served as one of the many delicious home-made pickles and chutneys, but I have not so far found a recipe.

See also:
Sloe gin (pp.170–2)
Elderberry wine syrup (pp.172–3)
Elderflower cordial (pp.120–1)
Blackberry jam (pp.138–40)
Rose petal ice cream (pp.140–1)
Nettle detox tea (p.112)
Mint and fruit ice cubes (p.120)
Mushroom-hunting (pp.162–5)

❀❀❀ *Hear the Dawn Chorus* ❀❀❀

Around the end of April set the alarm early – around 4.30 a.m. if you can bear it, wrap up warm and head for your local woods. Sit – or lie – down and listen; it's as simple as that. Keeping warm is crucial as you have to stay still so as not to startle the birds, so take a blanket or two and even a Thermos of coffee. In fact the only hard thing about this exercise is getting out of bed in the first place – which is why so few people do it. It is worth the effort, though, for the extraordinary sound of hundreds of birds all singing their hearts out at once, from the low, soft 'chook' and frequent 'pink pink pink' of the blackbird, the soothing coos and murmurs of doves and pigeons and familiar 'tik' or quick 'tick-ik-ik-ik' of the robin to the thrill of a warbling thrush or nightin-gale. Scientists seem baffled as to the 'purpose' of birdsong, and the more mystic among their number have even explained it as singing simply for the joy of it, which is a lovely notion. If you're able to persuade a child or two to accompany you on this early morning jaunt, they will never forget the experience.

And if you become addicted to the sound of birdsong – or, indeed, if the alarm fails or you fall back to sleep – an easier, if less magical option is to listen to birdsong on CD or on the radio. This can be a wonderfully soothing start to the day. A temporary station that broadcasts birdsong from an English country garden every day from 6 a.m. to midnight became a hit with half a million listeners earlier this year, and the company behind it has bowed to public pressure for better sound quality and has even upgraded the recording. Listeners have also launched campaigns to keep the station on air after fears it might be replaced with a commercial channel. (It currently appears as Birdsong on DAB digital radio; contact info@digitalone.co.uk for further details.) For more information on the dawn chorus – and on the annual International Dawn Chorus Day, sponsored by the Wildlife Trusts, visit www.idcd.info.

❧ *Observe Lent and Pancake Day* ❧

You don't have to be a Christian to honour Lent, the traditional period of abstinence between Shrove Tuesday and Easter that commemorates the forty days and forty nights Jesus spent fasting in the wilderness. We don't need to do without for that long – indeed, anything in excess of two days without food should only be done under medical supervision – but spring is a good time for a weekend detox (see pp.110–12), or to give up one of our vices for a while. If you want to give up something for Lent, the obvious choices include alcohol, coffee, cigarettes and chocolate. Unless you are incredibly strong-willed, you'll usually do better if you can find an appealing substitute for the offending habit: fruit cordials instead of alcohol, for instance, or a tasty herb tea or milky chai instead of coffee.

Start Lent in style with Pancake Day – and this may be easier to celebrate the weekend before Shrove Tuesday, especially if you are having people for lunch or supper. Everyone loves pancakes for pudding, either plain with sprinkled sugar and lemon, or dolled up with sliced fruit and chantilly cream. The custom stems from the practice of using up all the 'sinful' ingredients in the house in preparation for the ensuing period of abstinence (see basic recipe, opposite). So have a last glass of wine, square of chocolate or biscuit and relish every last drop or crumb. Thereafter, tick off the days as you go, and break your fast with whatever was your forbidden treat on Easter morning. Or, if doing without it hasn't been so bad, why not continue and give it up for good?

Pancakes

Makes about 8 pancakes.

110g plain flour
pinch of salt
1 free-range egg
300ml milk
splash of vegetable oil (helps prevent sticking)
oil or butter for cooking

Sieve the flour and salt into a mixing bowl. Add the egg and beat well with a fork till mixed together. Add the milk gradually, stirring with a whisk till you have a smooth batter (you can use an electric hand-held mixer). Add the oil.

Heat a little oil or butter in a non-stick frying pan. When it is hot but not burning, add a small ladleful of batter, swirling it around till the base of the pan is thinly covered. Pour any excess back into the bowl (the first pancake is always a bit of an experiment). Cook over a medium heat for a couple of minutes till the underside is cooked and golden brown. Shake the pan before tossing to make sure the pancake is free and ready to toss. Toss in the air – as high as you dare! Let the other side cook for a minute or so and pop on a plate in a low oven, covered with foil. Repeat till the batter is finished, and eat rolled or folded up with lemon juice and sugar.

❖ *Watch Buds Burst* ❖

'Look, Mummy, it's opened!' cried my young daughter as we sat down to eat one Saturday lunchtime. In front of her, in a jug of water, was the sprig of horse chestnut we had snapped off a tree in a friend's garden a week ago. Back then it had been hard to convince a small child that this bare twig, with its sticky brown buds, was worth taking home. Gradually, though, after a few days in our cosy kitchen, the dark scaly covering of the biggest bud began to split, revealing a fragment of folded, fuzzy grey-green leaf. Slowly the amount of green grew, until that day, when all three leaves emerged, still folded on the end of soft, silvery stalks, and looking for all the world like an old man of the woods, stretching with clenched fists after a long sleep. This comparison may sound fanciful, but anyone familiar with the nineteenth-century German photographer Karl Blossfeldt's work will know exactly what I mean. On our landing we have a copy of his photograph of just such a bud opening, and it makes me smile whenever I walk past.

It's a delight to share the joys of spring with children, but this everyday miracle can be enjoyed by us all; simply cut a few budding branches and bring them inside. Buds bursting open after the long cold winter are a powerful symbol of change and renewal that can bring new energy into your home and life. Raid a friend's garden if you don't have growth enough to spare in your own; think of it as a little light pruning, taking care to remove branches that are surplus to requirements, confusing the growth habit of the tree or threatening to cross and rub up against other branches on the shrub or tree. Add some wands of forsythia if you have it – to my mind those bright yellow flowers look more at home in a vase than in the border, and it's fun to watch the knobbly brown buds burst open in the warmth. On Easter Sunday, we hang our collection of bright painted eggs from the branches (see pp.102–3).

❧ *Find Some Spring Lamb(s)* ❧

Spotting the first lambs of spring is a joyful thrill. As winter softens into spring, the fields are full of hugely pregnant ewes who seem to get even larger and slower as the weeks wear on. I remember being pregnant myself at this time and sympathizing with them as they stood or lolled about in the grass waiting for D-Day. And then it happens – often, in mystic cosmic mode, around the time of a full moon. Next time you pass the field the energy has changed completely. The grass is dotted with squiggly, jumping white beings that hop about the field, lie curled up in the sun or stand on unsteady legs, nudging and nuzzling at their mothers' undersides for milk.

Whenever I see a field of new lambs I have to stop the car and stand and watch them for a while, even if it means I shall be late for an appointment. It's worth it for the sheer delight of taking in these tender new young lives, the beauty of their little faces and the gentle, though somewhat resigned and distracted, care of the ewes. Best of all is when the lambs suddenly jump up and gambol – yes, gambol is the word for it – across the grass, often leaping up and performing a touching little twist in mid-air.

If you live in the country, it's relatively easy to come across fields of new lambs; indeed, you might be friendly with a farmer who would let you come in and see the lambs at closer quarters, or maybe even watch some being born. There may be orphans or sickly lambs who need bottle-feeding, and this can be enormous fun for children. I remember as a child helping to look after the littlest, runt-like lambs on the farm where I grew up. My father used to come into the kitchen with some poor bedraggled, lifeless little thing in his arms, put it gently into a shoe-box and pop it into the bottom warming compartment of the Aga. Shortly afterwards – we took care to watch the clock! – a total transformation would have taken place. Out the little lamb would come, revived, dry and fluffy and hungry for milk.

Even if you live in town, try to get out at the weekend for a ride to spot some lambs, or visit a farm – those geared to receiving schools and other visitors may have feeding programmes children can help with, and probably Easter chicks to hold into the bargain. But you don't have to be a child to find pleasure in lambs – even the toughest old been-everywhere, done-everything face will soften in their presence, and they're a joy there for the taking. All you have to do is look at the right time and in the right place.

Lambs can appear in the fields as early as February and the season extends well after Easter, when the first lambs will already be putting on weight, developing into chubby little creatures with sturdy legs and surprisingly individual faces. And then, of course, there will come the time when you pass the field and they simply aren't there any more. And we all know where they've gone . . .

The vegetarians among you may find this in bad taste – for which my apologies. Indeed, I've heard of some people – Paul McCartney and his family among them – turning vegetarian as a result of watching the spring lambs from their window. But for me, any disappointment at the departure of the lambs from the fields is pretty much countered by the promise of new season's lamb in the shops. British lamb is among the best in the world, and those raised on salt marshes such as in East Kent and Sussex rank among the tastiest and most succulent. A large roast leg of lamb with redcurrant jelly and mint sauce made from the first sprigs of mint from the garden makes a great Easter lunch for family and friends – and is a further reason to give thanks for those lovely, lively little heralds of spring.

Mothering Sunday

Not 'Mother's Day', if you please – this may be what it's called in America, where the tradition, celebrated in May, is relatively short-lived – but Mothering Sunday, which dates back in the UK to the sixteenth century. For centuries, the middle or fourth Sunday in Lent has been devoted to honouring our mothers. As the one Sunday a year that men and women in service were allowed off duty, a tradition grew up for them to take gifts of cakes, eggs and flowers home to their families. The cake was often a Simnel cake, now associated almost entirely with Easter (see pp.100–101 for recipe); indeed, alternative names for Mothering Sunday include Simnel Sunday and Refreshment Sunday, the latter indicating a customary lapsing of the Lent vows for this 'halfway house' weekend. The flowers were sometimes hot-house lilies and so on, plucked from the greenhouses of the 'big houses' where the domestic staff were working, but more often just wildflowers picked from the meadows and hedgerows in the course of the long journey home on foot.

What is less known is that Mothering Sunday also refers to Christians celebrating and giving thanks to the 'Mother Church': there was a tradition for congregations to attend their nearest larger church or cathedral and to 'clip' or surround it by holding hands. This custom is currently being revived in the UK. To most of us, however, Mothering Sunday in church will continue to mean children coming back down the aisle bearing three short-stemmed daffodils and a sprig of greenery bound together with a damp tissue and a squeeze of silver foil.

Mothering Sunday is a lovely tradition to honour. If you are lucky enough to have a mother still alive, take her out to lunch, or go to her home, in the spirit of those in centuries past, bearing cakes and fragrant flowers. If you can avoid the crass commercialization of the shops, all the better: make your card, pick flowers from your garden, or plant up a tub or window box of pretty spring bulbs that she can enjoy. If you do send flowers, see the options on p.82. Other Mothering Sunday treats might include:

- a walk in the park with tea at a favourite nearby café
- a bird table or feeder with supplies of bird food to rig up near her window
- a voucher for a massage or aromatherapy session
- supplies of her favourite soap or toiletries
- a hand-made book with photographs and handwritten memories from your childhood

- a well-chosen book – of poetry, perhaps
- a cashmere jersey, scarf or wrap
- a fragment of a favourite poem or quote copied out by a calligrapher, with attractive illustrations. One of my favourites, first seen on a card made by a friend's daughter for Mothering Sunday, is this: 'A Mother holds her child's hand only for a short while, but holds her heart for ever'.

Sow Some Seeds

As the soil warms up, now is the time to start sowing seeds: vegetables for your kitchen garden and flowers for the border. Even if you're not a keen gardener, try just a few the first year, and soon you'll be hooked on growing from scratch. Watching a seed grow from a tiny dry speck to a small seedling and then a fully fledged plant – often putting on several feet of growth in the course of a single season – is still the closest thing to magic that I know. And it saves money, too.

For vegetables, try salad leaves, broad beans and courgettes for starters – they're all reliable and easy to grow. Tomatoes are also great; they need a little heat to germinate (an airing cupboard is fine) but are dead easy and hugely satisfying. For flowers, good choices to start with include nasturtiums (just push into the soil and forget), cosmos (in white or various shades of pink), pretty larkspur or nigella (love-in-a-mist) or *Cerinthe major* Purpurascens which, with its elegant peacock-blue bracts and electric-purple flowers, looks far more exotic and difficult to grow than, in fact, it is.

Many seeds can be sown in open ground once the soil is

warm enough (an old tradition has it that northerners used to bare their bottoms and sit on the soil to test its temperature) but can be started off inside on a sunny windowsill or in a greenhouse if you would rather. The advantages of starting in pots include warmer conditions and thus faster germination and growth, and a greater degree of safety from marauding slugs and snails; plant them out when they are three or so inches high and they stand more of a chance of survival. If you start off seeds inside, though, remember to 'harden off' before setting permanently outside; this means taking them outdoors for the day and in again at night (or opening and closing the lid of a cold frame) to acclimatize them gradually to outdoor conditions. It may seem a terrific faff, but ignore hardening off at your peril, as plants exposed to sudden changes in temperature often suffer what is known as a 'check' in growth, and can sometimes take weeks to recover.

Growing from seed also means you're no longer at the mercy of the garden centre for varieties available – for tomatoes, in particular, this is invaluable, as there are so many more varieties than the ubiquitous Moneymaker and Gardeners' Delight to try (Simpson's Seeds has an amazing choice – see p.99). You'll feel great come summer and autumn, when you'll be harvesting entire meals from produce you've grown yourself from seed. Particularly if you have children, or grandchildren, pumpkins can be the most tremendous fun to grow: sow two seeds per small pot and thin out to the strongest seedling before planting out in sunny fertile soil (some people swear by the tops of their compost heaps) and watering well. (See p.160 for a children's pumpkin party at Hallowe'en.)

For detailed advice on seed sowing, take a tip or two from those with a few decades of experience: a parent or grandparent, an elder at your allotment or, if all else fails, an author such as Alan Titchmarsh in his *How to be a Gardener* or John Cushnie in his helpful *How to Propagate*. However, most seed packets have clear enough instructions on the back; the crucial points are not to pack the soil in too tight, and not to over-water – if the soil is damp before sowing you shouldn't need to water again until the seedlings are quite sturdy. If and when you do water, do it sparingly from the base rather than pouring water on top of the soil in order to avoid disturbing the seed/seedlings and encouraging damping off disease.

In late summer and autumn, you can come full circle by collecting and storing your own seed (see pp.153–4). This subtle connection with the seasons can have far-reaching effects beyond the garden and/or kitchen. For me, it is a little window in a busy life through which I connect to farmers and tillers of the land across the continents and back through the centuries. It makes me feel resourceful, self-sufficient – and looked after, in quite a profound way, by the natural world. So give seed sowing a go. Even if all you have is a windowsill – and a child or grandchild or young friend to amuse – buy some mustard and cress seeds, help the children write their names with the seeds in blotting paper, keep moist and watch the seeds split open and grow. Paul Daniels, eat your heart out. It really is magic.

For seed suppliers see pp.98–9.

For suppliers of seedlings ready to plant see box on p.124.

Seed Suppliers

John Chambers Wildflower Seeds (01933 652562/ www.johnchamberswildflowerseeds.co.uk) supplies wildflower and grass seed, including many mixes for specific areas and even a 'wildflower windowbox' mixture.

The Organic Gardening Catalogue (0845 130 1304/ www.organiccatalogue.com) is the mail order arm of the excellent organic gardening association Garden Organic, and stocks a high percentage of organic seed including unusual salad leaves and several varieties of sweetcorn.

Plant World (01803 872939/www.plant-world-seeds.com) is a real plantsman's nursery near Newton Abbott in Devon, with a garden planted to represent the five continents, each area spilling over with exotic plants from those particular countries. The catalogue is full of flowering treats, and the seed always fresh and properly packaged.

Sarah Raven's Cutting Garden (0870 191 3430/ www.sarahraven.com) is a great source of both flower and kitchen garden seed, and thanks to Sarah's bold but unerring good taste, you are saved the trouble of sifting through pages of sickly yellows and salmon pinks: she stocks only the varieties she has grown and trialled at her gorgeous and abundant garden in East Sussex.

Secret Seeds (01398 331946/www.secretseeds.com) is a fantastic nursery based in Devon, offering seed for a wide variety of rare and unusual – and often extraordinarily beautiful – flowering plants. Check out their website for heart-stopping pictures.

Seeds of Italy (020 8427 5020/www.seedsofitaly.com) is a must for those who combine a love of gardening with a taste for Mediterranean cooking. Seeds for the ingredients of all your favourite dishes – including many varieties of basil, borlotti beans and crinkly dark green cavolo nero – are offered in their original attractive Franchi packaging.

Simpson's Seeds (01985 845004/www.simpsonsseeds.co.uk) is a family-run business specializing in seed (and young plants) of unusual tomato and pepper varieties, including some red-hot exotic chillis.

Suffolk Herbs (01376 572456/www.suffolkherbs.com) is another great source for organic gardeners, with seed for herbs, wildflowers and unusual vegetable varieties; the catalogue even offers alternative health products, dried herbs and spices and organic wines alongside.

Easter-Time Festivals

Falling on the first Sunday after the first full moon after the spring equinox, and celebrated with chickens, eggs, spring flowers and rabbits, Easter is more in touch with its pagan roots than most churchmen would have us believe. Whatever your religion, or lack of it, the four-day weekend is a good excuse to celebrate spring with gifts of food and home-made sweets, a traditional Easter cake and decorations, and an Easter egg hunt for children. Jewish Passover, of course, also falls at this time of year – this was the Last Supper that Jesus was celebrating when Judas betrayed him. If you have any Jewish friends, do beg an invitation to a Seder Night Supper. Traditionally open to non-Jews too, this is an ancient, dramatic and moving festival, involving many symbolic types of food, that tells the story of the flight from Egypt and the origins of their faith.

❧ *Make a Simnel Cake* ❧

Though now almost exclusively associated with Easter, Simnel cake was once a traditional part of Mothering Sunday (see p.93) and I like to honour this old custom by making it on the middle Sunday of Lent (Simnel Sunday or Mothering Sunday) and giving the cake a good couple of weeks to mature before eating it at Easter.

Simnel cake is basically a lighter version of Christmas cake, with the marzipan incorporated into the cake rather than covering it, and with special decorations. Traditionally, the eleven marzipan balls on top represent the twelve apostles minus Judas, who betrayed Jesus, and I always add a marzipan nest in the centre in which are arranged different coloured foil-covered chocolate eggs, and a larger cream egg clothed in a knitted yellow chicken suit my mother made. It's great to enjoy at home over the Easter weekend, or to take as a present if you are going to stay with others. Take care not to overcook it – the cake's best if it's still a little soft and squidgy in the middle. This recipe is my mother's, with a few small changes.

 MARGARET'S SIMNEL CAKE

225g butter
225g soft brown sugar
3 medium free-range eggs
3 tablespoons milk
350g self-raising flour
350g mixed dried fruit
50g peel

    110g natural glacé cherries
    1 teaspoon mixed spice
    1 tablespoon treacle

To decorate
    450g natural marzipan
    1 tablespoon jam, diluted with water
    beaten egg, to glaze

Preheat the oven to 150°C/300°F/gas mark 2. Grease and line a 20cm round springform cake tin. Cream the butter and sugar together then add the eggs and milk. Add the rest of the ingredients apart from the marzipan and stir well. Smooth half the mixture into the base of the tin. Divide the marzipan into thirds, rolling one third into a ball and using a rolling pin to make a 20cm round. Place on top of the mixture in the tin then add the remaining mixture. Bake on the bottom shelf of the oven for 1 hour; then lower the temperature to 140°C/275°F/gas mark 1 and bake for a further hour, removing when the top is brown, firm and just springy.

When the cake is cool, fashion one of the remaining thirds of the marzipan into a long sausage to stretch around the diameter of the cake, using diluted jam to secure it in place and a fork to squash it down and leave marks all around the edge. Position eleven marble-sized marzipan balls at regular intervals on the marzipan surround, and a nest of some sort in the centre. Brush the marzipan lightly with egg and glaze under the grill for just a moment till nicely browned. Wrap in foil to store.

On emerging from storage, the nest can then be filled with chocolate eggs, with perhaps a sprig or two of blossom, and the cake set on a pretty plate.

❧ *Have an Easter Egg Hunt* ❧

This hardly needs explaining, but here goes. An hour or two beforehand, take a variety of foil-covered chocolate eggs and other goodies and hide them in an easily definable area of your garden (or a park or paddock). Give each of the participating children half an old egg box in which to collect their loot and let them loose to search (older children who feel they ought to be too grown up for such games may still like to help the littler ones). In this age of equal opportunities, rather than each kid keep and consume their own stash, it seems to be the custom to pool the findings in a communal bowl and divide them up equally. However you do it, I've never known an Easter egg hunt to be anything other than a success – and it can also be adapted for other children's parties, from Hallowe'en to birthdays to Christmas. An added bonus is that, when doing a quiet bit of gardening in days to come, you might well come across the odd little chocolate treat, still edible in its foil paper wrapping.

❧ *Make an Egg Tree* ❧

My mother has had an 'Easter tree' since our childhood and hers, strung with decorated eggs ranging from splattered offerings from our childhood to intricate affairs bought on holidays all over the world, has inspired me to create my own. All you need is a few branches pruned from the garden or hedgerow and arranged in a jug, and enough decorated eggs – five or six will do to start with – to hang on them. If you have children at home or staying for the weekend, you can blow eggs with them (make a pinhole at either end and literally blow the contents out into a bowl for use as scrambled eggs or cake mix) and decorate them by dyeing with natural dyes, painting with paints or felt tips, or appliqué-ing with stickers or fragments of coloured fabric. A length of wool or ribbon threaded through the holes and anchored with a bead can create a loop for attaching to the 'tree' – or you can always stick the ribbon around the outside and tie in a bow at the top. Pick up other ready-decorated eggs made from everything from wood to plastic to padded fabric from shops and country craft fairs. Pack away in old egg boxes to keep safe for the rest of the year.

❦ *Plant a Herb Garden* ❦

This is a great job for spring, as the herbs can be bought relatively cheaply in small pots but will take off in time for summer. Plant as generously as your space and budget allow; the idea is to be able to pick handfuls of basil for making pesto, or mint for Moroccan-style tea, without feeling guilty about decimating your plants. Make sure you give your herbs the right conditions. Most herbs of Mediterranean origin (thyme, oregano, rosemary and so on) thrive on dry, well-drained soils, but others such as parsley, tarragon and basil need more moisture. Mint can cope with a fair amount of shade, but needs its roots restricted by a pot (which can be buried underground if you wish) to prevent it taking over.

Here are some tips for my top twelve garden herbs.

✳ *Basil* is one you definitely shouldn't be without: the scent of the leaves on even the tiniest seedling seems to exude all the essence of summer. It can be grown successfully from seed in early spring, using the warmth of an airing cupboard or propagator to aid germination, but you can cheat by buying potted basil from the supermarket, gently separating out the crowded little plants and re-potting in rich, well-draining soil in full sun. The first time you harvest, be sure to pinch out the growing tips to promote bushy growth. Grown among tomato plants, basil repels many pests and will benefit from the extra feeding and watering.

✳ *Bay* is often grown as smart clipped standard trees in pots to flank a front door, and you can use the prunings in the kitchen. I treat my small pyramid bay in the back garden this way; its twice-annual haircut keeps us in bay leaves for cooking all year, and the tree comes inside every Christmas as part of the decorations. Don't buy too small a plant; you'll be waiting for ever for a decent harvest, as bay is slow to grow. Like basil, it likes full sun and a sheltered position, particularly when young.

✳ *Chives* can be grown from seed, but a small plant or two, bought from the garden centre, will soon increase if the clumps are lifted and divided every few years in spring. They grow best when planted at least 6 inches from other plants and given rich, moist soil. (In poor soil the leaves turn yellow and then brown at the tips.) Keep well watered. The leaves can be cut to within an inch of the ground four times a year to maintain a good supply; cut just a section of the plant if you have only one. The flowers, too, can be added to salads. Garlic chives (or Chinese chives) can be grown in the same way; they have strappier leaves that taste of garlic. Grown beneath roses, chives deter aphids and other pests.

✳ *Coriander* in abundance is a boon for lovers of curries and Middle Eastern dishes. It can be grown easily enough from seed, but should be sown directly where it is to grow, as it dislikes disturbance. When put under any kind of stress, the seedlings bolt straight into flower, growing only the feathery top leaves and omitting to produce the larger lower growth which is most flavoursome for cooking. To keep coriander happy, give it light, well-drained soil in a sunny position and water well when young. Seed can also be harvested for use in the kitchen. An Indian gentleman at my allotment swore by rubbing the seed between his hands and soaking in a damp flannel overnight to promote better germination.

✳ *Dill* in the garden is great for making your own gravadlax or other fish dishes. The trick is to stop it from bolting; like coriander, it will miss out on the leaf production stage if disturbed or upset. Raise from seed in pots or plug trays or where it is to grow; it prefers well-drained poor soil in full sun. Protect from the wind and thin plants to 8 inches apart so they can spread. Push twiggy stakes around the seedlings to support them and water well in hot dry spells. Dill makes a good companion with chervil, the seeds of which will germinate and overwinter just as dill is giving up the ghost. The two herbs should coexist quite happily, re-seeding every year.

* *Mint* is a must for every garden. The family includes many different varieties including spearmint, peppermint, ginger mint, eau-de-cologne mint and apple mint, all of which have subtly different leaf shapes, textures and flavours. Grow a few and experiment with their use in mint sauce with roast lamb, chopped into tabbouleh and Middle Eastern salads, or crushed into drinks such as mojitos (see p.117) or Moroccan mint tea – just a sprig of young leaves crushed in the bottom of a glass with hot water and honey makes a delicious refreshing drink. Mint prefers full sun but will tolerate a fair amount of shade. Restrict its growth by growing in pots or a deep tin or plastic container sunk into the soil. Mint tastes best before it comes into flower, so keep cutting back to encourage bushy growth. Before it dies down in winter, bring a pot inside where it should continue to supply you with leaves till spring.

* *Marjoram* or *Oregano* are interchangeable terms for *Origanum vulgare*, whose spicy aromatic leaves are indispensable in Greek and Italian cooking, but there are many different varieties with subtly different uses. Pot marjoram (*O. onites*) is the one to choose if you want to use the leaves fresh, while the leaves of Greek marjoram (*O.v.* subsp. *hirtum*) keep their flavour best when dried. The golden oregano (*O.v.* Aureum) makes an attractive yellow splash in a herb garden and combines well with vegetables in the kitchen. Well-drained sunny dry soil is a must, and the plants grow well in containers.

* *Parsley* is one of those herbs you can never have enough of: it's worth setting aside a metre or so square for a mixture of flat-leafed and curly varieties. To cover this amount of ground it is cheaper to grow from seed, but you'll have to be patient – parsley seed takes 2–3 weeks with heat and 4–6 weeks without. Raise in pots or plug trays in early spring to avoid root disturbance and plant out only when the soil and air temperatures have begun to rise, and the seedlings are large enough to withstand slug damage. Cut the leaves down frequently to ensure bushy regrowth.

* *Rosemary*, like bay, can be grown as an attractive standard bush or tree; its mauvey-blue flowers look pretty in early summer and the scent of the leaves makes me long for roast lamb. It can be raised well from cuttings, but impatient gardeners will probably prefer to buy a potted plant. Give it well-drained soil in a sunny position, as befits its Mediterranean origins – against a south- or south-west-facing wall is ideal. Prune – quite hard, if you like – immediately after flowering; do not prune in autumn as new growth is susceptible to frost damage. Sprigs can be picked for cooking, however, all the year round.

* *Sage* is worth growing simply so you can nip out into the garden and pick enough leaves to make the simple butter and sage sauce (*burro e salvio*) to melt over fresh-cooked pasta or ravioli. It is also attractive enough to be grown for its appearance alone, though the most showy varieties, including purple and variegated types, don't have the best flavour. Plant in a pot or border in sunny, well-drained soil, prune well in spring to encourage young shoots with a strong flavour, and also after flowering in late summer to prevent the plants growing leggy.

* *Tarragon* is a treat in the garden for adding to chicken and fish dishes. Stuff a mixture of soft butter and chopped leaves beneath the skin of a chicken before roasting, or add just a few leaves to sliced courgettes before steaming. French tarragon (*Artemisia dracunculus*) is the type you want, rather than the less tasty but more vigorous Russian tarragon (*A. dracunculoides*) which is often wrongly labelled and sold in its stead. French tarragon cannot be grown from seed, and cuttings can be tricky, so buy a plant from a reputable herb nursery (such as Poyntzfield Herbs, see p.145) and plant in a warm, dry position. Remove the flowers, and pick leaves for cooking all year round.

* *Thyme* is an evergreen and will add immeasurably to your garden with its green, grey or golden leaves, its pretty flowers in all shades of pink through to white and dark purple, and the bees that will buzz around it when in bloom. On top of that, its culinary uses are many: add it to stocks and marinades, stick a few sprigs in an onion as a stuffing for chicken, or sprinkle in a pumpkin risotto. Different varieties of creeping thyme can be grown as a 'patchwork carpet' in a sunny spot, or in cracks (or intentional chequerboard gaps) between paving. It can also make a good ground cover for sun-loving trees and shrubs in pots. The crucial condition is well-drained soil and protection in harsh winters.

Do a Spot of Spring-Cleaning

Even if you have a cleaner, there will be corners of the house that she (or he) can never reach in the allocated time. To get your home really clean and fresh, set aside a weekend, or part

De-cluttering and Recycling

www.amazon.co.uk – for selling unwanted books and CDs.

www.carbootcalendar.com (01981 251633) – lists car boot sales throughout the UK.

www.freecycle.org – can put you in touch with locals who might want your waste stuff for free.

www.charityshops.org.uk (020 7255 4470) – lists more than 90 per cent of charity shops in the UK.

www.ebay.co.uk – the now-famous online auction site. Those who have mastered the art of photographing and registering their unwanted clutter swear by it, and some even make a reasonable income.

www.recycle-more.co.uk (08450 682572) – has general information on recycling.

www.computersforcharity.org.uk (01288 361199) – reconditions old computers to donate to other charities including Oxfam.

www.yell.co.uk – type in 'secondhand shops' and your postcode for a list of secondhand shops in your area.

Expert help – if all else fails, get the experts in: www.apdo-uk.co.uk is a nationwide directory of the 'de-cluttering experts' in your area.

of one, put on some great music and fill the fridge with rewards to be eked out at hourly intervals. (See p.285 for further suggestions.) De-clutter by filling a series of different bin bags for recycling, donating to charity, giving away through the excellent freecycle (see above), selling or exchanging at a market stall, car boot sale or swap shop with friends (see above and pp.270–1) or, as a last resort only, throwing away. If you can get it together with the necessary photography and computer skills, you can sell stuff on eBay (see p.109). You'll feel great when it's all done (particularly if you are luxuriating in a deep, hot, fragrant bath), and your house will be sparkling with vibrant new energy. I swear you can *feel* as well as see the difference in the place!

❧ *Go on a Spring Detox* ❧

While you're at it, why not spring-clean your body as well as your home? A good time for a quick detox is either during Lent, when you might be giving up alcohol or chocolate or some other vice anyway, or just after Easter, when you have gorged on chocolate and are starting to panic about baring all on a beach come summer. A weekend detox is not primarily about losing weight, though, it's about giving your body (and mind – these things are connected) a clear-out. I try to do this once in spring and once in autumn, carrying it on for a week if I can, and I guarantee you will have endless complimentary comments about your clear skin, bright eyes and general bushy-tailed-ness in the weeks that follow.

Simple weekend detox regime

You can buy one of the many books on the subject and follow their advice, but I find they involve a lot of shopping for obscure ingredients necessary to make complex but generally not very appealing meals. I now tend to begin with a day on nothing but a simple vegetable soup made by chopping up lots of organic vegetables, sweating them in a little oil and simmering them in water or a good stock such as Marigold's salt-free version. The nutrients from the veg leach into the soup, and because it is so pure and easy to digest it allows the body to focus on excreting existing toxins. On the second (or subsequent) day I might add some boiled organic brown rice, quinoa or barley, salads sprinkled with toasted pumpkin, sunflower and linseed seeds and, in the evening, a small amount of grilled fish or chicken. No red meat, no dairy, no caffeine, alcohol or chocolate, I'm afraid, and snacks and treats are confined to fresh raw fruit (best eaten alone rather than as part of a meal), carrot or cucumber sticks, or a few nuts and seeds. Drink lots of filtered water: filling a 2-litre jug or bottle at the beginning of each day is a good way to regulate your intake.

Yes, it is deathly dull, but if you know it is only for a couple of days, it's bearable. And combining the detox with some of the more luxurious ideas from the Stay In Bed All Day (pp.316–21) and Quiet Night In (pp.17–23) sections will make it all a little more bearable. Skin brushing before a shower or bath (pp.17–18) is great for stimulating toxin elimination, as is adding a handful or two of Epsom Salts to your bath (available from old-fashioned chemists or health food shops) and soaking for at least twenty minutes (add a few drops of grapefruit essential oil too). For a bit of well-deserved luxury, you could even book in for a massage with a qualified specialist in lymphatic drainage. Be prepared, however, for a nagging headache as the detox process begins – this can be quite fierce for coffee-lovers. Rest assured, after a while this is replaced by a lovely light feeling in your stomach that is all part of your reward.

The books all say, check with your doctor before going on

any kind of detox, and who am I to disagree? If you see a home-opath or herbalist (visit www.lemonbalmonline.com for ideas here) then it would be an excellent idea to enlist their advice on tablets, teas and potions that might help the process along. The following tea made from dried herbs helps support the organs involved with the eliminatory processes of detoxing. Marigold and cleavers are great cleansers for the lymphatic system, dan-delion root and burdock support the liver and digestion, and nettles are full of minerals for clear skin.

 DETOX TEA

> *25g dandelion root*
> *25g marigold flowers*
> *25g burdock root*
> *25g nettle leaves*

Mix the herbs together and store in an airtight jar. Use a tea-spoon per cup of boiling water. Infuse for 5–10 minutes and drink three or four cups a day, hot or cold.

Nettle tops (see section on foraging, p.84) also make an effective (and surprisingly sweet-tasting) spring detox tea and tonic. Gather them fresh in spring (use gloves), place in a jug, fill with cold water, cover and leave overnight. Strain and drink the pink liquid first thing in the morning throughout spring.

3.

Seasonal Pleasures: Summer

*T*here's that wonderful feeling of freedom at the start of summer – and the illusion that the warm weather, long languid days and sense of space stretching ahead will continue for ever and ever. This is going to be the year, I tell myself, when we will have lots of picnics, keep on top of weeds in the garden, go to the beach whenever we have a spare moment and fill the freezer and larder with home-made ice cream, jams, cakes and puddings made from home-grown or pick-your-own produce. Salad leaves seem to spring up overnight in the vegetable garden, tiny courgettes turn to torpedos when your back is turned, tomatoes and strawberries are cropping in abundance. Meanwhile the seaside, wildflower meadows and shady woods are beckoning to be enjoyed. Make the most of the long warm days by decamping as much of your life as possible outside, going on picnics, swimming in the sea, lakes and rivers, and cooking and sleeping under the stars. Time to throw a midsummer party, make ice cream and cocktails, pick fruit and flowers, go beachcombing and catch the sunshine with crystals strung at windows. In our increasingly unpredictable weather, we have to grab our chance at summer whenever it chooses to appear. Before you know it, we'll be in dry, dusty late August, looking forward to the cooler, slower pleasures that autumn holds . . .

✿ *Celebrate Midsummer* ✿

The longest day – or a weekend round about then, towards the end of June – is a great excuse for a party. And don't I know it? This is exactly when my birthday falls, and I usually have to compete with half a dozen weddings or other celebrations on this date, not to mention the World Cup, European Cup or whatever other sporting event is at its nail-biting peak at this time. Never mind – it doesn't stop us. We even had a telly room for football devotees one year, and the dancing in the streets when England actually won a match only added to the fun. The great thing about summer parties is that you can spill outside (weather permitting) so you can be freer with the numbers you invite, and people don't expect hot food which makes catering much easier. The important items to get right are the lighting in the garden – loads of pin-prick white fairy lights in the trees and around pergolas and sitting areas always look lovely, and those large foil-encased candles can be good for lining paths if you are confident your guests won't swish past in flowing robes and set themselves alight – and the drinks. The Cox & Cox catalogue has great outdoor lights and lots of other lovely things for outdoor and indoor parties (0870 442 4787/www.coxandcox.co.uk). With drinks, champagne or Prosecco always go down well, but summer cocktails – both with and without alcohol – are great fun and always appreciated. Here are a few favourites.

✽ *Serve Summer Cocktails* ✽

✽ *Mojito*: I became converted to mojitos in Havana, Cuba, where the best ones in the world are supposed to be served in Ernest Hemingway's old hangout, La Bodeguita del Medio. Since then, I have to say they have been superseded, in my book, by my husband's own rather splendid version, flavoured with mint from a bed of different varieties I planted at my allotment for this purpose. A mojito is one of those cocktails that have to be mixed in individual glasses.

> *mint leaves*
> *1 part freshly squeezed lime juice*
> *white sugar to taste – 1 teaspoon is enough*
> *2 parts good white rum*
> *ice cubes*
> *sparkling water*

Put 6–8 fresh mint leaves in the bottom of a tumbler with the lime juice and sugar. Crush the mint with a pestle to release its flavour and scent. Add the rum, then fill the glass with ice cubes and top with the sparkling water. Decorate with a sprig of mint.

✽ *Strawberry bellini*: The peach bellini served at Harry's Bar in Venice is an all-time classic, but I like this version using strawberry purée or liqueur. It works equally well with pink champagne – and you can certainly make the money go further by using Prosecco instead. This is similar to the lovely ones served in the restaurant at Petersham Nurseries in Richmond in summer (0208 940 5230/www.petershamnurseries.com to book a table).

1 bottle of champagne or Prosecco
225g fresh strawberries, puréed and strained

Open the wine and let it stand in an ice bucket for 5 minutes. Pour the puréed fruit into a glass jug and carefully pour in the wine, stirring gently to combine. Serve in champagne flutes – chilled in the freezer for 20 minutes if possible.

If you are short on time, placing a small strawberry in the bottom of each glass and using pink champagne is a good second-best.

✳ *Pimm's*: This was the great summer drink when I was at university, and I can still remember bumping into one renegade friend bearing a cardboard box full of all the ingredients for Pimm's when I was meant to be heading for the Backs with my books to revise. I seem to recall that the books were forgotten for that day. Pimm's is like that.

1 bottle of traditional Pimm's No. 1
2 bottles of good lemonade
orange, lemon and cucumber slices
1 small bunch fresh mint
borage flowers

For a jug of Pimm's, place plenty of ice in the jug, and add 2 parts lemonade to 1 part Pimm's. Thinly slice an orange, a lemon and half a cucumber and add to the mix along with the mint leaves.

To mix in individual glasses, place 3 ice cubes, 1 slice each of orange, lemon and cucumber, a sprig of mint and a few borage flowers in each tumbler, and pour on 1 part Pimm's to 2 parts lemonade.

A somewhat stronger drink can be made using 5 parts lemonade, 2 parts Pimm's and 1 part gin.

✳ *Blood-orange Campari*: This is simply gorgeous – the essence of Mediterranean summer. Pretend you are on a beach in Capri or the south of France. I also like to think that all that fresh orange juice must counteract the unhealthiness of the alcohol.

> *blood oranges*
> *Campari*
> *caster sugar and soda (optional)*

Mix 2 parts freshly squeezed blood orange juice to 1 part Campari, pour over ice and decorate the glasses with orange slices. You can add a spoonful of sugar if it tastes too bitter but, to me, that is the whole point of Campari, and the sweetness of the blood oranges balances it perfectly. Likewise, a squirt or two of soda water makes a longer drink, but I find the melting ice enough.

✳ *Non-alcoholic drinks*: One of the nicest things in summer is to have jugs of filtered tap water on the table, with ice cubes, sprigs of mint and a squeeze of lemon added. It's amazing how these little additions add a note of luxury. Iced tea is another fine thing to have in the fridge; just a pitcher of weak tea flavoured with honey or a little sugar and lemon is a great refresher, with lots of ice cubes added. But my all-time favourite has to be elderflower cordial – and if you don't want to make your own (see below) there are lots of good cordial concentrates on the market by the likes of Belvoir and Duchy Organics. Just add sparkling water and lots of ice – perhaps the fruity and herby ice cubes below.

* *Fruity and herby ice cubes*: These are dead easy, and an attractive treat to add to summer drinks, both alcoholic and teetotal. Children in particular love waiting for the ice to melt and release the fruit – or, in the case of my daughter, who has inherited her father's capacity to crunch ice with her teeth, chomp their way through to it.

All you do is place a small piece of fruit – a raspberry for instance, or segment of strawberry or watermelon – and/or a sprig of mint in each section of an ice-cube tray, add water to the top and freeze. Using filtered water ensures the ice cubes are beautifully clear. Consume within a month.

❋ *Make Elderflower Cordial* ❋

The distinctive smell of elderflowers is the very essence of summer – and luckily it can be distilled without too much trouble into a delicious syrup or cordial that keeps for at least a year. There are lots of recipes for using elderflowers (and elderberries, see pp.172–3) in Ria Loohuizen's excellent book *The Elder: In History, Myth and Cookery* but this is my tried and trusted method, which has the virtue of not needing precisely measured amounts.

Pick the elderflowers on a dry day, when the flowers are fully open but not yet going over – ones with yellowish, creamy stamens are the most flavourful. Use secateurs or scissors to cut the flowers cleanly without damaging the plant, and carry in a bag or shallow basket – not plastic, which will give rise to condensation and decay.

Remove as much of the stalk as possible and place the flowers in a large bucket or other container. Pour in just enough cold water to cover, put on a lid or some sort of cover and leave for 2–3 days. Strain the liquid through a muslin cloth into a large preserving pan; the flowers can go on the compost heap. Measure the pan of liquid and add 750g sugar and 1 tablespoon citric acid per litre. Heat gently, stirring all the time, while the sugar dissolves completely. Don't let it boil – some recipes specify boiling, but it does lead to a loss of flavour and fragrance. Pour (using a funnel) into sterilized bottles (just out of a hot wash in the dishwasher will do) with tight screwtops, and store in a dark, cool place, where it should last for a year.

As well as a base for soft drinks – just add sparkling water and ice cubes for the classic summer drink – this syrup can also be used to make sorbets, flavour gooseberry fools and pour over pancakes or fruit salad.

❋ *Sleep Under the Stars* ❋

The night sky on a clear summer's evening is an awe-inspiring sight – if only we take the time and trouble to look. If the stars were to appear only once every ten or hundred years, everyone would travel from near and far to the best observation spots and camp out to appreciate them to the full, but because they can be seen almost every night, we tend to take this ready-made miracle for granted. Anyone can stop for a moment – on stepping out of their car in the dark, or walking out into the garden after supper – to look up and take in some of the beauty overhead. For a truly mind-blowing experience, however, you need not only a clear sky, but to be somewhere without artificial street lighting: ideally in the remote countryside, far from the hazy light smog that hovers above and around all cities and conurbations. It's only then that you can see not only the large stars and major planets, but all the myriad smaller (or more distant) stars and galaxies in between. Look at it regularly and you begin to realize how the night sky is by no means static; the stars move across the sky (or, rather, the earth rotates) throughout the course of the night, and appear in different configurations during the progression of the seasons. At certain times of the year (late August in our part of the UK) there may be meteor showers – magical cascades of falling stars that are well worth wrapping up and camping out for. Keep an eye open in the news, or check out weather websites or the local press for other seasonal events such as comets and eclipses that may also be exciting.

Most people can pick out the Pole Star, the Plough, Cassiopeia (the big 'W') and Orion with his belt and sword; indeed, one of my earliest memories as a young child is sitting outside with my father on the farm, snuggled up to his plaid shirt late on a summer's night while he taught me some of the stars and their names. If you want to know more, there are endless books on the subject, but to get a good and entertaining grounding, check out your local observatory (via www.regionalobservatories.org.uk), where enthusiastic volunteers will be all too keen to teach you what you want to know, with the aid of powerful telescopes; some run courses or special teaching evenings at specific times of the year.

But the stars are one of those areas where knowledge is by no means everything. You don't have to be able to name and identify the stars to be filled with a sense of their beauty and wonder. Just get out there and look. Rather than stand with your head crooked back uncomfortably, get comfortable. Lie down – like John Gordon Sinclair and Clare Grogan in *Gregory's Girl* (you can even dance if you like) – but ideally on a camping mattress or yoga mat and under a cosy blanket or quilt. Bring pillows and cushions. Make sure you're warm enough to remain for a while – all night if you feel like it – and keep some citronella oil or similar handy if midges or mosquitoes are a problem. Then simply lose yourself, as humans have been doing almost since life began, in the timeless, fathomless splendour overhead.

Sleeping under the stars is a wonderful experience, whether alone, with a loved one, or with children – wonderful in very different ways, of course. In hotter climates, where the weather is more reliable, people regularly move their mattresses – even their entire beds on occasion – out into the garden or on to roof terraces or balconies off the bedroom, and it's worth thinking about this when a week of unbroken good weather is forecast. A friend of mine regularly sleeps out on her deck with her three teenage daughters whenever there's a full moon; and with a houseful of guests in high summer, this is one way to sort out the sleeping quarters. Just make sure everyone is safe and happy and able to slip inside again easily at the first drop of rain or panic at some unidentified rustling in the bushes.

Be prepared to be awoken early, of course. Sunrise can be as early as 4.30 in high summer – but you will be in the front row seats to appreciate it, and the dawn chorus, too. If you can brew up some tea or coffee while you're waiting, all the better. To my mind, sleeping under the stars in this way takes some beating. Camping in tents and camper vans can be great fun (see pp.247–52) but needs quite a bit of organization. Whereas sleeping outside in your garden, with nothing between your own face and the heavens, is raw, romantic, sensual, immediate – and as far removed from orange nylon and tangled guy ropes as wild swimming is from indoor pools.

❋ *Grow Your Own Salad* ❋

There is nothing like stepping out into your garden (or balcony or roof terrace) and picking your own salad leaves for supper. The tastiest cut-and-come-again types are eaten when the leaves are still small and so don't need a lot of space; you can grow them in a window box, old wooden packing case or apple crate lined with plastic sacks (with holes cut for drainage). Sow up until July, or when the weather gets very hot – most lettuce does not like hot temperatures and will either not germinate or bolt very fast. But some leaves, such as rocket, can be sown through-out summer, and August/September sowings of hardy varieties will last well into autumn/early winter. If you are in a hurry, try the small seedling packs on p.125 that are ready to plant out.

Instant Vegetable Garden

If you forgot to sow seeds in spring (see p.95), or didn't feel confident enough to try, send off for 'starter packs' of salad greens and other vegetable seedlings – all ready to plant – from the following suppliers. Dig the plot one weekend, plant up the next, and enjoy for many weekends to come!

Fentongollan Vegetable Plants Catalogue (01872 520209/ www.flowerfarm.co.uk): A great range, reasonably priced and packed in 'mini greenhouse' packaging so seedlings can happily wait a week or more before planting out. Tried and tested varieties in several collections, plus packs of ten of everything from basil plants to pak choi.

Rocket Gardens (01209 831468/www.rocketgardens.co.uk): Supply organically-grown salad, herb and vegetable seedlings in various selections, for delivery in June.

Wiggly Wigglers (01981 500391/www.wigglywigglers.co.uk): Their excellent catalogue (more of a source book for organic gardeners) includes a new range of 'Ready-to-Plant Vegetable Plots' in different sizes and combinations, including a Salad Vegetable Plot, all available till the end of July.

❋ *Go Wild Swimming or Find a Lido* ❋

I've always preferred open-air swimming to the claustrophobic, chlorinated fug of public swimming baths, but reading Roger Deakin's *Waterlog: A Swimmer's Journey through Britain* made me even more convinced. His passionate and entertaining account takes him the length and breadth of the UK in search of places to swim out of doors, from the rivers and sea of his native Suffolk to a Yorkshire lido made for miners to rinse off the coal dust to the frightening foaming whirlpool of Corryvreckan off the west coast of Scotland. (It also includes an exchange between John Le Mesurier and Jeffrey Bernard that has made me laugh more than any other book, but that's another story.) Read it and see if you, too, are not inspired to head off for an outdoor swim that is free – in every sense of the word.

The sea is the obvious choice, of course, and the British Channel is probably the warmest, if not cleanest choice (see 01989 566017/www.goodbeachguide.co.uk) for our cleanest swimming beaches). Swimming in rural rivers is another great joy that seems to have died out in recent years, perhaps due to fears about safety and pollution. I used to swim off punts in the Cam outside Cambridge, and in some places (Deakin comes across a few in his book), a rotten old jetty or rusty springboard remains to show that others have enjoyed the same spots in the past. Take a picnic and a Thermos of tea or hot toddy to warm you up afterwards. And in *Iris* read John Bayley's account of river-swimming with his wife, Iris Murdoch, from their student days almost up until her death, for a taste of just how magical – and addictive – it can be. For further information check out www.river-swimming.co.uk, the website of the River and Lake Swimming Association.

For city dwellers, lidos are a great alternative; there is something bracing and cheerful about their streamlined 1930s architecture, and if you go in the early morning you can glide up and down on your back while surveying the shifting clouds, without the distraction of clamorous voices and dive-bombing kids. Some cities also have swimming ponds, with those in Henleaze in Bristol and Hampstead Heath in London particularly popular. Once you've got used to the squidgy mud at the bottom, and the odd strand of waterweed entwining itself around your foot, you'll be hooked; and there are usually large expanses of grass on which to loll about with a newspaper or book. This is *rus in urbis* at its most seductive and well worth investigating.

Wherever you live, check out all your outdoor swimming options – some might even be mentioned in Deakin's book. If you're used to heated pools you'll doubtless find the temperature on the chilly side, but you can always wear a wetsuit even if, in my opinion, this cuts out not only the cold but the whole sensual experience of 'wild' swimming. But there are unexpected paybacks. Doctors agree that regular spells of immersion in cold water can improve circulation, prevent colds and ward off depression – with salt water considered especially beneficial. If you look at some of the sprightly elders who brave the waters of London's Serpentine throughout the year, they certainly seem to prove this point. In the absence of lifeguards in remote places, do beware of powerful currents and other hazards.

If you really can't kick the heated pool habit, try to track down one in the open, although it may mean joining a club. When I lived in central London, I used to start my day with thirty minutes in the outdoor pool at the Oasis Sports Centre off Shaftesbury Avenue (020 7831 1804/www.gll.org); it seemed then to be one of the capital's best-kept secrets and was often almost empty. Cold days were actually the most thrilling. I can still remember the tingling contrast between the chilly air and warm water on entry, and the thrill of swimming along half shrouded in clouds of steam.

An enterprising website www. lidos.org.uk lists all lidos and open-air swimming pools in the UK with current opening times, and has links to other open-air swimming sites. Another useful site is www.out doorswimmingsociety.com.

❋ *Have a Picnic* ❋

The British seem particularly keen on picnics, whether it's a grand black tie affair with champagne at Glyndebourne, cold roast chicken and pork pies from the boot of a 4x4 at a point-to-point, or a children's birthday party in the park with cake, crisps and sausages on sticks – and plenty of umbrellas in case of a shower. We're all too happy to load up the hamper and take off to a city park or meadow in the country at the slightest excuse. Food and drink, we are prone to saying, tastes better in the open air. Even though the commonly used phrase for outdoor eating – 'al fresco' – is Italian, to a European this means an elegant table on a restaurant terrace, not lugging provisions miles through the mud to lounge uncomfortably on the ground.

Personally, I'm a great fan of picnics. A solitary picnic, armed with a few favourite treats, a half-bottle of wine and a book, is, for me, one of life's greatest pleasures. A picnic for two can be gloriously romantic, whether the menu and venue are meticulously planned or simply arise from a sunny afternoon and a spontaneous nature. Family picnics can be an enjoyable and economical way of eating out and doing something different – particularly if ball games and so on are packed too for playing once the food has gone down. And larger picnics can be a gloriously informal way of meeting up with a lot of people without having to fret about space, numbers and what to cook. If everyone brings a 'pot luck' item there always seems to be more than enough delicious fare, and children and extra guests can be accommodated with ease. A good friend of mine has held a birthday party as a picnic on Primrose Hill in London for the past twenty-five years, and it is now a much anticipated annual event that has grown to include her friends' children and, in some cases, children's children. Where once we used to have trouble locating the right group of people on the hill, there's no mistaking now the huge tribal gathering, complete with children playing French cricket (p.133) and rounders and women cooing over the latest new baby.

Where to have them

Picnics are a good last-minute standby to have up one's sleeve. On a car journey cross-country, just some good cheese, fresh bread and salad picked up en route, eaten off paper napkins on a rug in a field, is often preferable to taking a chance at a roadside pub or café – and you can choose your own view and company. I keep an old tartan rug (with tarpaulin underside – even on sunny days the grass can still be damp at lunchtime) in the boot of the car for just this purpose, plus a small rucksack with old cutlery and a few plates and cups. If you've got one of those devices that plug into the car cigarette lighter you can even brew up your own hot tea and coffee.

Picnic food is somehow always more exciting when packed by someone else. I can still remember the thrill of unwrapping picnic lunches packed by my grandmother on the farm as a child. High up in the hay barn, or hidden away in a camp made from fallen trees and hay bales, my cousin and I would tuck into sandwiches made with sliced white bread, a smear of Marmite and rather more Anchor butter than was ever good for anyone. (I still have a penchant for this combination, and have been known to tuck in shamelessly at children's parties, should it ever be on offer.) It can be a thoughtful gesture to pack a little picnic for friends or family who have come to lunch, or to stay for the weekend, and have a long journey home by car or public transport. Children, in particular, will appreciate a prettily packed snack, and it's also a good way of clearing the decks of leftover cheese, cakes and so on.

What to eat

When it comes to standard picnic fare, good standbys include:

- a whole roast chicken – the legs and wings can be torn off, but remember a carving knife to slice up the breast
- my Favourite Cheese Pie (dead-easy recipe on pp.51–2)
- a cold ham with a jar of home-made chutney or piccalilli (see pp.164–5)
- a large old-fashioned pork pie with proper crisp but greasy pastry and jelly inside (see p.266 for suppliers)
- a huge pile of shell-on prawns with garlic mayonnaise in which to dip them (on a hot day, and if you're travelling far, buy frozen prawns, which should be thawed but beautifully cold on your arrival – and remember a big bowl for the shells and wipes or flannels for cleaning hands)

- a crisp green salad with dressing in a separate jar; pasta salad with olives, cucumber, tuna and sweetcorn
- Scotch eggs or hard-boiled eggs, with paper twists of salt
- raw carrots and peppers cut into chunks with tubs of hummus and/or guacamole
- lots of good crusty fresh bread – baguettes are always good
- good old-fashioned sandwiches are somehow much nicer if packed in greaseproof paper and tied with string rather than squashed into foil or clingfilm (just don't include tomatoes unless you like soggy wet bread)
- for a picnic pudding, you can't beat something like a cheesecake (bought and packed in a cardboard box) and loads of fresh fruit
- watermelon travels well and is wonderfully refreshing on a hot summer's day. A rather wicked treat, to which a friend introduced me at a summer music festival where bringing one's own alcohol was not permitted, is to cut a hole in the top of the watermelon and upend a bottle of vodka into the fruit overnight

For a simple and stylish picnic that is easy to carry, pack everything in one of those Indian 'Tiffin' cases – seven or so shiny metal dishes that stack one on top of another and are secured with a carrying handle. I got mine from a car boot sale but Habitat (0844 499 1111/www.habitat.co.uk) and Toast (0844 557 5200/www.toast.co.uk) were selling similar ones recently. For picnics for large numbers, where you are providing all the food, you can keep things beautifully simple. For my own birthday parties in the park I used to buy sacks of freshly made bagels from the baker's in Brick Lane, split and fill them with combinations of smoked salmon, cream cheese and gherkins and serve alongside mounds of glossy dark cherries just in season. All this travelled well, and looked and tasted lovely. Be sure to remember lots of recycling bags in which to pack up all traces of the fun afterwards.

Year-round picnicking

But don't think you can only picnic on a summer's day with the sun shining and birds twittering in the trees. To be an exclusively fair-weather picnicker is to miss a lot of the fun. Some of my most memorable picnics – more of an outdoor snack in some cases, to be precise – have been in the dead of winter. Going to my allotment on New Year's Day with a Thermos of coffee and leftover Christmas cake was always a much enjoyed ritual with the friends with whom I shared the plot; cupping our hands around the beakers to keep warm, we'd survey the beds and make plans for the coming year through the steam rising up in front of our faces. And when, on a blustery afternoon last November, my three-year-old was adamant about taking our huge picnic hamper down to the sea, I'm so glad I gave in to her insistent pleas. As we cuddled up beneath a warm blanket, with hot tea for me, warm apple juice for her and a couple of flapjacks, watching the waves crashing and foaming on the shingle, I could not have felt happier and luckier to be there. That's the thing about picnics: there is often quite a bit of effort involved, and at times the entire idea might seem to be madness – but it's almost always worth it in the end.

Rules For French Cricket

This is a great group activity for all ages, after a picnic or as part of a day on a beach with large expanses of sand. All you need are a soft ball and a bat (a sturdy length of wood or driftwood will do). Everyone stands in a big circle around the person holding the bat. Basically, they all throw the ball at them, trying for a hit below the knees, while the batsman tries to defend themselves.

- If they defend a throw by hitting the ball away, they are allowed to turn to face the next assailant.
- If the ball goes past them without touching the bat then they cannot move their feet and therefore have to twist to protect throws from behind.
- If they hit the ball and another player catches it, that person becomes the batsman.
- If a player lands a hit on the batsman's legs they get to bat next.

❉ *Go Beachcombing* ❉

A whole day on the beach is a real treat in summer, even for people like us who spend a lot of time by the sea. The trick, especially when travelling from far afield, is to remember the items that really make life much easier (sun cream, food, lots to drink, enough towels, a windbreak if needed) without getting utterly bogged down. Some people like simply to lie and look at the clouds, or sit gazing out to sea; some are not happy unless they come equipped with snorkelling and surfing gear or ball games to play on the sand (see above for rules for French Cricket). Others like to go rock-pooling, shrimping or fishing for crabs, armed with bits of bacon on lengths of string.

Apart from swimming as much as I can, the only exercise I favour on the beach is a walk up and down the shoreline, looking for treasures. Strictly speaking, it is not advisable to take too much from beaches, but all manner of pebbles, shells and odd-shaped pieces of driftwood seem to make their way into our house, in pockets, buckets or beach bags. Some go straight out again, the prettiest enjoy a brief sojourn on a plate or bowl, while a few get incorporated into something a little more permanent. Almost everything finds its way back to the shore in the end, however. The important thing is to use and/or appreciate your finds and then return them – no one wants a load of dusty old shells and pebbles cluttering up the place. The following ideas for making use of beachcombings around the home are simple yet stylish and can easily be de-assembled and their components returned to the shore.

Pebbles

I have a bit of a thing about stones with holes in them or ones shaped like hearts. The former are strung on rope or string in multiples of thirteen – for luck, the locals on our beach tell me – and the latter are ranged in a row on a shelf in our bathroom. I love the endless different colours and textures: the pebbles where we live are either ochre, grey or white or endless permutations of the same. Pebbles with holes in can be used to hold incense sticks, with a shell or flat stone beneath to catch the ash. Larger stones can be used as door props, and I've known people drill holes in them to hold candles or night lights. Pebble mosaics for the garden look lovely – particularly in seaside locations – but a less permanent option is simply to arrange them in a simple spiral, either in the home or outside, as is done with great beauty at Kettle's Yard in Cambridge (p.61).

Driftwood

Fragments of driftwood, bleached silver-grey, are also good keepsakes; depending on their size they can be used on light-pulls, as door or window stops or to make simple garden stools or benches. I have a plan to find one in an interesting shape and get an artist friend to paint the name of our seaside house on it in white paint. A sturdy piece of driftwood can also be used as the handle of an impromptu kite or a bat for a game of French Cricket (p.133).

Shells

And then there are shells – from those tiny pinkish-striped ones that leave a trail along the low-tide mark to ridged white or soot-tinged cockles, midnight-blue mussels, pinky-white 'slipper shells' and larger whelks and winkles with their satisfying spirals. Wash them well, and arrange in patterns or ranged in lines along shelves, or cram into a glass vase to prop up dried allium or sea-kale seed-heads. Large flat oyster-type shells or scallop shells can be used as salt cellars, soap dishes or ashtrays. Children love playing with shells: younger ones glue them on to cheap wooden picture frames or embed them in plaster of Paris smeared on plant pots; older ones like threading the tiniest clam-type shells (which handily have a hole in just the right place) into necklaces or pendants, or sewing them on to thick card to make greetings cards.

Unusual finds

Occasionally there is a real thrill on the beach – a spate of spider-crabs shedding their old shells, for instance, a shark's skeleton, cleaned and bleached by the waves, or a line of bright orange starfish stretching for miles at low tide. I remember the surreal beauty of a favourite beach in western Scotland almost completely covered, one morning, in heart urchin cases, as fine, white and delicate as porcelain. Trying not to crush them as I walked, I picked some and brought them home, where, displayed in a glass cylindrical vase in my bedroom, they were as beautiful as any art installation. (Sadly they did not survive the last move.) They might have made a good lampstand, displayed in this way; indeed, I have often thought about doing something clever to back-light shells to bring out their colour further. Alas, I am not clever enough with electrics to do something about it; maybe you are.

Sea pictures

As a child on seaside holidays, I used to spend hours making intricate 'sea pictures', either landscapes or faces using seaweed as grass or hair, and shells and pebbles as houses, rocks, eyes, noses or other features. If you have children to amuse, offering a small prize for the best sea picture is a good way to keep them happy for a while. It's a slightly more unusual alternative to the old standbys of sandcastles (complete with moats and fairytale turrets made from wet sand trickled through fingers), intricate ball runs and life-sized boats, all fashioned from sand and awaiting transformation – and ultimate destruction – when the tide comes in.

Edible beachcombings

My favourite kind of beach finds are the edible ones: samphire from the salt estuaries (see p.84), scallops and caragheen sea-weed in Ireland, tiny shrimps from the sea and, if you're feeling brave, razor clams, which look rather like yellow slugs wriggling out of their long hinged shells, but taste delicious lightly fried in butter.

❋ *Pick Your Own* ❋

This is self-explanatory, really, but worth remembering as both a good cheap source of local fresh fruit, and a good day or after-noon out. There are two approaches: to plan ahead with military precision, knowing what you want to pick and how much of it you need and taking all the necessary containers and so on with you; and the ad hoc diversion en route to somewhere else. My family favoured the former option during my childhood, and a good chunk of my formative years was spent bending over bushes in fruit farms in various parts of Kent. It was a while before my sisters and I realized that, though gooseberries were the easiest to pick – gaining you the satisfaction of fast-filling punnets and brownie points from the parents – that did mean an interminable winter of gooseberry pies and crumbles. (Gooseberry fool in summer is one delicious thing; snot-green gooseberry purée throughout the winter is another.) But we also used to pick huge amounts of strawberries, which are pretty useless for freezing, and would make ourselves sick by gorging on them in the back seat all the way home.

I'd like to plan a pick your own day in the spirit of these

childhood jaunts, but for us it often seems to be a last-minute dash or diversion, having seen a sign by the side of the road on our way down to the sea or to stay the weekend with friends. If you have a cool box in the car, particularly the sort that can plug into the battery to keep cold, a good few pounds of fruit can be kept at their peak even in hot weather. If not, lots of newspaper wrapped around the containers provides good insulation. Make sure the fruit will travel without getting damaged; a huge pile of fresh local strawberries, raspberries or cherries is a great gift, and a tremendous treat in the middle of the table if you have friends coming round, or are planning a party – a soggy, smelly, oozing mess is not.

Just a few warnings: don't pick more than you can eat, carry, store or freeze; it is easy to get carried away – see note on goose-berries on the previous page. Take hats and wear suntan lotion: even if it does not seem particularly hot, hours out in the open will take their toll. Insect repellent – and appropriate remedies in case of stings – is a good precaution. Take plenty of water to drink, and stop for frequent breaks, walks and snacks or the entire operation will stop being fun. Then, when you get home, you can embark on either of the following pursuits.

❉   *Make Jam*   ❉

I have spent many sweltering summers bending over hot pre-serving pans and obsessively testing the fruit for pectin content and set, only to end up with a gloopy mess that refuses to set or goo that cuts like jelly – never anything in between. The suc-cesses of recent years have all been down to one thing, in my opinion: jam sugar. I now buy the special jam sugar, containing pectin (which is vital for getting the likes of strawberries to set), that is readily available in supermarkets and follow the instructions on the back of the bag, reducing the amount of sugar slightly and adding a little lemon. (Use preserving sugar for high-pectin fruit such as blackcurrants, plums or gooseberries.) This is my foolproof recipe, which I have used with strawberries, raspberries and blackberries with equal success. The key seems to be slow cooking before the sugar is added and very intense and short cooking thereafter. Heating the sugar first in a low oven also seems to help, and reduces the boiling time, too much of which can adversely affect the colour, flavour and set.

 FOOLPROOF JAM

This makes 7 375ml jars

> *1.3kg fruit, wiped clean and with stalks removed*
> *juice of 1 large lemon*
> *900g jam sugar (heated for 20 minutes in a low oven)*
> *knob of butter*
> *a stainless-steel preserving pan (aluminium can react with*
>   *acid fruit)*

Put a small tea plate in the fridge to cool. Place the fruit and lemon juice in a preserving pan and heat till the juices run. Mash the fruit down a bit with a potato masher and cook for a further 5 minutes but do not boil. Tip in the sugar and stir till completely dissolved, still not boiling. Add the knob of butter. Then, increase the heat and bring to a full rolling boil that cannot be stirred down. Start timing and boil for 4 minutes only. Remove from the heat and test for a set by dropping a teaspoonful on the cold plate, leaving for a minute and seeing if wrinkles form when you push the surface – if they do the jam is ready and can be poured into sterilized jars (fresh from a hot dishwasher will do), labelled and stored. If not, boil up the jam again and test a few minutes later. Making little lid covers from gingham or pretty floral fabric is hugely satisfying and transforms the workaday jars into lovely presents. Line them up on your shelves and swell with pride.

 ROSE PETAL JAM

A delicate pink jam made from rose petals can be used to flavour ice creams, sorbets and syllabubs, or to serve whipped up into cream to accompany a big bowl of strawberries. Its flavour and scent will evoke the hazy height of midsummer, even on a wet winter's day. This makes two or three small jars.

1 cup of sugar – jam sugar ensures the best set
2–3 tablespoons water
2 tablespoons strained lemon juice
1 cup of rose petals – wild roses or the most fragrant you can
   find, closely packed

Make a syrup by heating the sugar, water and lemon juice till the sugar has all dissolved. Add the rose petals and cook gently for 15 minutes – be sure not to boil too highly or for too long, as the delicate fragrance will be destroyed. Pour into sterilized small glass pots or jars, cover the surface with greaseproof paper circles and seal.

To add to ice cream, make a further batch of the same lemon and sugar syrup, boiling fast for 3 minutes this time and leaving to cool. Whip up 300ml thick cream, fold in a good dollop of rose petal jam and pour into an ice-cream maker or freeze in a pot until firm.

❋ *Make Your Own Ice Cream* ❋

Like baking a cake, making your own ice cream is terribly simple and time-effective, but gives the impression of having gone to immense trouble – so it's a great trick to have up your sleeve when entertaining visitors. It is possible to make perfectly serviceable ice cream without a machine, but all the endless stirring and taking out of the freezer can be a bit of a faff, so I'd definitely invest in an ice-cream maker. No need to get one of the huge plug-in ones; my middle-range Magimix requires no electricity beyond the freezer and has never let me down. You just need to place the base in the freezer overnight before making the ice cream.

There are extremely delicious recipes for old-fashioned vanilla and traditional rich chocolate ice cream that entail cooking and cooling an egg and milk custard, but for a quick and foolproof fruit ice cream (great for using up piles of pick your own) you can't beat the following simple recipe. The amount of sugar needed will depend on the type and sweetness of the fruit, so taste for sweetness before freezing.

BASIC FRUIT ICE CREAM

> *500g ripe soft fruit – strawberries and raspberries can be*
> *mashed and used raw, but blackberries and blackcurrants*
> *should be stewed with a little sugar and water till soft*
> *100g caster sugar*
> *300ml double cream (600ml for blackcurrants)*
> *juice of 1 lemon*

Mash the fruit with the sugar, cream and lemon juice, pour into the ice-cream maker and follow the makers' instructions – which usually involve around 10–15 minutes' intensive automatic churning. Take out of the freezer about 20 minutes before you need to serve it, to ensure it will be soft enough for spooning.

(See also p.141 for rose petal ice cream.)

❋ *Take the Inside Out* ❋

I've always rather liked the idea of decamping outside for the summer into an impromptu outdoor room. I remember interviewing the Italian fashion designer Alberta Ferretti in an open-sided tent-like structure she erects on her immaculate lawn from Easter to October every year and fills with white-covered sofas, comfortable floor cushions, rugs, throws and plants – everything, in fact, that one would ever want inside, but with that lovely light feeling of camping (and none of the discomfort). If wind or a shower threatened, she'd just let down the sides and light a little gas heater. Heaven. I think there was even a candelabra hanging on a lacy white tie from a branch of the tree outside.

We don't all have the budget – or the climate – to go to such extremes, but if your garden is big enough, erecting a temporary structure such as an attractive canvas tent, or even a yurt or tepee (see websites such as www.whitecanvastents.com, www.indiantents.com, www.thereallyinterestingtentcompany.co.uk and www.Tipi.co.uk) can create some extra room for weekend summer activities or guests, provide a focus for parties and generally make life feel more festive for a few months. (Technically speaking, structures such as tepees need planning permission if they are to be left standing for more than twenty-eight days. I'd have hoped that planning departments would be too busy tracking down ugly roof extensions and uPVC conservatories to be bothering with such things. But don't say I didn't warn you.)

If you don't have the room or inclination for a tent, making a garden of any size work as an extra room in the summer months is a great way of gaining the feeling of extra space. Create an outdoor eating area with an attractive outdoor table and chairs (The Cotswold Company (0844 984 0984/www.cotswoldco.com) does nice ones, but junk shop finds, repainted in subtly graduated blues, mauves and greys, look every bit as good) and a simple pergola above for shade. Grapevines provide good shade just when it's needed in high summer, and a gloriously sybaritic feel with bunches of ripening fruit dangling overhead. They can be intertwined with scented roses or jasmine, but while you wait for the plants to grow, you can make a simple yet stylish awning by throwing a banner of white or striped fabric over the top and securing with ties; sari silk would also look sensational. If you already have a seating area, jazz it up by treating the seats to new cushions or hanging pretty bunting or weaving white pin-prick fairy lights overhead (Cox & Cox (0870 442 4787/www.coxandcox.co.uk) is particularly good at attractive but practical outdoor accessories.) For lounging during the day, invest in one or two seriously good pieces. RE (01434 634567/www.re-foundobjects.com) has the smartest deckchairs around in jazzy south-of-France-inspired stripes while Odd's (01993 830674/www.oddlimited.com) 'Old Rocker' – a swinging seat upholstered in faded flowery canvas – is not only beautiful but comfortable enough to go to sleep in. To continue the fun on into intimate, atmospheric evenings, bring out piles of lovely old blankets and invest in a fire bowl (Toast's stunning new House & Home catalogue (0844 557 5200/www.toast.co.uk) has both).

❋ *Bring the Outdoors In* ❋

Summer is all about blurring the boundaries of the home: you can bring the indoors out, but you can also bring the outdoors in, with great style. Forget expensive cut flowers, flown in from halfway across the world and too often faded in just a few days, and plant yourself an indoor garden. Most garden plants will do fine for a few weeks inside and, given the right conditions, many will thrive. In light rooms, go for collections of aromatic herbs, which will not only scent the space but be useful for cooking or flavouring summer cocktails (see p.117). Choose the largest container you can find, so you can plant large enough amounts to be useful – small fiddly pots may look good on a windowsill but are hopeless for snipping off more than the odd leaf. Don't limit yourself to conventional pots: why not plant your herbs in an attractive old wooden packing crate, or even a battered suitcase with the lid open? Just make sure the plants have good drainage – you may have to stand a large tray beneath the planter to catch any drips. (For mail order herbs try Jekka's Herb Farm (01454 418878/www.jekkasherbfarm.com) or Poyntzfield Herb Nursery in Scotland (01381 610352/ www.poyntzfieldherbs.co.uk) whose range of 400 organically grown herbs comes beautifully wrapped.) Lavender would also make a stunning scented centrepiece on a dining or coffee table – again, so long as the light is good. Downderry Nurseries (01732 810081/www.downderry-nursery.co.uk) has lavenders from deepest purple through mauves and pinks to white, with all manner of different leaf shapes and shades, a combination of which would look lovely; when you've enjoyed them for a few weeks just plant them out in the garden. You could even bring a potted shrub or tree in from the garden for a short sojourn, covering any unsightly soil with a smart mulch of pebbles, shells, glass marbles or old corks.

And don't stop there. I once grew morning glories round my sitting room window to great effect, and screened my bathroom with sweet-smelling jasmine in a pot on the windowsill. Just remember that most plants will need more watering inside the house, so be sure to look out for signs of stress. For unusual and recycled containers try Plantstuff (0870 774 3366/www.plant stuff.com) or the quirky and excellent Pedlars (01330 850400/ www.pedlars.co.uk).

❋ *Revamp Your Home For Summer* ❋

It's easy to give your home a fresh new look and feel for summer in one weekend without resorting to full-scale decorating. Just as you peel off wintry clothes when the weather warms up, remove unnecessarily heavy layers from your windows and furnishings. Those heavy velvet curtains may have been great for keeping out winter draughts, but for now all that's needed is yards of floaty muslin or vibrant sari silk. Replace cosy throws on sofas with light-coloured linen or ticking (for a classic New England beach house look, you might want to invest in fitted linen-mix loose covers that are put on just for the summer and can simply be thrown in the washing machine when dirty). Even cushion covers can change; find pretty faded linen floral ones at Cabbages & Roses (020 7352 7333/www.cabbagesand roses.com) or make your own in breezy striped ticking from Ian Mankin (020 7722 0997/www.ianmankin.com). Take up heavy, dark-coloured rugs and revert to floorboards (paint in pastel green or blue for a fresh summery look) or replace with simple sisal runners. (The Cotswold Company (0844 984 0984/www.cotswoldco.com) has attractive coconut herringbone rugs.) And don't forget the flowers – armfuls of them, carried in from the garden if possible and arranged loosely in large jugs, or bought in bulk at discount from a wholesale flower market (see p.150 for more ideas).

❋ *Catch Rainbows* ❋

Make the most of the summer sunshine by hanging crystals on fishing wire at the windows to catch the light and send it dancing in rainbows round the room. This is simple, yet so effective – and children love it. A crystal with wire to hang it on can also be a nice present to take to someone who is ill in bed; apart from being beautiful to watch, I like to imagine that crystals, combined with sunshine, must have some sort of mystic healing power. You can buy crystals online at www.crystalcavern.com but it's much more fun to buy them yourself at a shop such as Mysteries in Covent Garden, London (020 7240 3688/ www.mysteries.co.uk) – just avert your eyes from all the dodgy dragon ornaments.

❋ *Visit a Garden – or Open Your Own* ❋

From early summer to around the end of September, Britain's many thousands of private back gardens are looking at their best. And you can visit the cream of the crop through the National Gardens Scheme, an organization founded more than eighty years ago in which garden-owners whose plots pass the strict inspection criteria can open their gardens to the public to raise money for a clutch of worthy charities. Buy *The Yellow Book*, which lists the gardens according to location and date, from good bookshops in early spring and plan trips in advance – or keep a copy in the car for last-minute diversions. Visiting gardens in your own locality is a great way of seeing how other gardeners cope with comparable conditions. And making a special visit to some of the more unusual examples – or pretty terraces or villages where a number of smaller gardens open on the same day – pays huge dividends in enjoyment and inspiration. There are sometimes very reasonably priced plant sales, too, not to mention home-baked cakes and tea.

If you have a garden and think it might be good enough to be included in the list, get in touch with your local organizer (listed in the front of *The Yellow Book*) and arrange for an inspection visit. The idea of opening to the public may seem daunting, but as someone who has done it for many years with what must be one of the smallest gardens on their books, let me assure you it is great fun, and the NGS does a lot to help, sending masses of bright yellow posters for you to tack up (and plastic covers to protect them from rain) and offering advice on the phone. You definitely make more money for the charities if you offer cakes and tea as well, so enlist a few friends and family members to man the refreshments stall (make the prices manageable multiples of 50p or £1 to save scrabbling about for change). You'll also need someone on the front door to take money and keep an eye on who's coming in and out (one year there was actually a queue outside our house, as the garden is so tiny, and my husband had to ward people off, requesting they take a look at the front garden first). Though it might seem lazy, you need to keep yourself free to answer endless questions about how long you've lived here and which plant is which (more organized types do a printout, but I have never got round to this). It's quite a full-on few hours for all concerned, but it is always great to meet other gardeners, and the feel-good factor at the end of having raised money for charity just by doing something you love doing anyway is well worth it. (Make sure you keep some cakes back, and something fizzy in the fridge to reward your workers with, though!) Contact the National Gardens Scheme on 01483 211535 or visit www.ngs.org for further information.

Incidentally, you don't have to go through the NGS to open your own garden. Clubbing together with gardening neighbours to open your gardens on the same day is a marvellous way to raise money for locally based charities, a new church roof and so on.

❋ *Get Out the Magnifying Glass* ❋

The following simple pleasure is best enjoyed in the privacy of your own garden, lest anyone spot you and think you've finally lost your marbles. I was introduced to it by the garden writer Mirabel Osler, who knows a thing or two about simple pleasures and enjoys them in great style. After a lovely lunch in her long, narrow Ludlow back garden, Mirabel darted inside and came out with two large magnifying glasses and led me about her garden, looking at different flowers through our glasses as we went. What a revelation. Gazing into the heart of a flower with a powerful magnifying glass can be truly mind-blowing. All the component parts – pistils, anthers, stigma and so on – become objects of mysterious, otherworldly beauty. The central boss of a *Magnolia grandiflora* is transformed into a Tamil temple, intricately carved in creamy white marble; the rose Golden Wings has stamens as intricately crafted as underwater coral; while an opulent oriental poppy in full bloom has you quoting Ted Hughes's poem, 'Big Poppy'. Every hair, every vein, every subtlest marking is magnified many times, making you look at the miracle of the flower's construction anew. And for a bee's-eye view worthy of a pyschedelic pop artist, peer up the spotted tunnel of a foxglove and wonder.

Children adore this simple yet absorbing exercise, and it is worth having quite a few magnifying glasses so they can all enjoy it at once – it can keep even a bunch of boisterous young boys quiet for ages. And if they grow bored of flowers, get them to look at insects and pond life, too.

For Mirabel Osler's own account of plants under the microscope, and many other garden pleasures, read her wonderful book, *In the Eye of the Garden*.

✻ *Pick Garden Flowers* ✻

Walking around a spring or summer garden, seeing what's in bloom and picking just enough to fill a vase for your desk or kitchen table is a lovely way to start a weekend day. The calm of the morning, the scent of dew on the grass and the flowers waking up in the sun combine to offer a gentle, sensory treat – do it barefoot for full effect, if, like me, you're a hippy at heart. Use sharp secateurs for the cleanest cut, and lay the flowers in a shallow trug or, if you are picking quite a few, plunge them straight into a florist's bucket of water to keep them at their best. Then, once indoors, cut a further inch or so off the bottom of the stems and arrange in whatever receptacle springs to hand or mind.

Don't confine yourself to jugs and vases, lovely though a plain jug of cherry blossom or Japanese vase of irises looks. I save interesting glass bottles for just a single allium, rose or dahlia; even attractive jam jars for simple bunches of bluebells, hyacinths or lily of the valley. You can pick up old jars and bottles very cheaply from junk shops; believe it or not, old-fashioned fish paste jars are particularly pretty for tiny posies of primroses, violets or nasturtiums. Wine glasses or coloured glass tumblers also make fine impromptu vases for a few select blooms. Best of all I love my collection of really tiny vases, only an inch high and shaped as spheres, rounded squares and cylinders, available from Designers Guild (020 7893 7400/ www.designersguild.com) and just big enough for one flower, sprig or leaf apiece. Even in the dead of winter, when it would be hard to fill even a small vase with flowers from the garden, there is always enough for these little vases, which sit in the middle of the kitchen table, amid candles and night lights, where they can be admired at close quarters.

I much prefer the wild abandon of garden flowers – and they seem to have a radiance that shop-bought flowers, often picked in bud and flown halfway around the world, have not. I'd far rather fill my house with jugs of apple blossom and frothing cow parsley than fancy florists' 'arrangements' (see pp.95 and 284). But at certain times of the year the pickings are scarce. A house without flowers is a house without life, in my book, so I do buy flowers, too – as locally and seasonally as I can. Tiny posies of snowdrops in winter, bunches of bright yellow daffodils, like pools of sunshine in spring (sacrilege before January, except for Paperwhite narcissi: see p.197), and then anemones, scented stocks and vivid dahlias in summer.

To decorate the house for a party, I get up early and join the professional florists at New Covent Garden Flower Market (020 7720 2211/www.cgma.gov.uk for details), where you can pick up large bunches or 'wraps' of fifty or more of the same flower for not much more than the price of a regular bunch in the shops (but remember to factor in the VAT and £4 parking fee). Arriving home with great boxes of flowers gives me a huge creative buzz. I feel like an artist with a new box of paints – the finished picture is not clear, but the colours and textures of the raw materials are endlessly inspiring.

It's always lovely to receive a bouquet of flowers, but sometimes the arrangements are too trussed-up and complex for my taste. But there's great fun to be had in taking it gently apart, separating the flowers into types and colours, cutting some down and making up several smaller, simpler bunches. Even flowers you don't normally like can be made to look beautiful somehow: carnations can look pretty and exotic floating in a shallow dish of water (pulling the calyx, or green casing, in which the flower sits helps loosen the petals for a fuller, more informal look) and individual gladioli florets can be used in the same way. (See p.82 for tips on sending the best cut flowers.)

Caring for cut flowers is key: change the water at least every other day and cut another inch or so off the stems after a few days to keep the flowers looking fresh. Even if a few blooms are fading, pick over the bunch, discard what's dead and keep what's not to extend the life of a bouquet – even down to floating individual blooms as above. And when it's time to get rid of your flowers, don't throw roses away. The petals can be strewn over lawns or on the surface of ponds for a party, or dried to make potpourri. Everything else can go on the compost heap, to decay down and help create the flowers of tomorrow.

Finally, though I would never normally recommend fake flowers in a million years, Bloom's catalogue (01949 845444/ www.bloom.uk.com) is a cut above naff silk roses and unconvincing lilies. The more 'false-looking' the flower in its natural state, the more successful the fake version. Trust me, Bloom's white orchids (complete with buds and roots bursting from a clear glass container) are realistic enough to fool even seasoned gardeners.

❋   *Save Seeds*   ❋

Seed-saving is a lovely late summer pursuit that seems to ritualize the passage into autumn and the turning of the cycles of the year. Seeds gathered now are the fruits of this year's flowers, to be stored over winter and sown next spring to blossom again as next summer's blooms. The practice can also save quite a bit of money, and keep alive memories of particular people and places. Why give your money to the seed catalogues when you can swap home-grown seed with friends? The process is simple, though it is worth remembering that the seed from certain plants, such as hellebores and umbellifers, has to be sown fresh, immediately after gathering, in order to have a chance of germinating.

During the course of the summer, look for especially fine flowers whose size, colour or flowering habit has been noticeably attractive or unusual. Instead of dead-heading them as you might the rest, mark them with a small length of coloured thread or ribbon tied around the stem. Later on, when the seed is on its way to drying, place a paper bag over the flower-head, cut the stem and tie around the base with string or raffia left long enough to hang it upside down in a warm dry place such as a shed or spare bedroom. When the seed-head is completely dry, simply shake the bag to make sure all the seeds are released.

Seeds need protecting from strong light and extremes of temperature. Save them in small brown envelopes, neatly labelled with the time and place of their picking. You could even get children to decorate the packets, by designing a border and adding a picture, either hand-drawn, potato-printed or cut out from a catalogue, on the front. Pretty packets of seed from your garden make a lovely little present, tucked in with a birthday card or a thank you letter – especially if the recipient has admired the plant in question. Though small and unassuming, a few packets of seed contain within them all the fire and colour and scent of summer.

4.

Seasonal Pleasures: Autumn

J 've never been able to understand people who find autumn depressing in that 'end-of-summer, back-to-school' kind of a way. The changing of the seasons is one of the most wonderful things about the British climate and, though I do adore a long hot summer (whatever happened to them?), it does all get a bit dried out and frayed at the edges come the end of August, when everyone's ready for a change. Quite apart from which – call me a swot if you like – I was always quite happy to go back to school.

There's a magical time – and it often seems to be early September – when late summer slips softly into autumn. It's not so much a change in the weather; our Indian summer sun can shine well into November and still laps like warm water on my back as I work in the garden. It's more of a shift in atmosphere: we wake up one morning to a crispness in the air, a sweet translucency in the light that simply were not here before. Rosehips wink in the hedgerows and flocks of starlings hang like clouds above the ripening elder bushes. Suddenly there are spiders' webs everywhere, strung with droplets of dew in the dawn. Though often, in the dog days of July and August, I harbour a childish wish that summer will never end, I invariably greet these golden days of early autumn with relief. I love the simple annual rituals they entail: slipping a soft wool jersey over suntanned skin; lighting the first log fire; stirring blackberries into jams and the last fat courgettes of the season into pickles and chutney; watching the leaves change colour and bringing some autumnal bounty indoors to decorate the house.

❧ *Mark the Autumn Festivals* ❧

Harvest festival

Autumn is a great time for celebrating. First comes Harvest Festival – a good excuse to go to church if you don't usually (see pp.312–14), sing along to 'We Plough the Fields and Scatter' and give thanks for the harvest, both literal and allegorical, that we've reaped in our own lives. The tradition of passing on surplus produce and provisions to needy families has continued through the ages, though rustling supermarket bags have all too often replaced the baskets of home-grown produce lining the steps up to the altar that I remember from my own country childhood. Though I can understand that most people on the breadline would far rather receive tinned goods and washing powder than any number of pumpkins and marrows, it would be good to see a revival in home-made food and fresh produce alongside – surely everyone loves a fruit cake and a bag of crispy apples?

Hallowe'en

Next up is Hallowe'en – a great excuse for a weekend party. We like to blame America for the recent commercialization of this wonderful pagan festival, but the trouble is that we have adopted only one small part of the transatlantic festivities and chosen to ignore the rest. When I was in the States one October, I found a celebration of autumn that went far beyond tacky trick-or-treating. No porch or doorway, from New York to New Orleans, was without its collection of colourful carved jack-o'-lanterns stacked up the steps, while piles of pumpkins were for sale on street corners, from bulbous monsters 5 feet across to tiddlers for ranging along windowsills. Punctuated by these enormous and improbable fruits, city life took on a jolly, festive feeling, and the scent of pumpkin pie and hot cider hung in the air.

Long before anyone terrorized the neighbourhood dressed as a spook, Hallowe'en was a pagan celebration to mark the end of the autumn harvest and the onset of winter. The Celtic New Year fell on 1 November, but the partying began the night before, with the decking of halls with seasonal produce and a communal harvest supper. As on the Mexican Day of the Dead, there was a belief that the gap between the worlds of the living and the dead was opened on this night, and food was left out for ghosts and roaming spirits, too. I like to keep aware of this, during all the foolish frenzy of Hallowe'en, and imagine loved ones who have passed on hovering, unseen, on the edge of it all. Whatever one's beliefs, autumn is a great time for a party, and it feels good to mark the changing of the seasons. Out in the garden, combine harvesting your remaining produce with a timely prune and tidy-up, and you'll have lots of lovely materials to bring inside for both decorating and cooking.

Hallowe'en wouldn't be Hallowe'en without pumpkin

lanterns, of course, though when I was a child we always used swedes or turnips, which smelled awful and wrinkled up to form horrible gummy grins. I still love the annual ritual of gouging out pumpkins and marking out the usual toothy grimace and triangle eyes to cut (always harder than you think) with a sharp knife. We've taken to growing our own in recent years, with great success. Pumpkin seeds are among the easiest to germinate and grow (see pp.95–9), and while they do need a fair amount of space, can be intercropped with sweetcorn, which looks good as well as keeping the weeds down and moisture in. Keep the plants happy with plenty of water and a good feed every so often – plus sunshine if they are to ripen from green to orange.

Last year's pair of seedlings (one as insurance in case the slugs ate the other) yielded a total of ten sizeable fruits, so we threw an impromptu pumpkin party for my daughter and some little friends on the Saturday before Hallowe'en. They all arrived in costumes (one witch was even on a home-made besom) and had great fun (with parental help, of course) carving their gruesome faces before rushing off around the garden in a Hallowe'en version of an Easter egg hunt, with foil-wrapped pumpkins and skeletons instead of eggs. There was plenty of pumpkin soup (from the scrapings of a lantern I'd prepared earlier) plus barbecued hot dogs and warm apple juice – and lashings of local cider for the grown-ups. It was such a success I think we'll make it an annual event. The line of finished lanterns, grinning from ear to ear and aglow from the light of the candles inside, was quite a sight to see before they were carefully picked up and cradled home.

Other traditional Hallowe'en games include bobbing for apples (easier and drier if the apples are small!), eating sticky buns strung from a washing line with hands behind backs, and peeling an apple keeping the peel in once piece and throwing it over the left shoulder – the fallen peel is supposed to form the initial of the person you will marry.

Bonfire Night

Bonfire Night almost seems to have been superseded by Hallowe'en, but it would be a great shame if this most idiosyncratic of English festivities were to die out. Maybe the idea of burning an effigy seems somehow pagan and arcane; at any rate, the energy put into guy-making in my own childhood seems now to be channelled into trick-or-treat gear. When did you last see children collecting a penny for the guy on the pavement? Perhaps it is time to revive the tradition: making a guy is rather like making a scarecrow, and a good way to use up old clothes and festering worn-out cushions.

But happily, in rural East Sussex where we live most of the time, the tradition of guy-making is still alive and well. Bonfire Night festivities begin there in early October and last well into November, with each town allocated a different night for its celebrations so it's possible to go on a tour of them all. There's an anarchic feel to it all, with drums and fiery torches ablaze into the night. And you can forget poor old Guy Fawkes: the effigies can take a range of forms, and in Lewes are famously modelled on the popularly agreed *bête noire* of the year, from David Beckham (when he mucked up the World Cup) to Osama bin Laden. And then there are the fireworks . . . See www.fireworks.co.uk/abt/bonfiresocieties.html for a list of local bonfire societies.

Whether you attend a municipal display or enjoy a roman candle or two in the privacy of your back garden, Bonfire Night – or the weekend before or after it – is also a good opportunity for a party. Everyone loves to sit round a fire in the darkness, drinking hot cider and tucking into hearty fare such as jacket potatoes or home-made minestrone (see pp.209–10), barbe-cued sausages, and gingerbread or baked apples for pudding. Or get together with your neighbours and have a joint bonfire, perhaps in the largest garden, or according to a rota, or on a piece of public land nearby, to which everyone contributes. We experienced something similar last autumn when an impromp-tu communal bonfire celebration evolved in our area: some neighbours started to build a bonfire the Saturday beforehand on commonly used land and it grew like Topsy throughout the week as more and more people added prunings, old pallets and so on from their own gardens. By Bonfire Night itself it was enormous, and we all stood around to watch it being lit and brought fireworks to share over home-made hot dogs and burg-ers. As is so often the case with communal enterprises (see p.67), the size of the fire, the quality of the fireworks and quan-tity of food and drink were far larger than if everyone had done their own individual thing. And the fun, it goes without saying, was all the more. I do hope we'll do it again this year.

❧ *Go Mushroom-hunting* ❧

The thrill of finding fresh field mushrooms in the grass is a perennial one, and it's worth getting up early on some misty, moisty autumn weekend morning to go to their favourite growing places before other would-be foragers do. Mushrooms literally appear overnight:

> *very*
> *Whitely, discreetly,*
> *Very quietly*

as in the famous Sylvia Plath poem, and I'd love to see speeded-up footage of them pushing through the leaf mould and soil. Depending on where you live you may also find meaty ceps, morels, with their honeycomb texture, golden, flower-like chanterelles and sinister black horns of plenty – even, if you're lucky, that holy grail of mushroom-hunters: a truffle.

On the Continent, people from all walks of life go out foraging in the woods and fields for mushrooms in the autumn. Over here, in spite of our love of cultivated mushrooms and the increasing fashionability of local 'wild food' in restaurant kitchens, an air of danger and caution still hangs over the idea of gathering wild fungi. In fact, of the 3,000 species of large-bodied fungi that grow in the British Isles, only twenty or so are seriously poisonous, and can be identified without too much trouble with the aid of a good field guide. For your first attempt, to avoid tummy aches or worse, and to find the best places, think about joining a 'fungal foray' organized by an expert; you'll find these advertised in the local press, or through your local natural history society or wildlife trust. This is not only a pleasant way to spend a few hours at the weekend, but it will also definitely instil you with more confidence to head out on your own, armed with a shallow basket and a good guide such as Antonio Carluccio's *Complete Mushroom Book* or the mushroom chapter in Richard Mabey's classic *Food for Free*. These not only instruct you on the best mushrooms to pick, but also offer tips on harvesting in such a way that does not kill off the spores needed for more mushrooms to grow.

The following are some good rules of thumb to observe when looking for wild mushrooms:

- Only pick and keep specimens you are absolutely sure of. When in doubt, leave it in or on the ground.
- Pull the whole mushroom, stalk and all, from the ground, twisting gently until it breaks free from the soil. You need the entire specimen, stalk, base and all, for identification purposes; you can then cut off the earthy base to avoid getting soil on the other mushrooms in your basket.
- Don't pick mushrooms that are so old they have started to decay or too young to have developed their trademark characteristics.
- Though moist weather is good, avoid picking on very wet days, when the flesh will be soggy and prone to decay.
- Collect your finds in an open basket, never a plastic bag which will accelerate decay.
- When you get home, go through the specimens once more and cut in half any you are unsure of to check for unwelcome characteristics such as poisonous white gills.
- Clean by brushing, wiping with a soft cloth or cutting away dirt – washing or peeling is unnecessary unless stated in your guide.
- Use all wild mushrooms within twenty-four hours of picking, unless you are going to dry them in a drying oven or by threading, thinly sliced, on to string.

Though initially suspicious, I have recently become a convert to wild mushrooms, helped along by the plates full of chanterelles and horns of plenty that our neighbours in the country have left, most generously, at our door. This generosity has not so far extended to sharing their sources with us, but I'm working on it . . .

◈ *Make Chutney* ◈

I love chutney – the combination of sweetness and vinegary sharpness is the perfect complement to cheese and cold meats, a spread that, with good bread and garden salad, makes up one of my all-time favourite meals. I love making it too; it feels good to use up a glut of produce from the veg plot, or turn an end-of-season bargain from the farmers' market into flavoursome jars to squirrel away on shelves or give as Christmas presents. The slow, rhythmic chopping and mixing is endlessly satisfying: it feels as if I'm stirring summer sunshine and memories into all the jars and bottles to pro-vide cheer through the winter ahead. But I'll admit that some chutneys are more appealing – particularly as presents – than others. Get the proportions slightly wrong and they will end up too vinegary; cook for too long (as most recipes recommend, in my opinion) and you'll be left with a textureless, sludgy dark brown mess. So here I've included my favourite recipe, which I'm asked for so often I keep it on my computer, ready to print out.

🍵 COURGETTE AND DILL PICKLE

Because they are salted and rinsed and only quickly cooked, the courgettes or cucumbers keep all their crispness, and the paper-thin slices, mingled with the mustard seeds and feathery wisps of dill, look lovely through the glass of the jar. This pickle is particularly good with smoked salmon or a mature cheddar sandwich. The following quantities make 4 450g jars.

3 large cucumbers or 6 courgettes
2 large onions
50g coarse salt
450g soft brown sugar
600ml cider vinegar
1 tablespoon whole mustard seeds
a large handful or packet of fresh dill

Slice the vegetables very thinly (ideally with a mandoline), layer with salt in a dish and weigh down with a heavy plate for at least 4 hours. Drain and rinse very well – you don't want any traces of salt to remain. Dissolve the sugar in the vinegar over a medium heat, add the sliced vegetables, seeds and dill and bring to the boil. After 1 minute, remove from the heat and drain, reserving the juices. Boil the juices to reduce by about a third or until syrupy. Put the vegetables in sterilized jars to three-quarters of an inch below the lid, cover with the juices (some will be soaked up) and seal. This can be eaten straight away, but has a better flavour if left for three months – if you can bear the wait! A jar of this, with ribbon around the neck or a circle of jaunty fabric tied round the lid, makes a most welcome present, either for Christmas, or to take to your hostess for dinner, along with a bottle of wine.

Wear Cashmere

It might seem strange to include cashmere in a book on simple pleasures, but I have always believed that a few of life's luxuries (good sofas, chocolate, shoes, wine) are worth sacrificing other, lesser pleasures for. I'd far rather buy one good cashmere jersey every year than three or four cheaper ones that will bring me far less joy. You can save a lot of money by buying in the sales from specialist cashmere companies such as Brora (0845 659 9944/www.brora.co.uk) or Pure (0844 848 1030/www. purecollection.com) who offer a better quality than department stores or supermarkets. Wearing cashmere is like silk underwear – a soft, sensual pleasure that makes you feel caressed and cosseted all day long. It even gives others pleasure when they give you a hug. There are many different weights of cashmere, and a bit of clever layering – sleeveless pullovers with a shirt and cardigan in winter, the same items on their own, or slipped over a dress or skirt in summer – means your favourites can be worn all year long. This has another important advantage: avoiding moth damage.

How to avoid moth damage

Moths are at their most active from April to October – just those months when heavy jerseys might be languishing, unworn, at the back of your wardrobe. And moths *love* cashmere. Just as slugs and snails will go for gourmet lettuce seedlings in a garden brimming with other greens, moths will seek out the one pair of cashmere socks in a wardrobe full of wool. And have you noticed how they never do their damage anywhere it might possibly go unnoticed – round the back of a jersey, for instance, or on the inside of a sleeve? No, the holes will always be right in the middle of the front, or on the neckline or cuffs. This – I have since learned from Mustafa, my dry cleaner, who could be on *Mastermind* with his special subject as the life-cycle and habits of moths – is because the creatures are attracted to food, sweat and saliva as well as the cashmere itself. (And don't worry: you don't have to be a dribbling, smelly slut who puts clothes away with half your dinner spilled down the front to get into trouble – just the slightest trace is enough to attract them.)

The big problem with moths is that once you have got them, they are there to stay unless you take drastic action. Having learned the hard way that moths are not going to be put off by a few hand-sewn sachets filled with lavender and cedar shavings, no matter how pretty the embroidery, getting rid of our moths involved dry cleaning every single item in the wardrobe and the use of some rather dubious industrial-strength chemicals while we went away on holiday for two weeks. I now keep my cashmere jerseys in individual plastic bags, with a strong-smelling lavender sachet in each (renew with a few drops of essential oil every few months). I have also discovered pheromone traps which attract both male and female moths using sex hormones, thus eliminating them before they have a chance to mate and lay eggs (it is the hatching grubs that do all the damage), and which are apparently effective. Good department stores will sell a variety of moth control products – or try the strangely compelling website Do It Yourself Pest Control Supplies (www.diypcs.co.uk) for all manner of traps and deterrents delivered to your door.

Caring for cashmere

I've always believed in not over-washing delicate clothes, but the moth problem made me think again. I either dry clean my cashmere or wash it by hand using a delicate shampoo made specially for cashmere. (The wool programme on a washing machine can end up giving you a felty finish.) Wash inside out, gently squeeze the items after rinsing, roll up in towels and place on top of a radiator for a day; then finish drying out flat, between fresh towels, on the floor. In the words of Lou on *Little Britain*, it's a bit of a kerfuffle, but worth it to preserve that lovely fluffy softness and freshness. It's a bit like caring for a pet.

Over the years, as older items start to get misshapen and (in spite of my efforts) a little moth-eaten, I sew or patch them up as efficiently and attractively as possible and relegate them to gardening wear. I read somewhere that Jade Jagger, that most exotic of creatures, does exactly this, which makes me feel glamorous in the garden, too.

One word of caution: cashmere can be addictive. Before my daughter was born, I bought her a tiny cashmere cardigan from Brora. In spite of the fact that it was full price, not in the sale, she got tremendous wear out of it – the 6–9-month size saw her from birth to nearly two and washed beautifully. But to this day, she will not have any other kind of wool next to her skin. Thus begins a lifetime of luxurious and expensive tastes . . .

Brew Hedgerow Tipples

I was making sloe gin long before I realized you could do the same with blackberries, damsons and elderberries – and use vodka instead of gin. And that cutting up quinces into quarters and steeping them for three months in brandy is a lot less fiddly than making quince jelly. (Do this and you will no longer be looking on a pile of mouldering fruit with a mixture of annoyance and guilt come next year.) The following are more methods/ideas than strict recipes. If you're serious about making hedgerow tipples, good books to get hold of include *First Steps in Winemaking* by C. J. J. Berry, *The Elder: in History, Myth and Cookery* by Ria Loohuizen and *A Hedgerow Cookbook* by Glennie Kindred.

SLOE GIN

Picking sloes and damsons is a lot easier if you take an old-fash-ioned walking stick with you for gently pulling down the spiky higher branches, where the best fruit will often be lurking just out of reach. You can use whatever hedgerow fruit you like in this recipe, but I find sloes and damsons the most delicious – and also love the jewel-bright colour they turn the gin.

assorted hedgerow fruit, well washed
sugar to taste: most recipes suggest a third fruit to a third
alcohol to a third sugar, but this can be too sweet for some
1 bottle of gin

To avoid the laborious process of pricking the fruit all over with a pin, which I did for many years, simply put the washed fruit into plastic bags and place in the freezer for a week, where the cold will do the job of breaking down the skins.

For containers, I tend to use old Kilner or Le Parfait jars, or those large glass jars in which pickling vinegar is sold. I fill each container nearly halfway with fruit, then add enough sugar to bring it up to halfway and fill to the top with gin (cheap supermarket stuff is fine if you can wait for a year, but if you're more impatient it might be worth splashing out on better quality). You can add a couple of cinnamon sticks or a few juniper berries for extra layers of flavour if you want; some people add a few drops of almond essence after two weeks. Place the jars somewhere in the kitchen where you will remember to shake or swirl the fruit around every other day for a total of two months.

When it is ready to bottle, pass the liquid through a doubled muslin several times to ensure all the particles that might compromise its clarity have been removed. The sozzled sloes will have to be discarded on to the compost heap, but the damsons are worth a try: a friend of mine swears by them, warmed, with vanilla ice cream.

Pour, using a funnel, into bottles – smaller pretty ones you have saved up over the year can be given as Christmas presents – and label. The gin is ready to drink after three months, but is best left for a year. Rotating your bottles and bringing last year's to the fore is a nice autumn ritual and you could even invite a few friends round to taste the first of last year's vintage.

Variations using this method include mulberry gin; blackberry vodka (with a vanilla pod added) and walnut vodka (which needs 2–3 years to mature).

 ## QUINCE BRANDY

This looks so lovely in its jar, with all the spices nestled around the fruit, that I don't bother decanting it. It makes a splendid present, and can be used to make mincemeat for mince pies, and added to Christmas pudding and other seasonal treats. The following is enough to fill a large 5-litre jar, which looks spectacular, or a number of smaller containers. It couldn't be easier – you don't even need to peel the fruit.

> *4–6 quinces*
> *4 bottles of cheap brandy*
> *2 large cinnamon sticks*
> *4 star anise*

Wipe the quinces clean and cut them into quarters without peeling. Place in a large clear glass jar and pour the brandy over to fill to the top. Wedge in the cinnamon sticks and star anise as attractively as you can and screw the lid up tight. Leave for at least six weeks before drinking – the longer the better.

 ## ELDERBERRY WINE SYRUP

This is more of a medicinal tipple, packed with vitamins and especially good for warding off colds and flu. At the height of the bird flu scare, I read about a herbal remedy made from elderberries that was claimed to offer a good defence for humans, and re-solved that autumn to make some of my own. To my amazement, the elder trees in my garden were stripped bare that year by the birds; in former years they had eaten about half of the berries and left the rest to rot. Could the birds, perhaps, have been in on the secret? A herbalist friend confirmed to me that this had been a common occurrence throughout the country that year – a fact that made the hairs on the back of my neck stand on end. The natural world may be far fuller of wisdom than we think.

500g elderberries
1 litre red wine
1kg sugar to 1 litre juice

Rinse the berries and take them off their stalks (this is easily done using a fork). Put them in a large preserving jar and pour the wine over them, leaving for 24 hours in the fridge.

The next day, stir the berry and wine mixture over a medium heat until it comes to the boil. (If you have a preserving pan with measurements on the side the job of calculating the sugar later will be easier.) Then strain immediately and discard the berries on the compost heap.

Stir in the correct amount of sugar over a low heat until it has all dissolved, and leave to boil for 3 minutes.

Pour into sterilized bottles (just out of a hot dishwasher is fine), label and keep in a cool place.

❧ *Go Fly a Kite* ❧

Kite-flying is a worthwhile activity in itself, but can also enhance others such as a picnic (pp.128–32), a walk (p.306) or a day on the beach (pp.133–7). Everyone loves a kite – even the sight of them fluttering against the clouds is cheering, while the feel of that tug of air lifting the flimsy contraption ever higher is exhilarating. There are kites for all levels of ability, from simple, single-line affairs that a child can control with no trouble, to complex power kites that can be engaged in bouts of skyborne ballet. You can spend anything from a few pounds to several hundred. A good kite shop is the place to go – or visit a website such as www.kiteshop.co.uk (0845 130 4791) – and have a good browse and a chat with an attendant if possible before making your decision. Then, I'd suggest keeping the kite in the back of the car, so that if it is ever perfect kite-flying weather, you are likely to have it with you, wherever you are. Kites also make great presents for people of all ages, by the way.

❦ *Festoon the House* ❦

The natural world looks so good at this time of year I find myself wanting to bring some of it inside. I love to find an hour or so on Saturday mornings to fill the house with jugs of hips, haws and berries from the native hedge that borders our garden – scarlet and orange rosehips, glossy black elderberries and smoky-blue-grey sloes – and string up swags of dried hops and tawny grapevines. For a dinner party, it can be fun to strew the table-top with brightly coloured leaves, and make small squashes and pumpkins into simple candle holders (dug out to the diameter of the candle and 5cm deep) arranged on a dish of nuts. And (though I haven't yet tried this myself) a friend carefully snips off the casings of Chinese lanterns (*Physalis alkekengi*) from around the berries and slips them on to plain white fairy lights – fiddly, but apparently well worth it, and just as pretty when the orange fades to a bleached white skeleton.

Another friend, Francine Raymond, who runs the Kitchen Garden (01359 268322/www.kitchen-garden-hens.co.uk) – a small business specializing in hen-keeping and gardening accoutrements – makes beautiful wreaths from dried autumn leaves glued on to simple wire frames. To make your own, from early autumn collect and dry colourful leaves between sheets of newspaper and place underneath your rugs for at least two weeks to dry properly, or less if in front of an Aga. Cherry leaves are good at holding their spectacular crimson and orange colours, while turkey oak, plane and acer have interesting shapes. When the leaves are dry attach them to the wire frames with a glue-gun, perhaps adding other bits and pieces such as gold leaf or crystal to jazz them up a little. By mixing the shapes and shades of leaf you can create some stunning effects. For inspiration look at Francine's illustrated journal, *All my Eggs in one Basket* (£22 incl. p&p from the website), or book yourself on to one of her home-made decoration courses held in her cosy Suffolk cottage in November each year.

With children around, gathering and creating autumn decorations is a useful way to have fun, and there are some great seasonal ideas in *Nature's Playground: Activities, Crafts and Games to Encourage Children to Get Outdoors* by Fiona Danks and Jo Schofield. Leaves, conkers, acorns, rosehips, feathers, grass plumes, 'helicopter' maple and honesty seed-heads can be threaded on to strings and hung from branches or wooden batons to make 'forest mobiles', or arranged within a twiggy frame to form Andy Goldsworthy-style pictures or 'magic carpets' on a table, floor or lawn. Coloured leaves and grasses can be stuck or stapled on to cardboard bandanas to make festive 'woodland crowns' or masks, while the more ambitious could even use an old shawl to make a leafy cloak. Be sure to use only non-toxic materials with younger children. Don't forget to save some seeds, hips and berries (including honesty seed-heads) in a cool, dry place for stringing on wire to make homespun Christmas decorations.

Bake Bread

Baking bread is a very soothing activity, ideal during autumn weekends when outdoor life makes fewer demands on your time. The magic worked by yeast, the supple feel of kneading dough and the blissful smell of baking loaves are all the more appealing when it's cold and wet outside. Bread-making is by no means an instant process, but the different stages can be fitted in between other tasks in the kitchen – emptying the dishwasher or washing machine, for instance, or preparing other food. Some people even find the kneading process has a meditative effect: the mind gets caught up in the rhythmic movements and so is kept in the present moment, unable to stray to other thoughts or worries. Whatever, the results are always worth the effort, filling the heart with real 'home pride'. Some brown breads can be terribly heavy, so this recipe, courtesy of a friend, uses a mixture of different flours for a lighter texture. It makes a 900g loaf.

🐢 LOVELY BROWN LOAF

1 teaspoon sugar
15g dried yeast
450ml warm water
225g strong white flour
450g strong brown flour
2 teaspoons salt
25g butter
beaten egg or milk to glaze (optional)

Mix the sugar and yeast with a quarter of the water in a small bowl and leave until frothy (15–20 minutes). Sift the flours and salt into a larger bowl, then cut the butter into small cubes and rub it into the flour to form a breadcrumb texture. Stir in the yeast mix and gradually add the remaining water, mixing and drawing the dough together with your hands to form a sticky ball. Tip on to a floured board and knead for 8–10 minutes until the dough is smooth and elastic. Oil or grease a 900g loaf tin, shape the dough to fit inside, and cover with an oiled plastic bag. Leave in a warm place to rise for about 1 hour, until the dough has doubled in size. Preheat the oven to 220°C/425°F/gas mark 7. Dust the top of the loaf with flour or brush with egg or milk and bake for 30–40 minutes until the loaf is golden and its base sounds hollow when tapped. Tip out and cool on a wire rack.

If the above sounds too much like hard work, you can always get a bread-making machine; some people swear by them (see p.230) and you can throw in all manner of tasty additions from nuts and seeds to olives, cranberries and other dried fruit. Or the following are all sources of great bread – check for your local stockists or to order online.

The All Natural Bakery:
(0870 803 0263/www.allnaturalbakery.co.uk)

Artisan Bread:
(01227 771881/www.artisanbread-abo.co.uk)

The Authentic Bread Company:
(01531 828181/www.authenticbread.co.uk)

Celtic Bakers:
(07903 763206/www.thecelticbakers.co.uk)

Flour Power City Bakery:
(020 8691 2288/www.flourpowercity.com)

Hobbs House Bakery:
(01454 329757/www.hobbshousebakery.co.uk)

The Village Bakery:
(01768 898437/www.village-bakery.com)

❧ *Clean a Beach* ❧

A summer of picnics, beaches and day-tripper debris leaves many of our beaches in poor shape, littered with rubbish that not only looks awful but can endanger beach and marine life. Help spruce things up, while taking in a beachside walk, by enlisting for one of the Marine Conservation Society's annual beach clean events – held on the third weekend in September

(01989 566017/www.mcsuk.org). Around 4,000 volunteers cleaned 354 beaches in 2007, clearing up more than 346,000 pieces of litter. Beach litter is steadily increasing (up by a staggering 126 per cent since the 1994 annual survey), with crisp packets, cigarette butts, plastic drinks bottles and cotton buds among the worst offenders. For information on how to take part in regular surveys (four weekends a year) of your local or favourite beach, visit www.adoptabeach.org.uk). If you don't join an organized event, keep a few spare plastic carriers in your pocket, or a bin bag in the car, for picking up litter when you see it on a walk – it will take hardly any time to fill and you'll feel good about having done something to help. Put it in a public bin or take it home to your own.

❦ *Light a Real Fire* ❦

Lighting the first fire of the season is one of the many little rituals that make autumn special and the prospect of winter more bearable. And there is almost nothing to beat a cosy Sunday afternoon in front of the fire with tea and a good book when autumn gales are howling. Not everyone has an open fire or a woodburner, I know – but if you have a fireplace that is disused I do urge you to get a chimney sweep in to look at it to see if it might be used. I guarantee you won't regret it. If you really don't think you can find time to lay a fire and sweep up the ash (and here, I have to confess, a fire-lighting husband does come in handy), what about one of the latest, state-of-the-art woodburners that run on a handful or two of pellets for hours on end and have glazed fronts so you can appreciate the glow? The gas/real-fire lookalike option is a very poor third, but better than nothing. Real flames are not only cheery and cosy, they connect us with the elements and ancient cultures and traditions.

One of the reasons I fell in love with my husband was that he had a real fire in his bedroom that he not only knew how to lay and light expertly, but would also sit and contemplate, wordlessly, while strumming the guitar. Heaven – and it still is. Here are Frank's top tips for flawless fires. (He is also quite keen on health and safety aspects, bless him.)

How To Lay the Perfect Fire

- Wear heavy gloves when making a fire: this stops you getting splinters from the kindling and sooty hands while laying it. Clear out any old ashes from your previous fire; partially burned bits of fuel can be reused, but get rid of all the ash. (Sprinkle it round your fruit trees and bushes for a high-potash feed – E.)
- Get yourself a nice bundle of good *dry* kindling wood. Be very careful if chopping your own kindling – even small axes can be dangerous.
- Forget firelighters – they are environmentally unfriendly, expensive, toxic and have to be stored safely and out of reach of children. Old newspapers are the answer: tear into narrow shreds about 1cm thick, ripping quite a few sheets at a time. Even better, use the remains of confidential documents spewed out by a shredder. The widespread method of crumpling paper into balls lights more slowly and doesn't allow the fire to breathe enough in the crucial early stages when it has to ignite the wood.
- To lay the fire, place shredded paper loosely at the bottom, then build up a good strong tower of kindling on top. Here it's

a case of 'Cowboys and Indians': I prefer a squarish 'log cabin' type structure while others prefer a 'tepee'. Place the smallest and thinnest pieces at the very bottom and the larger bits towards the top. A log cabin has the advantage of being sturdy enough to support the coal/smokeless fuel/wood you'll be placing on top, but build it up with plenty of gaps so the fire can breathe while lighting.

- If you are burning logs use small ones (or split larger ones) when lighting the fire; don't expect to set great trunks alight from kindling as it may burn out before the logs catch properly.

- If using coal or smokeless fuel, place it carefully on your tower of kindling with tongs or (better) gloved hands. Don't use too much to begin with: it's better to get a smaller amount properly lit and add more once it's burning well rather than tip on too big a load for the kindling to set alight.

- Then – preferably using a long-stemmed lighter designed for lighting gas hobs, or a taper or extra-long matches – light the shredded paper in several places along the bottom of the pyre.

- Put a good fire-guard in position: fires often crackle and spit out sparks in their early stages which could be dangerous, or at least spoil your rug.

- Keep a careful eye on the fire while it's taking light. The fuel or logs will tumble as the kindling burns up and bits can fall out. Assuming it's got good and hot with yellow flames dancing about for a while, don't be surprised if there's then an apparent lull after the kindling has burned out; the fuel/logs should have been lit and should soon be burning well.

- If the fire seems to be struggling, reach for your bellows (or blow carefully down a long cardboard packaging tube) to give it some air. If it's really struggling, add more kindling in strategic places to perk it up, but if you've followed these instructions you shouldn't have such problems.

- Add fuel to the fire gradually – not too much at once. Poke ash out from the bottom, but be careful not to lose the good stuff.

- If you are having problems – or if it's getting at all smoky in your room – your chimney might not be drawing properly. Get your friendly chimney sweep in – and be prepared to rush outside when asked, to see the brush sticking out of the chimney. They seem to want you to see that they have done a good job.

- Finally – and most importantly – be very careful throughout. Don't leave a fire unattended without putting a good guard in position, and do not let children play with or look after the fire or leave them on their own with it. Best to settle down in front of it and keep an eye on it all evening yourself. (Which can be used as a good excuse not to be able to nip to the shop/walk the dog/generally do anything else – E.) Make sure it has burned down safely and put the guard up before going to bed. Install smoke and carbon monoxide alarms in the room and around the house and check the batteries regularly.

5.

Seasonal Pleasures: Winter

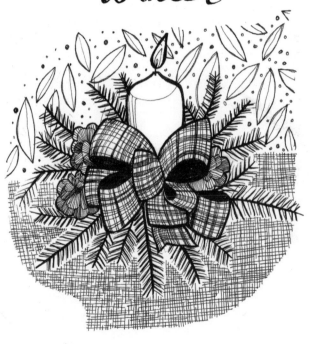

*A*s the evenings draw in, I find real satisfaction in simple pleasures such as lighting a wood fire, making the Christmas cake and inviting friends for tea after a brisk wintry walk. I used to find it unbearable when the clocks went back and it suddenly got dark at four o'clock in the afternoon, but I've started trying to celebrate this closing-in of things, as I've realized that life without proper seasons would, for me, be intolerable. Here in England, we may complain when the days become shorter, but we must spare a thought for those further north in the Scottish isles, Scandinavia and Iceland, where daylight is confined to just a few hours in mid-winter. And we can learn from them too. Winter in Nordic countries was traditionally the time for sitting around the fire making things, both home-made crafts and delicious culinary delicacies such as cured fish and gravadlax, many of which would be squirrelled away for Christmas. And though carving on walrus tusks or complex Norwegian knitting patterns may be beyond us, a little simple crochet or making our own Christmas cards can fulfil the same purpose.

December is, of course, inevitably dominated by Christmas, and it's easy to become grumbly and Scrooge-like and almost wish it was all over before it has begun. Here, again, the secret is to get ahead of yourself. There's a thin line between being smugly sorted and just avoiding the last-minute panic, and I've finally learned that if I start buying presents in late November, just as I see suitable things for the right person, try to make the Christmas cake and pudding on 'Stir-Up Sunday' at the start of Advent, and take in the odd carol concert with the children in my life, then the whole four weeks before Christmas can become a joyful build-up rather than a stressful nightmare.

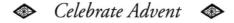

Celebrate Advent

The four weeks of Advent can be a great way to schedule for, and really enjoy, the run-up to Christmas. Whatever our faith, upbringing or age, we can all respond on some level to the symbolism of the Christmas story, and the sense of anticipation, not just of a big day of feasting and family and frantic present-opening, but of a birth of something young and good and perfect at this (for us in the northern hemisphere) very darkest and coldest time of the year.

Lighting Advent candles is a lovely tradition that can bring a spiritual dimension to the progression towards Christmas and impart a bit of magic to mealtimes throughout December. When I was a child we had one of those little brass ornaments with the nativity scene in the centre, the shepherds and wise men in a circle all around, and the angels tooting their trumpets on the periphery, which was made to rotate by lighting four small red candles, the heat of which made little overhead propellers spin around. My mother has since given me an attractive painted wooden version she found at a German crafts market, and it has become a much loved feature at our Christmas table. You can also find single tall Advent candles marked with the days of December which you light for just as long as it takes that day's section to burn down (usually around an hour). Or why not make your own centrepiece with four candles arranged in the centre of a wreath of evergreen foliage? There are plenty of evergreen herbs around in winter such as rosemary, lavender and sage, which make an aromatic alternative to the traditional, and slightly gloomy holly and ivy – and placing them in a ring bun tin with a hole in the middle works well. Light one candle every night for the first week of December, two in the second and so on; the natural progression means that the candles will burn down to different lengths, providing a really pretty centrepiece by Christmas Day.

Advent calendars are generally enjoyed by all. We often end up with two: one that satisfies my own insistence on some sort of reference to the nativity story, and one with the inevitable chocolates inside.

❖ *Christmas Books* ❖

Another lovely activity for Advent is to get out the Christmas books. In our house most of these are kept in the attic (in a mouse-proof box) with the Christmas decorations. We bring the books down a good two weeks before the decorations and keep them in a pile in the sitting room, taking time to look at one or two each day, and choosing a different one every night to read to my daughter in bed. Any of the titles below would make wonderful Christmas presents for godchildren or other children in your life, and would be enjoyed for many Christmases to come.

My daughter Mary's particular favourites, at age four, include:

🎄 *The Christmas Story* by Ian Beck, the traditional nativity story simply told with Beck's charming and sensitive illustrations.

🎄 *Harvey Slumfenburger's Christmas Present* by John Burningham, with his humorous illustrations I remember from earlier books from my own childhood.

🎄 *Happy Christmas Maisy* by Lucy Cousins, with its 'lift the flaps and pull the tabs' and Tallulah the chicken's 'Jingle Bells' pants.

🎄 *The Night Before Christmas* and other magical festive pop-up books by Robert Sabuda.

🎄 *Olive, the Other Reindeer* by Vivian Walsh, with J. Otto Seibold's distinctive illustrations, featuring Olive the dog who mis-hears the line in the song ('All of the other reindeer . . .') and ends up saving Santa's bacon.

And Christmas books aren't just for children. I like to dig out Laura Ingalls Wilder's *The Long Winter* for myself, and reread the Christmassy bits in *Little Women*, Winifred Foley's *A Child in the Forest* and other classics. Other lovely books to have about include Jan Pieńkowski's *The First Noël*, a beautiful piece of craftsmanship that pops out to form a carousel and can be hung up as a decoration, Dylan Thomas's *A Child's Christmas in Wales*, John S. Goodall's *An Edwardian Christmas*, with its pictures evoking the elegant extravagance of that era, and *The Oxford Book of Christmas Poems*.

To experience the true spirit of Christmas, you can't beat traditional Bible readings. I defy anyone, Christian or not, to find anything more thrilling and beautiful than Isaiah xi, 1–10 ('And the wolf shall dwell with the lamb, and the leopard shall lie down with the kid') or John i, 1–6 ('In the beginning was the Word, and the Word was with God, and the Word was God').

On a more prosaic level, don't forget the Christmas cookbooks. I like to have them out on the kitchen table quite early on in the proceedings, to help me make shopping lists and to gather ideas for Christmas cookies, chutneys and alcoholic treats to give away (see pp.192–4). *The Nantucket Holiday Table* by Susan Simon, *Elizabeth David's Christmas* and Frances Bissell's *The Scented Kitchen* are full of lovely ideas, and a particular favourite is Francine Raymond's beautiful ring-bound *A Christmas Journal* with its ideas for home-made natural decorations and presents as well as recipes for everything from pickled spiced quinces to champagne cocktail sorbet; there's even a cardboard pocket at the back for your own notes and recipes.

◈ *Christmas Cake* ◈

The best Christmas cake I've ever made is an adaptation of the one in Nigel Slater's *The Kitchen Diaries*, its moist ultra-fruitiness perfectly countered by the crunch of whole hazelnuts (p.190). Like him, I use pale natural marzipan rather than the bright yellow stuff, though I draw the line at his choice of golden icing sugar for the icing – I like my icing snowy-white, preferably drawn up into little peaks with a knife and decorated with an eccentric assortment of ornaments and 'Merry Christmas' handwritten in squeezy coloured icing. I try to make it on or as near as possible to what is commonly known as 'Stir-Up Sunday', the Sunday before Advent for which the collect (or prayer for the day) begins 'Stir up, we beseech thee', putting the first carols of the season on the CD player, and setting aside a good hour for the weighing, measuring and stirring and two and a half more for the cooking (if you start too late you're likely to fall asleep and burn it!). The tradition since my childhood is that everyone in the house at the time must have a stir and make a wish – do it on a weekend when you have visitors and you'll not only make stirring all those stiff ingredients less of a chore, but have some fun into the bargain.

 NUTTY CHRISTMAS CAKE

This recipe makes a cake that will give 12–16 slices, and is cooked in a 20cm cake tin, but can be scaled up – remember to increase the cooking time, though.

250g butter
125g soft light brown sugar
125g soft dark brown sugar
3 large free-range eggs
65g ground almonds
1kg dried fruit – I use roughly equal amounts of raisins,
    sultanas, prunes, apricots, cranberries, figs and glacé
    cherries (where necessary cut into small pieces)
100g shelled hazelnuts

    3 tablespoons brandy plus more to 'feed' the cake
    zest and juice of 1 orange
    zest of 1 lemon
    250g plain flour
    ½ teaspoon baking powder

To finish the cake
    1 tablespoon apricot jam
    750g natural marzipan
    600g royal icing sugar
    juice of a lemon

Line a tin (with a removable base) with baking parchment that comes 5cm or so above the rim. Preheat the oven to 160°C/325°F/gas mark 3. Beat the butter and sugars, either by hand or with an electric whisk, until pale and fluffy. Add the eggs one at a time (don't worry that it curdles) and slowly stir in the ground almonds, dried fruit, hazelnuts, brandy and fruit zest and juice. Sift the flour and baking powder and fold in lightly. Dollop the mixture into the tin and smooth the top. Bake in the middle of the oven for 1 hour, then reduce the temperature to 150°C/300°F/gas mark 2 for a further 90 minutes. Remove from the oven when a skewer comes out with no raw mixture attached and leave to cool on a rack, then wrap in foil and store in a cool place. Feed the cake with brandy every week till Christmas by spiking with a skewer in several places and adding a tablespoon or so of alcohol. A few days before Christmas, spread the cake with apricot jam diluted with a little water and cover with the natural marzipan. The following day, cover with stiff icing made with the royal icing sugar mixed with hot water and lemon juice till it stands in soft peaks. Decorate with springs of holy and tasteful red ribbon or jolly plastic reindeer and snowmen, as you choose.

◆ *Cooking Up Presents* ◆

I also like to cook things to give away as Christmas presents. Some of these will be the jams and chutneys made at the tail-end of summer and nicely matured for folk to enjoy with their Boxing Day leftovers (the recipe I get asked for most is the courgette and dill pickle on pp.166–7). 'Hedgerow tipples' such as sloe gin and quince brandy (see pp.170–2) also make great presents, decanted into attractive bottles and adorned with a festive ribbon and label. Biscuits are good fun: I do a basic gingerbread recipe (right) using cutters shaped as stars, Christmas trees, hearts, snowflakes and even (sent by a Swedish friend) reindeer, and decorate with plain white icing-sugar-and-water icing. Children love making and decorating biscuits – we use Smarties and silver crunchy balls for baubles on the Christmas trees. Arranged on paper plates when the icing is dry, the biscuits make lovely presents for teachers, neighbours, friends and relations or, if you make a hole pre-cooking to be threaded with red ribbon, can even double up as tree decorations.

When I was a child we would make endless batches of green and white peppermint creams and coconut ice (the main ingredient for both is pure icing sugar but, hey, it's Christmas), and I've carried on the tradition with my own daughter, making batches of coconut ice, coloured pale pink and shaped into mice, for families with children; use white chocolate buttons for ears, silver balls for eyes and dubious but nonetheless useful 'strawberry laces' for tails.

With a bit of ribbon and a handwritten label these simple offerings from the kitchen make great gifts; they take very little time, effort and expense, and, if you make them with children, can use up many a cheerful hour that might otherwise have been spent in front of a computer or TV screen. Without wanting to sound smug or soppy about it, there is something very heart-warming about making things yourself, in your own kitchen, perhaps from family recipes handed down over generations, to send out to the ones you love. And in my book, anything that helps teach children that presents don't need to be bought from the shops just has to be a good thing.

GINGERBREAD TREE BISCUITS

This recipe makes about 20 biscuits – see previous page for ideas for decorating, giving as presents or hanging as tree decorations.

350g plain flour
2 teaspoons ground ginger
1 teaspoon bicarbonate of soda
100g butter in small cubes
175g soft light brown sugar
1 medium free-range egg
4 tablespoons golden syrup
cutters, icing and decorations as required
2 greased baking trays

Preheat the oven to 190°C/375°F/gas mark 5. Sift the flour, ginger and bicarbonate of soda into a large bowl. Rub in the butter with your fingers until the mixture resembles fine breadcrumbs. Stir in the sugar. Break the egg into a separate bowl, add the syrup and beat well, then stir into the dry ingredients. Mix to a dough and knead till smooth. Roll out the dough to a thickness of 5mm on a floured board (do this in two lots if easier). Cut out as many shapes as possible and place them on the baking trays, rolling out the remaining dough again for a further batch. If you are making tree decorations, now is the time to make a hole for the ribbon – larger than you think as they tend to close up while cooking. Bake for 12–15 minutes till golden brown. Leave them on the trays to cool for 5 minutes then carefully lift on to a wire rack to cool completely. Decorate as you wish – white glacé icing lattice-style on heart shapes looks pretty, or let the kids loose with the silver balls and sprinkles.

Home-made Presents, Wrapping and Cards

Presents

Offerings from the kitchen, prettily packaged in your nicest jars with jolly fabric tops or a ribbon around the neck and a hand-written label, or wrapped in tissue paper twists, make marvellous presents (see previous pages). Other ideas that don't involve trekking round the shops and contributing to consumer hell include:

Pots or bowls of planted-up bulbs such as fragrant Paperwhite narcissi (pp.197–200)

 A framed photo or small photograph album of a holiday or event shared with the recipient over the past year (see pp.46–7 for more ideas for gifts using photographs)

 A custom-made calendar featuring family photographs (use a site such as www.photobox.co.uk)

 A compilation CD of specially chosen music

 A voucher for a massage, reflexology session or similar treat from a local practitioner

 Handwritten vouchers that you devise yourself are also great fun and can be customized according to the recipient's age, sex and relationship to you. For girlfriends, how about a night out at a 'girls' film' followed by sushi for two; for children, a sleepover for three friends with pizza thrown in; and for partners, anything from an extended weekend lie-in to (if you think you can survive it) smiling waitress service for him and ten mates next time they are round to watch the football? For a truly great present for an old friend, new mother or particularly deserving partner, you could even create a little booklet of assorted vouchers – this works best if you have nice writing or can draw or make them look attractive in some way.

Wrapping

If you're making a lot of presents, the last thing you want to do is go out to the shops and spend all the money you've saved on cards, wrapping and ribbon that are as unbiodegradable as they are expensive. In the old days, it was enough just to find some wrapping paper, cut it to size and sellotape around the gift in question. Now there are enormous sections of department stores devoted to 'gift wrapping', and we are expected to buy not only wrapping paper and cards that can cost as much as £5 apiece, but also all manner of fancy ribbons and other adornments, plus a further box or bag in which to present it all.

Well, I'm not buying into that. The UK uses 8,000 tonnes of wrapping paper every year just on Christmas presents – the equivalent of 50,000 trees. On the premise that the more overtly 'manufactured' the product, the more environmental damage it causes, it's best to keep things simple. I'm a great fan of brown paper. This might sound spartan, but it can be jollied up by stamping or painting a design or the recipient's name in bright colours – children will enjoy doing this. Or, if you've squirrelled away some paper from Christmases past, cut just a broad band to wrap around the centre as a colourful contrast. Tissue paper always looks good and biodegrades fast – you can add it straight to the compost heap without shredding. One year I even used old newspapers to wrap presents, just the black and white pages, jazzed up with stars hand-drawn with a chunky silver pen, and, for smaller gifts, pages from glossy magazines. Trust me, it actually looked quite smart.

The key when scrimping on paper is to use lots of pretty, reusable ribbon. To supplement a drawer of recycled ribbons from presents, bunches of flowers and the like, I buy spools of silver and dark red ribbon, lightly wired to keep its shape, from florists' suppliers, but standard haberdasher's stuff does just as well. It ought to cost no more than you'd spend on shop-bought paper. Another option is to make the wrapping part of the present, and pop your home-made gifts into pack-away shopping bags. Those from Carry-a-bag (cotton in a variety of styles) and Onya (parachute fabric in bright colours folding into keyring-sized pouches) – see p.268 for more details – are particularly attractive and could be secured with a big silver bow.

Cards

If you have the time and inclination to make cards – and young children can always be begged or bribed into a session of potato stamping or paper snowflake-making – home-made offerings are always well received. Hand-made cards get pride of place on our main mantelpiece, with favourites from former years, such as the cut-out white card Christmas tree or tiny model sheep on a snowy field of cotton wool, being wheeled out again and again. If time is short – and heaven knows it often is at this time of year – how about customizing a family photograph, or a picture of your house or garden in the snow? If you do buy cards, make sure they are charity ones, and that the cause concerned does receive a good percentage of the price; www.christmas-cards.org.uk allows you to choose designs from sixty or so charities, and claims that 100 per cent of the purchase price goes to the charities.

 Paperwhite Narcissi

December is also when the first Paperwhite narcissi bulbs begin to bloom about the house, their small star-like blooms filling an entire room with their scent. Growing in glass bowls filled with pebbles, they look extremely elegant, but are, in fact, almost effortless; if you order enough bulbs and keep planting them in succession you can have fragrant flowers right the way through till spring. Unlike most bulbs, which need a period in the dark and cold before flowering, Paperwhite narcissi are specially forced to bloom five to six weeks after planting, and need only water to grow. Since seeing them grown this way in a garden shop in Manhattan a decade or more ago, I have always done the following. Do try it for yourself.

In late summer, when placing my bulb order, I add on 100 Paperwhite narcissi bulbs (200 if I am planning on planting them up as presents). (I buy them wholesale from De Jager (01622 840229) but Peter Nyssen (0161 747 4000/www. peternyssen.com) and others do a discount the more bulbs you buy. You can pick them up in smaller bags from the garden centre, but this works out much more expensive). When the bulbs arrive, unpack them and place, green shoots upwards, in rows on one of those coloured plastic milk crates (the container needs to have plenty of air circulating as you may end up with bulbs two or three deep). Keep this in a cold, dark, frost-free place such as a shed or a basement, but handy so you can raid it for fresh bulbs throughout the winter months. To have flowers for Christmas, fill a shallow glass bowl with pebbles – grey Scottish beach pebbles of the type you buy from garden centres look lovely, or you can substitute white, jade green or other decorative mixes. I have two large shallow bowls 22 inches across which take twenty or so bulbs each, and six or seven smaller ones, some round and some square, which fit between three and seven each. Arrange the bulbs, closely grouped, on the surface of the pebbles, and add a couple of 1-inch lengths of artists' charcoal – this magically stops the water from smelling.

Then pour in enough water *just* to touch the bases of the bulbs. (This is important – if the bases stand too long submerged in water they will rot, but if they are too far away the roots will not grow.)

Over the next week or so, you should see the green shoots begin to put on more growth, and the bases of the bulbs start to sprout spidery white roots, which will weave their way among the pebbles, anchoring the plants in place. In another week or two buds will swell between the leaves. Progress is pleasingly fast, and in a warm house you can almost see the stems growing. Just make sure the roots, but not the bases of the bulbs, are in contact with water. Too much heat too soon and you'll get too much leaf and stem growth with the tiny flowers waving way ahead, so it's best to start them off in a cool room – or even outside – and bring into the warm when you want to bring them into bloom. With several bowls on the go at once, you can stagger them to bloom when you want, taking them outside to delay the growth or prolong the flowering, or moving them nearer a radiator to chivvy them along. In their later stages, the tall stems may need staking, or tying up with raffia or lengths of ribbon so they don't collapse. Using hazel or other twigs with catkins as supports looks especially pretty.

When giving the bulbs as presents you ideally want the shoots a couple of inches high with the buds just showing; you can keep them outside for weeks at this stage. Or give them 'dry', with the bulbs arranged on top of the pebbles, a pretty ribbon around the bowl and simple instructions handwritten on a luggage label – that way, the recipient can start off the flowers in their own time.

The only snag with forced bulbs is that they don't tend to flower well again the following year. I've tried feeding mine as the foliage dies down, but they've usually come up 'blind' (without blooms), so I usually compost the bulbs and buy new each year. I can't imagine winters without them now, and the pure white flowers are an especially welcome contrast in the visual cacophony that is Christmas.

◆ *Build a Film Library* ◆

Way back in the dim and distant video age, I visited a house where the owner had a personal library of his favourite films on video, all in matching white covers with handwritten labels. I resolved to do the same myself. Ten years on, I don't so much mind that I never got around to it, as technology has changed and DVDs take up a fraction of the space. The latest models of digiboxes and other recording devices make recording from the television much simpler than it once was, so I've finally begun building my own personal film library by recording the old black and white films that are often on the telly on a weekday afternoon. Now, when I fancy an old Cary Grant movie on a wet Sunday, or a friend comes to stay who has never seen Powell and Pressburger's wonderful *I Know Where I'm Going!*, I simply search out the DVD (not hard as I have only ten so far) and put it on. A good supply of Disney features, from *Dumbo* to *101 Dalmatians*, can be a life-saver when children come to stay, or to dangle as a carrot instead of the TV. And keep a good film reference book nearby for when people want to know the date it was made or start arguing over the name of that ubiquitous character actor. Remember, of course, that you are only permitted to copy a film for personal use. And make sure the covers – either soft plastic pouches or see-through boxes – are attractive (you can customize your own inner cards) and have all the information on that you need.

Top films for a rainy sunday afternoon

All About Eve: 1950s style and savage wit make this an all-time great, with Bette Davis superb as the ageing Broadway star threatened by a sweetly self-effacing but ruthlessly ambitious starlet.

Breakfast at Tiffany's: Poignant, stylish, funny and heartbreaking, this is a movie I will never ever tire of. Audrey Hepburn is heavenly throughout, and I've never managed *not* to cry at the end. Released in 1961.

Don't Look Back: Stylish and often very funny documentary following Bob Dylan and hangers-on on his controversial 1965 tour of the UK – stinging performances and off-the-cuff one-liners.

Don't Look Now: Death, grief, psychics, sex and ultimately more death in Venice in this 1973 cult classic, with superb performances from Julie Christie, Donald Sutherland and the astonishing city itself.

Harold and Maude: Cult 1971 favourite featuring a death-fixated teenager's romance with an eighty-year-old (Ruth Gordon in fine form) who lives in a railway carriage. Surprisingly joyous.

I Capture the Castle: The 2003 film is not a patch on the book, but a worthy attempt at portraying eccentric family life – and burgeoning romance – in a crumbling castle. Great 1920s costumes.

I Know Where I'm Going!: Powell and Pressburger's haunting 1945 tale of unexpected romance in the Hebrides – romance, comedy, bleak and beautiful scenery, deerhounds, whirlpools.

It's a Wonderful Life: Frank Capra's ultimate feel-good movie (1946) with James Stewart as the family man saved from suicide by elderly angel Clarence. Small-town American comedy at its best.

LA Confidential: Intriguing 1997 thriller full of surprises and set in the corrupt but stylish LA of the early 1950s. Great performances from Kim Basinger and Russell Crowe.

My Life as a Dog: This tender 1985 Swedish rites-of-passage movie makes me cry and laugh in equal measure while never slipping into sentimentality. You can almost speak Swedish by the end.

The Night of the Hunter: Weird but often wonderful black and white 1955 thriller featuring Robert Mitchum as a psychopathic preacher in pursuit of two children. Trippy moonlit river boat scene.

O Brother, Where Art Thou?: George Clooney even manages to look hunky in a beard and dungarees in this good-humoured 2000 romp with fantastic bluegrass music throughout.

The Philadelphia Story: Katharine Hepburn, Cary Grant *and* James Stewart – what more could you want? Top-notch script and performances in 'Hollywood's most wise and sparkling comedy' made in 1940.

Top Hat: The Fred Astaire and Ginger Rogers classic from 1935, full of gaiety and charm after all these years, with a plot complicated enough to keep your interest between songs.

◈ *Feed the Birds* ◈

You don't need to be a 'twitcher', spending the weekend closeted in a hide and clothed in an old anorak, to enjoy watching birds. Just the birds in your garden or near your house should keep you wonderfully entertained, as long as you provide them with adequate food and water and places to perch and nest. According to the latest advice from wildlife experts, we should be feeding the birds year round, but winter is the time when they need it most, and when watching their antics through the window will be most entertaining. A feeder of some sort is vital, and whether you choose a traditional bird table, or smaller feeders strung from the trees or some other support depends largely on the space at your disposal. I've used everything from elaborate 'bird theatres' with a variety of feeding stations and perches arranged in a row, to branches strung with fat balls, peanut rings and a range of attractive natural foods, to tiny glass-fronted seed trays with suckers that stick directly to your windowpane. All have been successful. What's crucial is that you position the feeders where you can sit and watch without disturbing the birds (they'll become quite bold after a while but can explode into flight if scared by sudden movement) and that you refill them regularly.

Get yourself a basic identification guide – I swear by my old *Observer* book – and take it from there. You may be surprised by what you see. Though our native birds are under threat in their natural habitats, forced out of the countryside by intensive farming methods, many are finding far more amenable homes in Britain's million acres of back gardens. Wrens, for instance, are far more common in our towns than they used to be, and I was enchanted one afternoon to see a flock – a charm? – of tiny goldcrests flitting about my London garden. Furthermore, the effect of climate change on migration patterns means that exotic birds such as hoopoes and oriels are more frequently sighted here, not to mention the green parakeets, escapees from zoos and their descendants, that have colonized parts of London.

A range of different feeders and types of food is the best way to attract a wide variety of birds. Tits, sparrows and nuthatches are among the most acrobatic, and enjoy dangling upside down for the tastiest morsels, while blackbirds and robins prefer a flat surface on which to feed. Some birds like peanuts, and robins in particular like live mealworms (see opposite); goldfinches fight over teasel or black nyger seed, while thrushes love apples, and robins and wrens go for chunks of old cheese.

A tree strung with well-designed smaller feeders can make a decorative garden feature. My little apple tree with its bobbing fat balls, coconut slices and peanut baskets looks as festive as an outdoor Christmas tree, and I hope that visiting birds will snap up any lurking pests while passing. Taller trees can take larger feeders that need less frequent filling; CJ Wild Bird Foods (see opposite) has one that is 120cm long and takes 3.5kg food. Or why not imitate Pam Lewis's 'bird theatre' at her wonderful wildlife garden, Sticky Wicket in Dorset (01300 345476/ www.stickywicketgarden.co.uk)? Outside her kitchen window is a pergola strung with beautiful woven willow feeders and roosting pockets that she makes herself; see her book, *Sticky*

Wicket, for more ideas and information on her winter willow-weaving courses.

Companies such as CJ Wild Bird Foods (0800 731 2820/ www.birdfood.co.uk) and Wiggly Wigglers (01981 500391/ www.wigglywigglers.co.uk) sell a wide selection of good-looking bird feeders, nesting boxes and so on, plus various feed mixes to keep different kinds of birds happy, including mealworms and other live food. Clean feeders regularly with mild detergent (wearing gloves) to avoid a build-up of dirt that could lead to disease, and be sure to provide water, too.

Planting trees, shrubs and flowers whose berries and seedheads will also supply the birds with food over the winter is another attractive option, of course; and planting a native 'tapestry' hedge of brambles, blackthorn, hawthorn, hazel, dog roses and guelder rose will look lovely, as well as providing the birds with food, shelter and nesting opportunities, and you with the wherewithal to make the 'hedgerow tipples' on pp.170–3. So your goodness to God's creatures will not go unrewarded.

◈ *Make Marmalade* ◈

Good home-made marmalade is a simple yet luxurious treat: an everyday alchemy of oranges, water and sugar. Making it is a perfect job for a cold, rainy weekend. Closeted in a warm steamy kitchen, with fragrant fumes rising from a bubbling pan, you'll feel cosy and virtuous. And the end product, even though I have yet to achieve absolute perfection in my own efforts, is always heaps better than the shop-bought stuff. It's crucial to use proper, bitter Seville oranges, which are only around in the shops from December to February. (Many organic box schemes will deliver them, too.) The following recipe is cooked long and slow which makes for a more reliable 'set' on modern stoves, and results in a dark, chunky and pleasantly sticky texture. It does, however, take time over an entire weekend for all the various stages.

 CHUNKY MARMALADE

Makes about 7 500ml jars

> *1.3kg Seville oranges*
> *2 lemons*
> *3 litres water*
> *2.7kg granulated sugar*

You'll also need a preserving pan (stainless steel not aluminium, which reacts with the fruit), a 38cm piece of muslin, a nylon sieve, some foil and sterilized preserving jars (hot from the dishwasher is fine in my book).

Wash the fruit, place in the pan with water and bring to a gentle simmer. Cover with a lid of double foil, folding the edges firmly over the rim, and poach gently for 3 hours. Remove from the heat and allow to cool enough to handle. Lift the fruit out into a colander placed over a bowl, cut in half and scoop out the flesh and pips into a medium saucepan. Reserve the orange peel but discard that of the lemons. Add 600ml of the poaching liquid to the fruit pulp and simmer on a medium heat for 10 minutes then strain into a bowl through a nylon sieve lined with muslin. Meanwhile, cut the orange peel into chunky strips and return to the preserving pan. When the pulp is cool, gather up the corners of the muslin, twist into a ball and squeeze hard with your hands to extract all the pectin-rich juices into the preserving pan. Really go at it, till all you have left is the pithy membrane of the fruit, which can go in the compost. Leave the pan of liquid and peel overnight, covered with a clean tea towel.

The following day, empty the sugar into a large roasting tin lined with foil and warm for 10 minutes in an oven preheated to 160°C/325°F/gas mark 3. Warm the preserving pan and its contents over a gentle heat before adding the warmed sugar, stirring well with a large wooden spoon until all the sugar crystals have dissolved. (On no account let the liquid boil until the sugar is dissolved – keep checking the back of the spoon for crystals.) When all the sugar is dissolved, turn up the heat and let the marmalade bubble away gently for 3 hours before testing for a set by spooning a teaspoonful of liquid on to a cool plate – once the surface wrinkles it is done. Keep checking at 15-minute intervals and, once setting point is reached, remove the pan from the heat and let it cool for 30 minutes before ladling through a funnel into warm sterilized jars. Seal while hot and label when cold. With pretty jars and circles of fabric tied around the top, home-made marmalade makes a great present – at Christmas or throughout the year. You'll never buy the shop stuff again if you can help it!

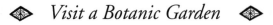

Visit a Botanic Garden

Botanic gardens are fantastic places to visit all year round, but are particularly attractive on a winter weekend. Many have areas or walks that have been planted specifically to look good in the winter months, with snowdrops and other early spring bulbs, scarlet stems of dogwoods and scented blooms of daphnes, wintersweet and witch hazel appearing on bare branches (the one in Cambridge is particularly impressive).

More alluring still, especially in a real cold snap, are those with glasshouses. There can be few more pleasant ways to take refuge from freezing winds than to wander for an hour or two among beautiful exotic plants in a steamy, jungle-like atmosphere. Many, such as the Palm Houses at Kew and Edinburgh, are breathtaking examples of Victorian architecture, and there may be a series of houses, leading you from the hot steamy habitats of tropical palms and orchids to lush ferneries or arid landscapes studded with succulents, cacti and spiky agaves. There may be splashing fountains damp with moss, or still pools covered with water lilies – the pads of the amazing *Nymphaea amazonica* can be 8 feet or more across. These artificial exotic landscapes can be wonderful places to walk with a friend, chatting as you go, but are also great to explore alone, allowing yourself time to look closely at the plants and flowers, learn from the labels and visual displays and absorb the unusual atmosphere. Sometimes, as at Kew's famous Palm House, there is a spiral cast-iron staircase to an upper walkway, giving a parrot's eye view down on the leafy canopy below.

Other places such as the Living Rainforest, just off the M4 in Berkshire (01635 202444/www.livingrainforest.org), have simulated thunderstorms and monkey cries, with birds and butterflies flitting about the branches. Watch the sunshine slanting through the leaves of a banana palm, turning them brightest lime green, and check out the tiny hands of embryonic fruit; admire the newly emerging fronds of tree ferns, tightly curled like a shepherd's crook; see how everyday staples such as coffee, cocoa and ginger grow in the wild. And if you have enjoyed your visit, make a donation, or pledge to help protect the real-life endangered habitats around the world. To find your nearest botanic garden, visit Wikipedia (en.wikipedia.org/wiki/botanical_garden) which has a list of all the botanic gardens in the UK (and, indeed, in the world) with links to their websites and details.

Make Minestrone

A good hearty soup is wonderful in winter: fantastically welcoming if you have friends coming for lunch, or to stay for the weekend, and also good just to have in a huge vat in the fridge to decant and heat up by the bowlful as required. Though there are many good seasonal recipes to be found in various cookery books, my favourite is still the minestrone I learned to cook when an au pair in Italy. The combination of good fresh vegetables, cooked in stock along with borlotti beans and pasta is totally delicious. Sure, it involves peeling and dicing a few vegetables, but I find the process rather soothing. Put on the radio or some good music and it is done in no time.

ITALIAN MINESTRONE

This makes 4 bowlfuls – double the quantities for larger numbers.

25g butter or olive oil
1 onion, sliced
1 rasher of streaky bacon, chopped
1 carrot, diced
2 sticks of celery, chopped
75g borlotti beans, soaked overnight and drained (or half a tin)
bouquet garni
1.5 litres good beef or chicken stock
1 leek, sliced
2 tomatoes, quartered (or half a tin)
a handful of frozen peas
a handful of pasta shells
salt and ground black pepper
chopped parsley
crusty bread and grated Parmesan cheese to serve

Heat the oil or butter and lightly fry the onion, bacon, carrot and celery. Add the beans and bouquet garni, pour the stock over, bring slowly to the boil and simmer, covered, for 1 hour. Add the leek, tomatoes, peas and pasta shells and simmer for a further 20 minutes. Season with salt and pepper to taste, sprinkle on some chopped parsley and serve with crusty bread and grated Parmesan.

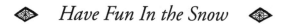

Have Fun In the Snow

We have so little snow in this country now, it's worth dropping everything to get out and enjoy it when it comes. Go tobogganing. Make a snowman or snow angels (lie down in the snow and move your arms up and down and legs out to the side to make an imprint). Build an igloo out of snow bricks, if you have enough snow. Drop hot maple syrup on to a bowl of snow to make snow candy (remember Laura Ingalls Wilder's *Little House in the Big Woods*?). Create a snow lantern by hollowing out a cylinder of snow and placing night lights within. And enjoy coming back to hot cocoa and crumpets in front of the fire (see pp.179–82).

Learn to Knit or Crochet

It sounds corny, but the long winter evenings and weekends are a great time to learn a new skill. Knitting and crocheting have been enjoying a bit of a fashion revival in recent years, with knitting clubs with names like Stitch 'n' Bitch enticing women who not long ago would never have been seen dead wielding a knitting needle; even supermodels have been snapped crocheting backstage at the fashion shows. Finding someone to teach you is your best bet, and many older people will be only too pleased to pass on their skills. There is a whole generation whose mothers were either too feminist or too busy to think of teaching knitting and sewing to their children, so the revival has come just in time. If you can't find a real live teacher, try the following websites:

Rowan (www.knitrowan.com) for details of knitting and crochet workshops and courses; Knitchicks (www.knitchicks. co.uk) to link up with a knitting group near you and the UK Hand Knitting Association (www.ukhandknitting.com) for more courses and general information on knitting and crochet. Begin with something easy like a scarf or small squares that can be stitched together to make a cushion cover or blanket, and use reasonably thick yarn so that you can see what you are doing and be encouraged by your swift progress.

◈ *Out With the Old and In With the New* ◈

We always leave our Christmas cards and decorations up until Twelfth Night, which as I calculate it is the evening of 6 January; it's supposed to be bad luck to keep them up after then, and anyway the tree is usually on its last legs and I'm looking forward to getting the house back into some sort of order. The weekend before Twelfth Night is a good time to give a party: the house is still festive, people are less frantic than before Christmas, and seem keen to socialize, even if some will have given up drinking for January. If you're clearing up after a party, you might as well take down the decorations too, rather than do it in a hurry, mid-week. I like to make a little ritual of it, putting on some Christmas music for the last time as I take down each of the tree decorations, wrapping the more fragile ones in tissue paper, and pack them all away into their bags and boxes. (Incidentally, do protect your decorations from moths and mice – the idea of them feasting on my knitted nativity is just too horrible to think about.) The cards are put in the recycling, except for the prettiest hand-made ones, which I keep from year to year, and other nice ones which can be cut up and used as tags. The tree and wreath and any interior greenery end up on the pavement for the council to collect (if yours doesn't do this, many garden centres and supermarkets will take them). When everything has been taken down and packed away, my house looks heaps bigger and less cluttered – a feeling that lasts precisely two days.

The end of the year is also a good time to go through new and old calendars and diaries, transferring birthdays, holiday plans, school inset days and any other important dates. As I do it, I like to look back over the events of the past year as I see them written down, remembering the birthday parties, the weekends away with friends, or when others came to stay, the trips abroad, the festivities at Easter, Midsummer or Hallowe'en. (It's nice if you can relive some of these memories with a friend or partner – the best I can do is to get my husband to grunt in occasional agreement from his book and armchair, but I like to think he secretly enjoys it, too.)

Somewhere in my old diary, there will usually be a short list of wishes and resolutions for that year, and it can be fun to review what has happened and assess the strength of one's resolve before writing down new lists for the year ahead. I think New Year's resolutions are great, but seem to do better with positive resolves than with endless lists of 'No more' this or that. 'More exercise' is always a good one; more meditation; more having people to supper. In an old diary from my twenties I found scrawled the admirably ambitious resolutions, 'More Holidays and More Sex' but sadly I didn't have time to trawl through the rest of the diary to see how I fared with them.

Make a bit of a ritual of it. If you *are* giving up drinking, for instance, pour yourself a glass or two of really good wine or enjoy a dram of malt whisky. Turn the light down low and burn some candles. Without, I hope, sounding too corny, I find all this a really rewarding way of saying goodbye to the old year and hello to the new.

6.

Having Guests and Going Away

⟋ *Having Friends to Stay* ⟍

H aving family and good friends to stay for a weekend is, for me, one of the real joys of life. The luxury of two or three full days spent in the company of those you love is something very special, and enables you to get up to date with their lives, become properly acquainted with their new partners or children and just hang out without the pressures of work tomorrow and who's driving home. Having house guests is inevitably hard work, however (unless you have paid help), particularly if you do it properly. It is all very well being laid-back and relaxed about things, but arriving to unmade-up beds and a meal that is quite clearly being scraped together from the contents of the store-cupboard can feel incredibly unwelcoming. Hospitality – that old-fashioned word – seems an important part of life to me, and here are a few tips on making it easier, gleaned from many years of having friends and family to stay, both in London and at the seaside.

Make them welcome

It doesn't take much to make guests feel warmly welcome. Showing them into a lovely spare room is a good start. Making up beds is much more pleasurable if you have lots of lovely bed-linen (see pp.319–20). Give guests a couple of pillows each, plus extra blankets or quilts on the end of the bed in case they feel the cold, and a hot-water bottle with a warm cover in winter. A bedside table with a lamp (check the bulb works), alarm clock and space for a glass of water and a book is essential, as is somewhere to hang a few clothes and, if they are staying longer than a night or two, a drawer or two in which to unpack. A small bunch of flowers – maybe picked from your own garden – is always a lovely touch, as is selecting a few books or magazines for the bedside that you think might be of interest. A radio would also be great – and will save having the news/football results on at full blast through the rest of the house.

In an ideal world, your guest would have their own bathroom, perfectly equipped with fluffy towels, flannels, toothpaste and new toothbrushes in packets (amazing how many people forget theirs) and nice things to put in the bath. If they are sharing the family bathroom, however, make sure they have somewhere to hang their towels (I have white towels for us and pale green for guests, so they can easily identify their own) and keep their washbag.

What to feed them

When it comes to feeding guests, I've learned a few tricks that make people feel incredibly fussed over but actually take very little time, expense and effort. These include making a cake (a big fruit cake or flapjacks (see p.30) always go down well after walks), home-made ice cream (easier than pie if you have even the most basic ice-cream maker: see p.141) and a proper cooked breakfast on Sunday morning (stretching this into a brunch with coffee, croissants and orange juice too can actually involve you in one less meal to prepare (see pp.299–305 for more ideas). If people are arriving on Friday evening, I like to do something warming and welcoming like a casserole, which also won't ruin if they are delayed. Similarly, for lunch arrivals on a Saturday, home-made soup, salad and plenty of good cheese and/or a home-cooked ham can be eaten at any time, and provide useful leftovers for snacks at other times (amazing how hungry men and teenage boys, in particular, can get, especially after walks or swimming). It's my rule that one meal over the weekend will not be cooked by me. Unless you have a wonderful guest who offers to cook (see p.224), this will mean lunch in a pub or a takeaway, but don't for a minute feel guilty: such outings are part of the fun you are providing. Good fish and chips by the sea, or a curry in town, can be a real treat – and your guests will be happy that you're having some 'time off'.

That only leaves one other meal, and I think it is important to make this special. It doesn't have to be elaborate, however; quite the contrary. The idea is to produce it all effortlessly, with good humour and a minimum of fuss. My tips are a roast during winter – good organic local meat and vegetables in season practically cook themselves, and if you're lucky you'll get a hand with the peeling and chopping – and a barbecue in summer. Men seem to love barbecues, so this is a crafty way of delegating most of the work. Send them out into the garden with a few beers, a good work surface and enough cooking implements and foil etc. and they will hardly even notice they are helping. Butterflied and marinaded leg of lamb always goes down well (get your butcher to take the bone out), as do good sausages or fresh-caught fish (often best cooked in foil to stop them falling apart). Then all you need is a few big bowls of salads, including a good green one and something like couscous or potato salad which you can make in advance. (I try to make up a good salad dressing in a jar before people come and keep it in the fridge to avoid last-minute fussing, but making dressing is a good job for a guest if you give them all the ingredients they'll need.) As for pudding, there's the home-made ice cream (see p.219) which can go with a big home-made pudding, a shop-bought pie or tart (if you have a local WI you can even pretend it's home-made if you want) or fruit salad and biscuits depending on appetite, inclination, time of year and so on. Try to do all the shopping beforehand – or make a trip to your local farm shop or farmers' market part of the fun. No matter how much your guests might offer to be of help, they won't thank you for a Saturday morning spent trundling down supermarket aisles.

What to do with them

When it comes to entertaining, I think it's best to think up a few possibilities beforehand and sound them out on your guests when they arrive. People do seem to dread being bored, but to find your every waking hour planned in advance and organized by your hosts can be exhausting. Personally, I do very little other than suggest a good walk (along the beach or in woods in the country; round a proper good big park in town) and perhaps a trip to a gallery, museum or farm – whatever is likely to be of most interest or novelty to your visitors. Even a poke around local antiques shops can be fun for some; not everyone has to do the same thing, after all, and arrangements may be tempered by the age, health, sex and sporting inclinations of those involved. Don't forget that the chance to participate in your own routines might be interesting – a trip to the local farm to buy meat, or to accompany you and/or children to yoga/riding/dance classes or whatever may be enjoyable, especially for godparents or grandparents of the children involved. It may be possible for visiting children or adults to participate in classes if they wish: ask them in advance if you need to book.

Whatever you have done, whenever you come back home, have lots of tea (good big teapot essential), biscuits and home-made cake (see p.219) on hand, and stock up with apple or other juice for kids. Such teatimes, warming cold hands on mugs and talking about the day's events, are often some of the happiest memories of my weekends with friends.

Bedtime conundrums

Bedtime is another opportunity to make your guests feel cared for. Few will refuse a hot-water bottle in winter, and it's a nice surprise to find one secretly slipped into your bed, especially in a cold house. Offer people a cup of tea before retiring or a glass of water in their room and make sure they know where tea and coffee etc. are for the morning. Timing can be a conundrum, however. Is it rude to go off to bed before your guests? On the whole, I think so, really, unless they are such old friends or family that it doesn't matter; or they're an old friend of your spouse and you think they might relish a bit of one-on-one together; or you are ill, have a young child who wakes early, or an early appointment the next day, in which case by all means make your excuses. If your guests seem intent on staying up much longer than you can last out, I think it's fine to head off after a certain point; night-time rituals such as letting out the dog and setting the breakfast table can give them warning of your intentions, and offering them tea or opening another bottle of wine will show you feel okay about it (and hopefully prevent them raiding your own supplies – see p.227).

Keep calm and carry on

It's important when hosting house guests not to overdo it. In the early days of having friends to stay at the seaside, I frequently used to overstretch myself and would often feel exhausted and even slightly resentful by Sunday evening – the last thing anybody wants. We've learned now not to invite people for too many weekends on the trot; except for high summer, we now try to keep every other weekend for ourselves and local friends. And I make sure I get enough time alone to keep myself sane. Nipping out for a quick dog walk, half an hour's gardening or to look at the stars can be a real life-saver, as can a surreptitious phone call to another friend on the mobile or in the privacy of your bedroom. Whatever you need, within reason, I say. Unless you are gone for hours on end, your guests will probably not even notice. A happy, relaxed hostess is one of the keys to a happy weekend, so taking care of yourself is taking care of everyone. Don't let anybody tell you otherwise.

❧ *Being the Perfect Guest* ❧

The boot's on the other foot, and you're off to stay with other people for the weekend. Here, based on many years' experience with a beach house that gets extremely popular in summer (with people we have hardly seen in years ringing up as they 'just happen to be in the area'), are our own top tips on being the perfect guest.

DO

✳ Arrange a rough time for your arrival, and if you're running much over that, ring your hosts to warn you may be late. It's all much easier now with mobile phones, and your hosts will be relieved to hear they have time to take the dog for a walk/nip to the shops/have another drink before you all arrive.

✳ Arrive bearing gift(s)! It's all very well apologizing for not having had the time/seen anywhere suitable on the way, and promising to buy wine later, but bringing at least a small token with you is a kind acknowledgement of the effort involved in having people to stay. Flowers are always lovely, the less garage-y the better, and good chocolate and/or bottle(s) of wine, especially if you're big drinkers yourselves. I also usually bring something small for the children of the house: a game that can keep them all occupied for an hour or two will be popular with everyone; toys with particularly annoying noises will only ensure that you'll be brought something worse when they come to stay with you. Especially welcome – and if you're staying longer than a night or two you can up the ante a little – are items your hosts will not be able to find in their immediate surroundings (smart bath oils from Jo Malone and the like for rural folk; local cheeses, smoked fish and other goodies if you're travelling from the country to the town). But you don't have to spend a lot of money. A bunch of flowers from your own garden and a home-made cake are the absolute tops with me.

* Offer to bring sleeping bags for the children. This cuts down on laundry enormously and can actually add to the fun for the children.

* Keep offering to help, especially with clearing tables and washing up. Only expect to be waited on hand, foot and finger if you are recovering from an illness, relationship break-up, bereavement or the like.

* If you are staying for more than a night or two, offer to cook for your hosts. One of our friends once arrived from Leeds with all the ingredients for a curry which he cooked with great finesse on the Saturday night, which was a real treat for all.

* Or, if you prefer, insist on paying for everyone if a pub lunch/fish and chips is on the cards.

* Try to keep the place tidy. This is particularly important if you are taking children to visit tidy people who don't have kids of their own. Keep your possessions in your room and clear away children's toys when they have finished playing with them.

* Ask about the family's routines, such as rising times in the morning and do your best to fit in with them, particularly if everyone's sharing the same bathroom. This might involve hanging back till those who have games fixtures or appointments to go to have finished, or

getting up a little earlier to nip in quickly first. If you are likely to be up inordinately early, or frequently get up in the night, do warn your hosts, unless you fancy being attacked with a blunt instrument in the early hours.

✳ Leave your room as you found it and offer to strip the bed.

✳ Take all your possessions back with you: forgetting loads of stuff can leave your hosts with the time and expense involved in packaging it all up and sending it back.

✳ Send a handwritten thank you card or letter (see pp.33–7). People who are otherwise flawless guests can blot their copybook in one fell swoop by forgetting a thank you letter. Mention specific moments that gave you most pleasure, and make it clear how much you enjoyed spending time with your hosts themselves. Additional offerings from children are particularly prized in my book. You might even add a CD of music or a book you think they might like (even this one!). And if an unexpected event such as pre-paid theatre tickets or a child vomiting all over the sheets makes you feel especially beholden, then a box of chocolates (see p.267), bunch of flowers or even a plant for the garden sent by post (see p.82) would be a kind gesture, and ensure your swift return!

DON'T

✳ Arrive with a hangover and spend the weekend moaning about your symptoms. The new girlfriend of a friend of my husband's once did this and almost all we heard of her the whole weekend was her constant demands for the hapless fellow to bring her more water and aspirin.

✳ Assume you can bring your pet dog, cat or whatever without warning. I speak as a dog owner myself here; people who do not have pets can really panic about having an unfamiliar creature in their house, and even if they have animals themselves, these may not get along with new arrivals.

* Bring horribly infectious diseases, nits and dog fleas into your host's home (see above).

* Expect your hosts to play early morning baby-sitter to your rampaging children every morning while you lie in bed till noon. I love spending time with children who come to stay, and time alone with a niece, nephew or godchild can be particularly special. I treasure memories of one particular beach walk with a five-year-old in the early morning when the water was way out and we found a string of starfish right along the tideline. But before I had my daughter, I would sometimes be up for hours supervising four or five kids before their parents emerged – fine for one morning, but not three in a row, thanks. The only exceptions are single parents, to whom I'm always happy to give a break.

* Drain the hot water cistern by having a long luxurious bath without checking first; most systems can cope with lots of baths if given enough warning. The hungover guest mentioned on the previous page blotted her copybook still further on another occasion by taking thirty minutes to shave her legs in the shower, thus emptying the tank when my husband was trying to get ready to be best man at a wedding. She has not been back.

* Leave the loo seat up (men) or, worse, fail to clear up after yourselves or your children properly.

* Forget to warn hosts of food allergies or fads – they may also have forgotten you are vegetarian. If you (or any of your children) are a really fussy eater, it's thoughtful to come prepared with some of your own supplies.

✳ Have rows with your spouse. Even behind closed doors they will probably be audible, and the atmosphere affects everyone.

✳ Spend endless time texting or on your mobile phone. If you have to make calls, do it outside or in private.

✳ Clutter the house more than you can help. Try to confine your possessions to your own quarters or, if you're sleeping in a room that is used during the day, in the bag you arrived with.

✳ Expect to be entertained and organized every minute of the day. Be resourceful: come equipped with books and toys (and DVDs) for children, get out maps and take an interest in the local area. It might be that you could introduce your hosts to something *they* don't know about.

✳ Go to bed way before your hosts (this smacks of boredom in their company unless you have a good excuse) or long after they themselves have done the rounds of offering tea, making hot-water bottles and so on and finally slipped off themselves.

✳ Help yourself to the contents of the wine rack after your host has gone to bed.

✳ Forget to send a thank you note – see p.225.

◁▷ *A Word on Weekend Homes* ◁▷

It's everyone's dream to have a bolthole in a contrasting place to escape to at weekends. City-dwellers long for a cabin in the mountains or a cottage by the sea; for country types it's a tiny, central pied-à-terre in town to overnight in after theatre or shopping trips. But is having two homes really all it's cracked up to be?

Having lived the so-called dream for several years now, I

know it can certainly be magical: the best of both worlds. I love the fact that my daughter has grown up equally familiar with the buzzing energy of London and the still, silent beauty of the stars and the sea at night. And yet, all this does not come without its drawbacks: traffic jams on the way there and back; two gardens to look after; the feeling of permanently loading and unloading the car and living out of badly packed bags; the new take on 'food miles' clocked up by that cabbage that's gone up and down the motorway so many times uneaten it's lost its appeal. The list could go on – but it's an unspoken rule that you can only really ever moan about having two houses with someone else in the same position. It seems so wilfully ungrateful otherwise. And in our case, the ups have so far outweighed the downs that the few irks and inconveniences have definitely been worth it. The following tips and observations might help if you frequently spend weekends in a different place, or are considering buying or renting a weekend home.

- The ideal weekend house should be situated within a couple of hours (well within, if possible) of your home. Any more than that and you will not only get fed up with the amount of time you spend in the car, but clock up hideous petrol bills and a heinous carbon footprint.
- See if you can avoid travelling at rush hours, to cut down on time spent in the car or on crowded trains. The only positive aspects of the travelling time are that there are beautiful views of the countryside to be enjoyed from the car window (most attentively by non-drivers, naturally), and the journey can be valuable for having the sort of conversation (about finances, for instance, or

where and when to take a holiday) that it can otherwise be difficult to engage one's spouse in when they are not strapped to a
seat and unable to escape.

If you are thinking of buying a weekend property, rent in the area
first. Not only do you get to see how and if the arrangement
works for you, but you also learn about the ins and outs of the
locality and can sniff out any properties that might be coming on
to the market – some of the most magical places never make it to
estate agents' windows.

Unless you are lucky enough to have people to take care of the
properties in your absence, I think having two abodes only really works if one place is extremely small and simple. Otherwise,
alongside all the fun and enjoyment you envisage yourself
having, you are just signing yourself up for two lots of house and
garden maintenance, and will resent the fact that you spend
every weekend mowing the lawn/touching up the paintwork
rather than lazing on the beach/strolling in the mountains.

The simple place doesn't *have* to be the place where you spend
least time: I know people who hole up in a tiny flat in London
all week and are then only too happy to spend weekends in the
country tending their 2-acre garden, as that is what they love best
in the world. But you don't want two great unwieldy properties
on your hands; the experience is supposed to be life-enhancing,
not exhausting.

Make sure that the weekend place is comfortable and cosy, particularly if you will be using it a lot in winter. There are timer
devices on the market, not at all difficult to install, that allow you
to programme central heating by remote control to come on an
hour or so before you arrive – a real modern luxury if ever there

was one. If you have an open fire or woodburner, leave plenty of dry logs ready.

Avoid 'empty cupboard syndrome' on arrival by keeping a freezer stocked with standby supplies of bread, milk and so on – even the odd frozen pizza. You don't want to be the classic 'out-of-towners' arriving laden with supermarket bags rather than using the local shops, but village shop opening hours may be erratic and there's no pleasure in waking up without coffee and fresh bread to hand. (A bread-maker can be handy – pop a few ingredients in the machine and awake the next morning to the aroma of baking pervading the house.)

A larder well stocked with long-lasting basics is also essential; make sure you have the means to knock up an impromptu risotto and the other store-cupboard standbys on pp.256–7, a batch of flapjacks (p.30) or home-baked scones (pp.30–2) and you'll always be able to cook at any hour or cope with unexpected visitors in style.

A good barbecue keeps cooking simple in summer: buying good local meat or fish is an enjoyable way to support producers in your area (see pp.261–2), and cooking outside has the double advantage of being both fun and an attractive pastime for men (see p.220 for ideas).

Have 'two of everything' – from clothes to toiletries in the bathroom – to cut down on the packing palaver. Though the initial outlay might seem expensive, it pays off in the end, as the clothes, cleansers, shampoo, shoes and so on all have just as long a life, only split between two places.

Lots of towels and good bed-linen are vital (see pp.20 and 319–20 for the best suppliers). Get into the habit of making up the spare bedroom again whenever you strip the sheets: that way you'll always feel prepared to welcome visitors. Keep the linen for each room in a chest at the end of the bed to ensure no tedious confusion when it comes to finding the right size and colour. Put soaps or lavender bags in among them to keep them smelling fresh.

Unless you can allow yourselves the luxury of a cleaner in your weekend place, try to adopt a quick and well-rehearsed routine for tidying, cleaning and packing up when heading home. Arriving next time to an untidy house is extremely dispiriting, and leaving crumbs and unwashed cups and the like in an uninhabited place for days on end is not only unpleasant but will also encourage mice, or worse. At the same time, though, driving home is exhausting enough, without having spent the last couple of hours scrubbing floors and cleaning the fridge. So try to keep on top of jobs in a way that doesn't dominate your weekend; plenty of storage and a good, efficient hoover help.

However, if you can afford a cleaner, and can find someone local to help, you will never look back, especially if you have lots of visitors; your cleaner may also be happy to help with the beds and washing and put the odd pint of milk in the fridge.

The other key to enjoying a weekend home is *not* to fill it constantly with other people. Of course, it is great to share your place with family and friends, but not every weekend. You'll only really feel on top of both your lives, and equipped with enough energy to cope with a houseful of visitors, if you keep some quality time there to yourself.

❧ *Renting a Weekend Cottage* ❧

If you enjoy seeing different parts of the country, and just want the odd weekend away with friends, renting a house or cottage may well be the answer. There is something very exciting about arriving somewhere new – whether with your partner, a friend or large group – to stay for a few days. Everything is new for all of you, and the whole exercise has the air of an adventure. Allocating the best bedroom to the person/people who did the organizing, and then on a first-come, first-choice basis seems to avoid any arguments on the subject, and assigning each person/couple a different meal to plan has worked well in my experience. (Indeed, my husband and I first bonded over making a huge cooked Sunday brunch, including his mean Bloody Marys (p.305), for ten others at a Landmark Trust house in Devon; the others, all being couples, had decided that we were the least in need of a lie-in.) Here are some good sources of places to rent for weekends:

* *The Landmark Trust* (01628 825925/www.landmarktrust. org.uk) is a building preservation charity that rescues historic and architecturally interesting buildings and their surroundings from neglect and rents them out at reasonable rates. Some are truly stunning and in breathtaking places – and many can accommodate large numbers.

* *National Trust Cottages* (0844 800 2070/www.nationaltrust cottages.co.uk) has a unique collection of over 320 properties in outstanding locations in England, Wales and Northern Ireland;

they even have a last-minute bookings service. Similar properties are available in Scotland belonging to the National Trust for Scotland (0131 243 9331/www.ntsholidays.com).

✳ *Portmeirion* (01766 770000/www.portmeirion-village.com) will rent you one of the unique picturesque cottages in the Italianate Welsh model village built by Clough Williams-Ellis and made famous as the setting for the cult TV series *The Prisoner* in the 1960s.

✳ *Helpful Holidays* (01647 433593/www.helpfulholidays.com) has a wide range of properties to rent in Devon, Dorset, Cornwall and Somerset, from cosy cottages for two to much larger houses that would suit several families. Their telephone service really does live up to their name.

✳ *Rural Retreats* (01386 701177/www.ruralretreats.co.uk) rents holiday cottages with style. No psychedelic carpets, nylon sheets or frilly loo roll holders here – properties have been strictly vetted for tasteful furnishings, privacy and so on – and there's a hamper of food on the table, a bottle of wine chilling in the fridge and a real fire (in winter) ready to light on arrival.

✳ *Alastair Sawday's Special Places to Stay* (01275 395431/www. sawdays.co.uk) has a section on self-catering, alongside hotels, inns and B&Bs, all selected on account of stunning or unusual locations and a high standard of furnishings, food and general care.

Incidentally, another approach that works well, particularly for families, is to find a cottage you love and stick to it, booking up for several weekends and longer holidays per year. This makes it feel much more like 'your place', but without the extra mortgage and maintenance costs. And knowing the cottage in advance makes packing – and deciding what to do while there – much easier.

⟨⟩ *City Breaks and Country Hotels* ⟨⟩

Where to stay

For Bridget Jones, the weekend break in a country hotel was the ultimate in desirability, but personally, I'd far rather go and stay with friends or rough it in a tent than pay through the nose for a lot of unnecessary frills and fussing. Similarly, I've never been too keen on B&Bs, whether it's the nylon sheets and smelly showers at the bottom of the market or the smug air of 'aren't we wonderful?' at the top. Being a guest in someone else's house is one thing when you know them, but quite another when you are complete strangers, and I've never quite mastered the friendly chat over breakfast, either with the owners or, God help us, with fellow guests. There are some amazing places, however, in Alastair Sawday's *Special Places to Stay* (see p.233), so don't let me put you off.

✳ *Hotels*: Far preferable to me is the anonymity of a hotel – the old-fashioned kind with a well-stocked bar and roaring real fires if at all possible. Recommendations from like-minded friends is the best way to find somewhere you'll like, though the plethora of 'city style guides' to hit the bookshops recently usually seems to include more traditional venues as well as those designed by Philippe Starck and the like, where you can't find the way in and the bar's so full of beautiful young people you end up raiding the mini bar in your room. If I see a hotel I like the look of in a magazine or colour supplement I cut it out and keep it in files marked 'Places to Stay (UK)' and 'Places to Stay (Europe)' and 'Abroad' – which sounds a bit anal but has served me well over the years.

I'd normally avoid the big chains like the plague, but in city centres they can occasionally be a good option, as the business clients on whom they rely during the week have gone home and there are often some rather good deals. We once spent a surprisingly pleasant few days at one bang in the centre of Glasgow, where staff didn't blink twice at our lilac camper van in the car park, nor our large hairy lurcher accompanying us up and down in the lift. (Incidentally, a book called *Pets Welcome!* by Anne Cuthbertson is vital reading if you travel with a dog – or even, as the book makes clear, a cat, bird or other kind of pet (the mind boggles). Entries range from bog-standard B&Bs where dogs are welcome to sleep in the rooms to hotels that seem more geared to dogs than humans. I remember a hilarious one in Cornwall where packets of dog snacks were stacked next to crisps in the bar and the conversation was strictly confined to canine topics.) The website www.petsarewelcome.co.uk (01873 840750) is also useful.

✳ *Home from home*: Renting a flat for a weekend away might seem an unnecessary luxury, but can actually work out cheaper than a good hotel and has the undoubted advantage of making you feel as if you really do live in the place. I have done this (albeit for slightly longer than a strict weekend) in Paris, Rome, Venice and New York, and have loved it every time. For me, a big part of visiting a city is checking out their food markets and delis, and having your own place means you can bring delicious packages back to your 'home' to eat in style, rather than have to smuggle them into rooms that are not equipped with plates, spoons and so on. There's also the privacy of one's own breakfast unencumbered by the need for social chit-chat, plus the possibility of saving so much money by the odd home-cooked lunch or supper that you can afford to eat out somewhere swanky (remember that for many famous restaurants you'll have to book weeks in advance). You can also entertain guests, if you have friends in the city, which is particularly fun if you feel that you are always eating at their homes and long to return the hospitality. I love this way of living in a city, and have come to regard 'my' flats in central Rome and the West Village/Meat-Packing District of New York almost as additional homes. See websites such as www.citysonnet.com, www.athomeny.com and www.affordablenewyorkcity.com (for New York), and www.myhabitat.com for Paris, Italy and the UK.

* *Home-swapping*: This is another possibility and can be enormous fun, with everything from eco-houses and houseboats to crenellated castles on offer. You often swap vehicles too. Visit www.homelink.org.uk.

What to do

When it comes to what to do on a weekend away or city break abroad, I'm a great believer in not trying to cram in too much. Call me lazy if you like, but I always feel I absorb much more of a place's essence by strolling its streets, browsing its small shops and markets and lingering over a latte in a café than by dashing hither and thither ticking cultural 'must-sees' off a list. One gallery or church and perhaps one museum per day is more than enough – and means you have time to appreciate them without becoming exhausted or overloading your brain. Visit the large famous galleries and museums by all means, but make a beeline for just one collection or a handful of paintings you've been longing to see, rather than trying to cram it all in. Walking rather than using the lifts is a good way to absorb some of the rest as you go, as is breaking your visit with tea or lunch in the café. But make sure you leave time to take in one or two of the lesser-known delights: museums where the collection is housed in a former home are always my favourites, with Sir John Soane's Museum, Leighton House and the Wallace Collection in London, Kettle's Yard in Cambridge, the Frick in New York and the splendid Jacquemart-André in Paris all well worth a visit. (For more on enjoying museums see pp.57–62)

If the weather's fine, a picnic in a park is a fun way to enjoy both the park and some local produce – and do some people-watching. Pack yourself a little picnic gleaned from trips to a deli and food or farmers' market with some freshly baked bread and head for the open space of your choice. Whether it's

Central Park in New York, the lovely Place des Vosges or Luxembourg Gardens in Paris, you'll have a great time – and see a whole different side to the city. Italian parks on a Sunday are packed with families, dressed in their best church-going clothes and enjoying the showing off as much as, if not more than, the fresh air. Paris has probably the best and most comical selection of small dogs being walked, some in perfect designer outfits, while in America there's baseball to watch, and skateboards and roller-bladers to dodge. Park life is a hugely underrated pleasure, either at home or abroad. Lou Reed knew it when he penned 'Perfect Day', as did Bob Dylan in 'Simple Twist of Fate', not to mention Blur's 'Parklife'.

For visitors or travellers on a budget, teatime offers a good opportunity to take in the delights of the grand hotels and restaurants that might otherwise be off-limits. Some places can be unexpectedly quiet in the afternoons. I remember a wonderful afternoon in Harry's Bar in Venice (heaving every evening as everybody throngs there for a bellini) where, as almost the only customer, I was fussed over delightfully with the best egg and salmon sandwiches ever. Try to make room for some local colour: check out the street markets and junk shops, find out where the locals go for a great (and probably cheap) swim or Turkish bath; ask about local food festivals, fetes and other celebrations that might be a little off the beaten track. (For more on the latter, check out websites such as www.whatson when.com, www.2camels.com and www.Culture-England.com before you leave.)

When dusk gathers, go somewhere with a great view for drinks: watching the lights coming on and twinkling across the cityscape far below is always a thrill, and places like the Hilton in Park Lane, London and the Rainbow Room at the Rockefeller Center in Manhattan may seem obvious but they do have immense style. (Do remember that many such places have a dress code, so it's always safer to ring first to check.) If you spend all your money on cocktails, so be it. This may be the evening to sample the local fast food option – be it noodles, falafel or fish and chips – on your way back to bed.

Green Holidays

Fancy staying in an eco-house, or combining your weekend away with some voluntary work? To find out more about eco-tourism holidays, visit www.responsibletravel.com (01273 600030). Other useful sites include www.tourismconcern.org.uk and www.ethicaltraveler.org. For eco-breaks in the UK, visit www.greentraveller.co.uk (for green holidays and places to stay) and www.organicplacestostay.co.uk (for hotels, B&Bs and guest houses serving organic food) or the Green Tourist Business Scheme (GTBS), www.green-business.co.uk. Also see the courses at the Centre for Alternative Technology in Wales (p.240).

⟨⟩ *Go British* ⟨⟩

As the expense and environmental acceptability of foreign travel are called into question, why not stay closer to home? Thanks to decades of cheap air travel, many of us are less acquainted with our own great cities and countryside than with those of other countries. Time now to explore Britain, whether it's

Weekend Courses

Going away for the weekend can be combined with learning something new if you sign up for one of the many weekend courses now available in everything from angling and art appreciation to yoga. Here are just a few ideas:

Crafts: There are all manner of crafts courses throughout the country, but check out those held by painter, felter, beader and general all-round craftswoman Juju Vail – often held in spectacular locations – detailed on her blog www.jujulovespolkadots.typepad.com.

Eco Living: The Centre for Alternative Technology (CAT) in Machynlleth, North Wales, offers residential courses in everything from organic gardening to installing solar heating systems and making your own bio-diesel. Contact CAT on 01654 705981/www.cat.org.uk – and you may be able to stay in one of their eco-cabins.

Gardening: Large gardens open to the public may hold weekend courses in general gardening. Acclaimed ex-London garden designer Ruth Collier holds weekend courses in garden design from her new home in Dorset (07875 774502/ www.couturegardens.com), while Pamela Woods of Sacred Gardens can teach you how to make the most unprepossessing urban plot into a sanctuary for the soul (01453 885903/ www.sacredgardens.co.uk).

Rock Climbing: The National Mountain Centre in Wales (01690 720214/www.pyb.co.uk) offers weekend courses for those who have had some experience of indoor rock climbing but want to take it out of doors. The British Mountaineering Council (0161 445 6111/www.thebmc.co.uk) has information on more general courses.

Sewing: Learn how to make everything from clothes and

curtains to impressive roman blinds: info from Sewing Tuition (01608 644877/www.sewing-tuition.co.uk).

Surfing: You're never too old to start, and many forty-some-things of my aquaintance now swear by it. Devon and Cornwall are the places to go and the British Surfing Association (01637 876474/www.britsurf.co.uk) gives a list of accredited schools.

Wilderness skills: Come the apocalypse, you'll know how to survive if you learn bushcraft skills (01283 730851/ www.woodlandsurvivalcrafts.co.uk), everything from lighting a fire without matches to tracking and searching for wild food and water.

Writing: City Lit in London (020 7831 7831/www.citylit.ac.uk) offers a Write a Short Story in a Weekend course, while New Writing Patnership (01603 877177/www.newwritingpartner ship.org.uk) runs residential weekends in various locations, from poetry and prose to writing for radio with acclaimed published writers.

Upholstery: Sounds dull, but can save you shed-loads of money and help you revamp market finds. Tresithick Upholstery (01726 884500/www.tresithickrestorations.co.uk) offers beginners courses on a beautiful Cornish estate near Truro.

rediscovering the delights of bucket-and-spade seaside holidays, walking in Wales or Cumbria, sailing around the Norfolk Broads, travelling by barge along the waterways or enjoying the stylish new cafés, restaurants and theatres in regenerated towns like Bath, Bournemouth (yes, Bournemouth!) and Glasgow. There are just so many possibilities – far too many to list here. But just for starters, think of Hadrian's Wall, Durham Cathedral, the Giant's Causeway and the wild, unfrequented Northumbrian coast – not to mention the Orkneys, Outer Hebrides and many remote and beautiful islands around the coast of Scotland. Even smaller market towns and resorts – Broadstairs, Burnham Market, Lewes and Rye, to name but a random handful – make great bases for exploring the surrounding coast and/or countryside.

Britain has changed a lot in recent years. Gone are the days of not being able to find a cappuccino or a decent salad outside London. Cafés and restaurants celebrating simple, seasonal food are cropping up everywhere, with organic pubs and restaurants right on the beach from Kent to Cornwall and beyond. Provincial hotels and B&Bs no longer mean close proximity to swirly patterned carpets and brushed nylon bedding – you can stay in great style and comfort if you know where to look (see pp.233–239). So, get out a good atlas and plan your next trip! Every country and town in Britain has a tourist board (www.enjoyengland.com, www.visitscotland. com, www. visitwales.com, www.discovernorthernireland.com and www.discoverireland.com are good places to start) and the internet offers endless research opportunities. Browse books such as *The Rough Guide to Britain* and *The Time Out Guide to*

Weekend Breaks in Britain and Ireland, and once you have cho-sen a destination, ask friends who live there or know the area for recommendations for places to stay and things to do. Keep a file of places you'd like to visit.

The other great advantage of travelling within the UK is that, unlike the delays and discomfort that often accompany air travel, the journey itself can be part of the fun. It doesn't even have to mean hours cramped up in the car. See the following places for ideas on train travel and renting unusual or 'green' vehicles.

❧ *Forget the Car!* ❧

More and more city folk are forgoing the hassle and expense of buying, insuring and taxing their own car and renting cars through companies such as easyCar (08710 500444/www.easy car.com) or Streetcar (0845 644 8475/www.streetcar.co.uk) by the hour, day, week or month, for everything from the Saturday shop to weekends away or even longer holidays. Not only does this usually work out cheaper overall, but cars are always new (reassuring, particularly if your own is not) and the cover for breakdowns good. To rent a 'green car' compare the deals offered by the various rental companies on 'dual fuel' models such as the Toyota Prius at http://www.greencar site.co.uk/green-car-hire.htm. For classic cars and other unusu-al options, see the box, pp.246–7.

<svg></svg> *Let the Train Take the Strain* <svg></svg>

Instead of beginning a weekend away by packing up the car and spending hours stuck in traffic, why not go by train? Even factoring in a taxi to the mainline station (a necessary luxury if you have loads of luggage), the fares can be surprisingly reasonable if you are together enough to book well in advance – and family and/or student railcards will help. Going by coach is obviously the cheapest option of all, but can be cramped and queasy-making and somehow makes me feel like a student again. The lovely thing about trains is that they do, in the words of the advert, 'take the strain' and, unless you are unlucky enough to be caught up in awful delays, make the journey a part of the fun. Some routes – Bristol Temple Meads to Weymouth, Shrewsbury to Aberystwyth, Edinburgh to Dundee and the wonderful West Highland Line – are worth travelling on purely for the pleasure of watching the panorama unfold through the window.

Book a table seat so you can spread out and have space to read the paper, enjoy a picnic, even use a laptop or play board games. (If you want peace and quiet, remember to book the Quiet Car.) Personally, I find that dividing the time between reading, snoozing and looking out of the window suits me fine – and with a small child in tow, the inevitable trips up and down the carriages to loos and the buffet car can even be enjoyable. Travelling by train keeps your carbon footprint low, and you'll end up taking less luggage too.

One of the nicest ways to extend your holiday time is to use the overnight sleeper service. For far-afield travel to the Scottish Highlands and Cornwall – even parts of Europe – this really

makes sense, and there is something rather romantic about setting off in your cosy cabin late at night and arriving as the sun rises.
I have used the Scotrail service many times, even with a small child
and dog in tow, and though I can't say I had the best night's sleep
(you are rumbling along at 90 miles an hour, there are the noisy
jolts and bumps as different carriages are connected and discon-
nected at Crewe in the early hours, and I had both dog and child
deciding to join me in my bunk), the service is fine. You get a
breakfast of sorts delivered an hour or so before your final destination, but nonetheless I'd recommend heading straight for a good
breakfast when you arrive. The Royal Highland Hotel right next to
Inverness station is rigged out in fine style with tartan carpets and
open fires and offers everything from porridge and kippers to a full
fried breakfast, with the seagulls squawking in the air overhead.

For further information on the Caledonian Sleeper service
to Scotland contact 0845 601 5929/www.firstgroup. com/scotrail
and for the Night Riviera from London Paddington to Pen-
zance contact 0845 700 0125/www.firstgreatwestern.co.uk.

For all other information on train services in the UK try the
excellent Man in Seat 61 (www.seat61.com) which has won
many awards for its free advice on planning and booking travel by train – and boat – within the UK and beyond.

Alastair Sawday's *Go Slow England: Special Places to Stay,
Slow Travel and Slow Food* has other slow travel ideas.

And at the other end, if you need a car, you can rent one for
the duration of your trip (see p.246). But for something a bit
more unusual, how about a vintage, split-screen camper van or
a stylish Morgan sports car for the weekend? Both could be waiting for you at the station when you arrive (see over for details).

Renting a Vehicle

Rent a vintage VW Camper Van: Scooby Campers (0131 467 1312/www.scoobycampers.com) has a small but lovingly restored fleet of vintage VW camper vans for hire (both with beds and without) for travel in and around Scotland (hire starts in Edinburgh). Snail Trail (01767 600440/www.snailtrail.co.uk) is another camper van hire company, based in Bedfordshire; all their vans have new engines and have been flawlessly restored in pastel colours and named Betty, Pearl and so on – some even have their own blogs, detailing their travels. Rentadub (07971 096518/www.rentadub.co.uk) offers camper vans – and convertible Beetles – for hire in Cornwall and the West Country.

Hire a Morgan: If you are going to Cornwall, how about stepping off the train and hiring a Morgan sports car for the weekend? What fun to come down on the train – either the sleeper or late afternoon with dinner in the Pullman – and pick up a beautiful classic car in which to tootle round the coast with the roof down? Check out Perranwell Garage (01872 863037/www.perranwell.co.uk) and go to the 'Morgan hire' link on the website.

VW Beetles and Mini Coopers: If you fancy beetling about in a Beetle, or other smaller stylish model, Cool Cars 4 Hire (0208 811 1106/www.coolcars4hire.co.uk) is based in London and offers various smaller cars for hire, such as VW Beetle convertibles and Mini Coopers – even Smart Cars – while Rentadub offers VW Beetles along with their camper vans (see above).

Other classic car hire: Other companies offering classic car hire – Morgans, Porsches, E-type Jags, Karmann Ghias, MGBs, you name it – include:

Lakes and Dales Classic Car Hire (01768 879091/www.lakesanddales.co.uk/Classiccar)

Dream Car Hire (0844 800 0195/www.dreamcarhire.com)

Classic Car Hire (www.classiccarhire.co.uk)

The Open Road (0845 070 5142/www.theopenroad.co.uk)

Land Rovers: If you are going into rough terrain, why not hire a Land Rover or other off-road vehicle? Land Rover Car Hire Locator (www.carpages.co.uk/info/landroverhire.asp) helps you find one from car rental companies throughout the UK, including at major airports.

◆ *Camping* ◆

I used to love camping. It was our regular childhood holiday, either in old-fashioned canvas bell-tents in a field at the foot of the Brecon Beacons in Wales, or in vast campsites in France where the ready-pitched tent came as part of the package – less romantic, perhaps, but every bit as fun for a child. One of the few things I liked about being a Girl Guide was the twice- or thrice-yearly camps, where we learned to pitch and strike proper ridgepole tents, make handy gadgets from lashed-together wood on which to balance our washing-up bowls and keep our bedding dry, and cook corned-beef hash and other hearty fare on fires we'd lit ourselves. Looking back, I still think all the dubious marching about in uniform and pledging to crown and country was worth it just for that. Since then, I have spent many happy nights under canvas – at music festivals and road protest sites, after parties in the country, and in places like Scotland where you are still permitted to pitch a tent in open country or by the sea. I can't say they have ever been the most comfortable of nights: in fact, I can remember quite a few where I have not slept at all owing to a snoring companion, the tent flapping in the wind, *Blair Witch*-type nightmares or, worst of all, the rain coming in. But it was usually worth the ordeal for the total joy of a fine dawn under canvas – one of life's great cheap pleasures: the filtered light and dappled shadows, that strange and specific camping smell, the delight of unfastening the front entrance to frame the morning view and savour the fresh air, the promise of freshly brewed coffee and a fried breakfast. I still think camping is a wonderful activity – not least because it reminds us of how little we actually need in order to be happy. Shelter from the rain and sun, good food simply cooked, a few friends and a beautiful view – that does it for me.

So why don't I do it nowadays? Reader, I married a non-camper. And, not to put too fine a point on it, I got older and more attached to my home comforts.

Camper vans

A rather successful compromise was an ancient lilac VW camper van which took us on many happy trips through Devon and Cornwall and all the way around the coast of Scotland one summer, and made for rather more in the style and comfort stakes at Glastonbury and the like. Known to the cognoscenti as a 'Devon' model (it's hard not to get sucked into the enthusiasts' jargon), the van had a smart striped sideways pop-up roof and a table and bench seat that turned into a reasonably comfortable bed (if you didn't mind having to turn over whenever the other person did). It had a small sink (that ran off a bottle of water), a fridge and a little gas cooker that tucked away behind the front passenger seat. Not being the most adept at lighting a campfire in the wind, I loved this little cooker, and used to rustle up everything from porridge to a fry-up to a pretty

Games For Car Journeys

Arms and Legs

Divide into teams (or individuals) responsible for left and right sides of the car. Each team (or person) has to look out for pubs on their side of the road and take note of the name. Points are awarded per limb (e.g.: Jolly Farmer = 4; King's Arms = 2; Fox and Hounds = 12 (plurals are set at 2 unless otherwise specified); Rose & Crown = 0. Anyone's head, e.g. the King's Head, Queen's Head = –5). Set a time limit or number of points to reach to win. (If possible, exclude the driver from this game. Not only should their eyes be firmly on the road, there is also the risk of cheating by altering the route to their team's advantage.)

Car Snooker

Start with a white van, car or police car and proceed by spotting cars in the order of a snooker game (yellow, green, brown, blue, pink, black) with a white one in between each one. Rumour has it that the police use this game when deciding what cars to stop for random speed checks. (To remember the order of the colours, memorize the mnemonic You Go Brown Before Potting Black.)

Car Cricket

Divide into two teams. The batting team/person has to spot a red car in order to start, then scores 'runs' by counting up silver and white cars before the other team/person gets them out by spotting a Land Rover (substitute another type of vehicle in areas where Land Rovers are either too numerous or unfeasibly scarce). Keep a score till the journey ends, the cars run out or boredom sets in.

mean risotto on it, while Frank strummed his guitar (these were the pre-ukulele days) in the back. Indeed, when the camper van broke down, as they are all prone to, and ours did more than most, it was often the cooker that saved our spirits, as we brewed up a cuppa while waiting for the RAC.

After a good ten years' hard service, our camper van is now parked in the garden of our seaside home, rusting quietly in the sea air and (I'm told) beyond feasible roadworthy repair. But it still doubles up as a great little greenhouse for raising seedlings, and I'm plotting an interior revamp that might give it a second life as an emergency extra bedroom. They're not cheap, neither to buy nor to maintain, but camper vans are great fun and I would recommend them to anyone who likes the spontaneity of taking to the open road with a map and a few possessions and Kris Kristofferson's 'Me and Bobby McGee' on the CD player. You don't even have to splash out on your own: they are available for hire at quite reasonable cost (see box, p.246).

Camping Kit

- A bedroll including a thin inflatable mattress (www.thermarest.com/00 353 21 462 1400) or thick yoga mat, sleeping bag or duvet, blankets and sheets, and comfortable cushions or pillow. Silk linings (available from camping shops) are good for cold nights.
- Wind-up torch – or torch and spare batteries.
- Basic cooking utensils, crockery and cutlery, etc.
- Good coffee and coffee-making kit.
- Box of matches.
- Camping gas or know-how to build a good fire.
- Swiss Army knife and corkscrew.
- Compass and Ordnance Survey map(s).
- Guitar (or ukulele – see pp.37–9).
- Bottle of good whisky (nothing like a wee dram to get you off to sleep in the inevitable slight discomfort).
- A good book – poems or ghost stories ideal.

Some Great British Campsites

Applecross Camp Site, Applecross, Wester Ross, Scotland (01520 744268/www.applecross.uk.com): Hillside site with amazing views out over the sea to Skye. A polytunnel café with its own bakery adds immeasurably to the appeal, and the wonderful Applecross Inn is just down the road.

Arthur's Field at Treloan Farm in Cornwall (01872 580989/ www.coastalfarmholidays.co.uk): An idyllic site that dates back to the 1930s. It overlooks the sea in Gerrans in an area of outstanding natural beauty, with a lovely beach nearby and sailing on the Percuil River.

Caerfai Farm, St Davids, Pembrokeshire (01437 720548/ www.cawscaerfai.co.uk): Farm site, powered by solar, geothermal, wind and biomass energy. Pitches are large and uncramped, with ocean views, and stunning Caerfai Bay is a five-minute walk along the coastal path.

Low Wray, Windermere, Lake District (015394 32810): A magical wooded and grassy site right on the shores of Lake Windermere, with the Drunken Duck pub just a short walk away.

Tom's Field, Langton Matravers, Dorset (01929 427110/ www.tomsfieldcamping.co.uk): A mature and sheltered, no-frills site with bags of rustic charm and spectacular views out to sea and the coastal path nearby.

Troytown Farm, St Agnes, Isles of Scilly (01720 422360/ www.troytown.co.uk): The Scillies are made for camping and this, the UK's most south-westerly site, has breathtaking views of the Atlantic, the roar of which also helps drown the noise of fellow campers. Farm shop, including own ice cream, on site.

For more, check out the campsite reviews on www.thehappy campers.co.uk and www.ukcampsite.co.uk, buy *Cool Camping* by travel writer Jonathan Knight (there is now a regional series) and check out his own website, www.coolcamping.co.uk

7.

A New Approach to Chores

$\mathcal{A}$ s someone who is self-employed, I know I'm lucky not to have to fit all the week's chores into two short work-free days, but it still amazes me how many people are prepared to spend a large chunk of their weekend queuing in a supermarket, trawling the aisles of DIY stores or immersed in the duller end of domestic duties. Now I know there *are* people for whom shopping for shoes, digging up potatoes or doing a nice bit of grouting equals Big Time Fun, and when it comes to gardening I am one of them, so we'll leave people to spend their precious time as they wish. But it seems to me that many of us head to the high street on a Saturday almost on automatic pilot. So if, like me, you'd rather spend your free time in more enjoyable ways, it's worth investigating alternative methods of getting chores done. Or, on occasion, not getting them done. All of which might end up being more fun, cheaper and better for the planet.

☺ *Shop-free Weekend* ☺

Simply as an experiment, try setting yourself the challenge of a shopping-free weekend. On one level this is dead easy: buy in the basics such as bread, milk and a few vegetables a day or so beforehand (even easier if you grow your own or have a veggie box delivered), get yourself invited out to eat at least once, and scour your kitchen cupboards for a Store-Cupboard Challenge to use up as many existing supplies as you can. Trust me, it really is amazing what you can knock up with a few bags of pulses, cans of tuna or tomatoes, stock cubes and risotto rice. You might even find yourself using up that bag of bread flour just before its use-by date (see p.177 for bread recipe). Here are a few of my favourite Store-Cupboard Standbys:

RISOTTO

The best risotto uses a good chicken stock, and I often have some handy from a roast chicken carcass (a great weekend standby); if you keep frozen home-made chicken stock in your freezer, so much the better. A good bouillon mix with a handful of fresh garden herbs and a bay leaf is a passable last resort. A few rashers of bacon are flavourful, and can be fried along with the onions in stage one; otherwise it is just a matter of seeing what you have in the cupboard or crisper drawer of the fridge. Mushrooms and frozen peas are a good standby or, if the cupboard is bare but you have some saffron strands, fear not, as you have all you need for a classic *risotto alla Milanese*.

Basic risotto (per person)

1 tablespoon olive oil
knob of butter
½ onion, finely chopped
1 good handful of arborio risotto rice

splash of white wine (optional)
300ml chicken or vegetable stock – kept at boiling point
second knob of butter
1 tablespoon or so grated Parmesan

Heat the olive oil and butter in a heavy-bottomed pan and add the onion, stirring for 5 minutes or so till transparent (you can also add a rasher or two of sliced bacon at this stage). Tip in the rice and stir until coated in the oil and butter. Pour in the wine, if using, and cook for several minutes. Then add the stock to the rice, one ladleful at a time, and stir well until it has been absorbed. Add more in stages until the rice seems just al dente – cooked and creamy in consistency, but still with a tiny bit of bite in the centre – which should take 15–20 minutes. Any other ingredients such as cooked vegetables can be added at this stage, along with milled pepper. Remove from the heat and stir in the second knob of butter and Parmesan and beat the risotto well with a spoon to get the desired consistency – soft and creamy (never solid). Serve with more Parmesan, if liked.

🍵 PEA AND PESTO SOUP

This is incredibly easy – the store-cupboard version by necessity uses pesto in a jar, but the 'fresh' stuff from a chiller cabinet or delicatessen makes a huge difference. This serves 2–3 and is great with garlic bread (keep a supply in the freezer).

> *750ml water*
> *375g frozen peas*
> *2 spring onions, trimmed but whole (omit if you have not got)*
> *1 teaspoon Maldon salt or ½ teaspoon table salt*
> *½ teaspoon lime juice (from a bottle if no fresh limes)*
> *4 tablespoons pesto (ideally 'fresh' but if not from a jar)*

Bring the water to the boil (or boil a kettle first and measure it out). Add the frozen peas, spring onions, salt and lime juice and return to the boil for 5 minutes. Remove and discard the spring onions and whizz up the peas and their liquid with the pesto using a hand-held blender.

🍵 THREE BEAN TUNA SALAD

Consisting largely of the contents of tins, this is the classic store-cupboard standby, but none the less delicious for that, particularly if you can lay your hands on some fresh parsley and olives. This feeds 4.

> *1 tin each of haricot, kidney and borlotti beans (if you have some*
> *French green beans, substitute for one of the tins of beans)*
> *1 onion, ideally red, finely chopped*
> *black olives, if possible*

1 tin of tuna in brine
dressing made from 2 parts extra virgin olive oil to 1 of
*   balsamic vinegar, 1 teaspoon runny honey, 1 teaspoon*
*   mustard, 1 clove of garlic, crushed and all mixed together*
fresh parsley, roughly chopped

Drain the beans and place in a salad bowl with the chopped raw onion, olives and flaked-up tuna. Pour over the dressing, mix well and sprinkle with parsley. This is good with warm crusty bread, and improves on being kept in the fridge overnight.

The Favourite Cheese Pie (pp.51–2) is another tasty possibility, if you have frozen pastry, eggs and cheese to hand.

Raid your own kitchen garden if you've got one – even in the dead of winter there might be a leek or two, or a handful of fresh parsley. Otherwise, beg a few veg from a friend with an allotment in return for an hour's weeding, or go on an afternoon's foraging for wild food (see pp.83–6). You may end up fitter and having had more fun, as well as with a few more pounds in your pocket. You may even discover a new hobby or feel such satisfaction from your new-found resourcefulness that you'll be inspired to make permanent changes in your shopping habits. Whatever you do, it has got to beat standing in a supermarket queue.

◎ *Alternative Food Shopping* ◎

Sure, supermarket shopping is convenient, but I'd far rather spend a little more time doing my food shopping in a way that is not only more enjoyable but also leaves me with a better taste in my mouth – even before I've eaten the goods. To my mind, supermarkets superseded their optimum size years ago – or am I alone in finding the places grim and soulless, the distances one has to push one's trolley quite exhausting, and being faced with no fewer than forty-five types of rice a wholly unnecessary stress?

Home delivery

Buying from supermarkets online seems a good solution in theory, but those I know who do it are frequently frustrated by having to stay at home to receive the delivery, and finding many items either have an impossibly short shelf life, or have been replaced by totally unsuitable substitutes. The newer breed of organic food delivery companies such as Abel & Cole (0845 262 6262/www.abelandcole.co.uk) and Riverford Organics (0845 600 2311/www.riverford.co.uk) now deliver organic wine, rice and pasta, recycled loo paper and right-on cleaning products along with the organic veggie box and fruit bags, which is a great way to get in the basics alongside regular supplies of fruit and veg – all of which can be heavy and unwieldy to carry. I used Abel & Cole a lot when I was pregnant and had given up my allotment and didn't want to be out and about carrying heavy bags.

But as someone who genuinely loves food, I found I missed being able to look at, choose and occasionally even sample the produce. Like any old-time veggie-boxer I was also beginning to get fed up with the challenge of finding yet another use for swede in January, and strawberries that went mouldy if we didn't eat them almost on the doorstep. For me the way to do it is to make a monthly supermarket trip or home order for basic staples (to be honest, I let my husband go whenever I can – he claims to enjoy it) and do the rest at smaller local shops or markets. But everyone's needs and inclinations will be different. Here are a few of my favourite alternatives.

Farmers' markets

I can still remember the thrill of walking round my first farmers' market, in Union Square in New York, back in the early 1990s. It was heartening to see colourful stacks of corn and autumn squashes piled up against a backdrop of grey urban buildings, and the figures of the farmers – in dungarees and donkey jackets and with ruddy, weather-beaten faces – looked similarly splendid and incongruous beside the suited city slickers. I spent a happy hour or two browsing the stalls, sipping hot spiced cider and buying freshly baked bread, jars of honey and armfuls of garden flowers to bring back to the little apartment I was renting. Someone should do this in the UK, I remember thinking – and sure enough, in time, people like Henrietta Green at London's Borough Market and Carla Carlisle at Wyken Hall in Suffolk did just that. Nowadays almost everyone has access to a farmers' market or farm shop, where fresh, seasonal local produce can be bought directly from the people who grow or rear it – and I can't think of a better or more enjoyable way to shop. Food miles are kept to the minimum, as are the middle-man's profits, and the produce just has to be fresher. (The madness of carrots being grown in Cornwall, driven hundreds of miles across the country to be packaged and then transported back to supermarkets in the West Country that was highlighted in recent reports cannot be a practice anyone would wish to support.) And shopping like this can be a sociable event, too. At our weekly farmers' market in the country I frequently bump into friends and neighbours and am introduced to new faces; and it's also fun to chat to the producers and build up a relationship with your favourites.

Farm shops

You don't have to live in the country to frequent a farm shop. Look out for them on journeys that take you through rural areas – many do a great line in home-baked cakes and puddings too, as well as lovely cut flowers. Famous ones such as the glamorous Daylesford Organics in Gloucestershire (01608 731700/ www.daylesfordorganic.com) are well worth a detour, but there are plenty of smaller (and much cheaper) gems quietly carrying on in other corners of the country. And at certain times of the year, keep an eye open for the temporary fruit and veg stands that line the rural roadsides: bundles of asparagus in Worcestershire in late April and May, and punnets of strawberries and glossy cherries in Kent and Sussex in July are beautiful bargains not to be missed. Picking your own is another option worth considering, particularly if you have a freezer (see pp.137–8).

Shopping for alcohol

Some swear by cross-Channel trips to stock up on beer and wine as an alternative to the supermarket run – and if you book ahead, and combine it with lunch in an attractive seaside town such as Le Touquet or Boulogne, or even a night in a local auberge, this can be a fun way to get the booze in over the course of a weekend. If all you're doing is tipping straight off the ferry or out of the Chunnel into a hypermarket and trundling your clanking cargo straight home, however, I'd forget it. You have to do a hell of a lot of shopping – for a wedding or large party, for instance – to make the expense and unpleasantness of the travelling worth it, in my book. Online shopping for alcohol is now much easier than it was (see pp.266–7), and this can ease the pressure on time, trolley space and triceps.

But I've recently discovered what I consider the most enjoyable alternative: Buying British. Gone are the days when English wine was a laughable affair: sparkling wine from Kent (Chapel Down, see p.266) and Suffolk (Wyken Vineyards, 01359 250262/www.wykenvineyards.co.uk – sadly no mail order) is now served at the poshest parties, even at Buckingham Palace. And, fuelled by the effects of climate change, top French viticulturalists have been making trips across the Channel, and offering substantial sums to farmers for prize south-facing slopes. Cider – which the British make particularly well from the West Country through to Kent and East Anglia – has never been so fashionable. And a host of micro-breweries are offering delicious alternatives to the usual can of lager. (My favourite is Wyken Vineyards' low-fizz Good Dog Ale (see above), which bears a black Labrador on the label and the slogan: 'Makes You Want to Sit and Stay'.)

Buying British certainly cuts down the 'booze miles', and it can also be great fun. Check out the vineyard or brewery nearest you – some have shops and restaurants attached and offer a tour of the site combined with tastings and lunch, which can provide a pleasant focus for a weekend in the country.

Brewing your own is another enjoyable alternative, but

requires more in the way of instructions than is possible in a book of this nature. Visit www.homewinemaking.co.uk or check out a book like *First Steps in Winemaking* by C.J.J. Berry for further information. And look at the recipes for hedgerow tipples on pp.170–3.

Water

Buying bottled water is not only expensive and unwieldy, it's also dodgy on health and environmental grounds. Research has proved that not only is much bottled water little better for you than most tap water but that toxic phelates can leach out of the plastic and into the contents if stored incorrectly. And what exactly happens to the many millions of empty bottles we dispose of every year? It's becoming increasingly trendy to ask for tap water in restaurants, but if you really don't trust your supplies at home, buy a filter that is simply installed beneath the sink (try The Fresh Water Filter Company 020 8558 7495/ www.freshwaterfilter.com); the £250 or so cost will quite quickly be recouped and, to my mind, is well worth it.

Smaller local shops

For other food items, shop at smaller stores and markets. People on the Continent have always shopped thus, stopping off on their way to or from work to fill a string bag with fresh beans and salad or buy a bit of fish or meat for their evening meal, a habit I picked up in Italy. To me, it's a pleasure that adds to the spontaneity of life, deciding what to cook depending on what the butcher or fishmonger has at its best that day and looking at the recipe books afterwards, if necessary, rather than deciding on a recipe and making a list first. Even in my part of south London (glorious to me but often deemed insalubrious) it's possible to get all the ingredients for a dinner party – from fresh shell-on prawns and hunks of Parmesan or pecorino cheese to organic chocolates and the juiciest honey mangoes – by simply walking from the Portuguese deli (tiny but packed to the gunwales) through the colourful Caribbean market to our local health food shop. And for the odd more rarefied treat, there are specialist shops and mail-order suppliers such as Rococo for hand-made lavender-flavoured chocolate or the Hebridean Smokehouse for salmon straight from the lochside smokery (see pp.266–7).

The joy of shopping in smaller, more frequent amounts is that there is much less to carry at a time, which means you can leave the car at home. Having the odd fold-up shopping bag or rucksack on one's person (Onya Bags, see p.268, are my favourites) makes life easier and more guilt-free – or how about a trolley on wheels? Don't laugh: I've been weathering the old-lady jokes for years with my trusty woven wicker model and am now rather gratified to find the things have actually become trendy. For more alternatives to plastic bags, see below.

Alternatives to plastic bags

According to the makers of Onya Bags, one reusable bag has the potential to eliminate 1,000 plastic bags, which are wasteful to produce, clog up landfill sites, litter our countryside and beaches and endanger birds and marine life. All good reasons to invest in a few and – most importantly – keep at least one on you at all times. The holy grail, it seems to me, is a bag that is

Internet Food and Alcohol Shopping

Berry Bros & Rudd (0870 900 4300/www.bbr.com), the old-school vintner based in St James's, London SW1, offers a surprisingly friendly and easy-to-use ordering service with plenty of advice available.

Black Isle Brewery (01463 811871/www.blackislebrewery.com) has an excellent range of organic beers in brown bottles with distinctive graphic labels.

Booths Wine (0800 197 0066/www.booths-wine.co.uk) offers pre-mixed cases of its best wines while also allowing you to choose your own combination of any twelve bottles by price, country, grape, colour/style etc. For those who know exactly what they want, its sister company Everywine (0800 072 0011/www.everywine.co.uk), sells virtually every wine online in same-wine cases.

Elizabeth Botham & Sons, Whitby (01947 602823/www.botham.co.uk) sells Yorkshire specialities, from fruity Yorkshire brack, own-blend teas and home-made jam from the owner's Victorian tearoom to Whitby kippers, Harrogate toffee and Wensleydale cheese.

Chapel Down Vineyard (01580 763033/www.englishwinesgroup.com) has an efficient mail order service, often with selected wines on special offer. Their sparkling wines are particularly good – try the award-winning Pinot Reserve 2002 and Vintage Brut 2002. Also good for unusual English beers and cider, including the fiendishly strong Biddenden Cider.

Forman and Field (020 8525 2352/www.formanandfield.com) supplies fresh seasonal British food including Mrs King's Pork Pies – quite the best pork pies in the world, with crisp traditional pastry (complete with jelly) encasing marvellously meaty innards. Available in several sizes, they keep for a fortnight and make a cheery present for a meat-lover.

Fortnum and Mason (0845 300 1707/www.fortnumand mason.com) is the undisputed master of the hamper, from tuck-shop treats for children at £30 to top-of-the-range luxury at £300-plus, all packed in beautiful F&M wicker hampers.

Hebridean Smokehouse (01876 580209/www.hebrideansmoke house.com) farms salmon and sea trout without chemicals in pristine Atlantic waters, smokes them over peat then slices and packages by hand.

Holker Food Hall (015395 59084/www.holkerfoodhall.co.uk) sells salt-marsh-reared lamb, venison and shorthorn beef raised by tenants of the Holker Estate in Norfolk.

Isle of Wight Bacon Company (01983 840210/ www.isleofwightbacon.co.uk) produces dry-cured bacon and ham and five types of sausages from naturally reared free-range pigs.

Lynher Dairies Cheese Company (01872 870789/ www.lynher dairies.co.uk) sells three delicious different Cornish cheeses, which arrive beautifully wrapped in nettle or wild garlic leaves.

Neal's Yard Dairy (020 7500 7653/www.nealsyarddairy.co.uk) has a huge range of British cheeses of tip-top quality; try the Montgomery cheddar, Ragstone goat's cheese, Graham Kirkham's creamy Lancashire and famous Colston Bassett Stilton, or sample one of its regional or themed selections. Tell them when you want to eat it and they'll choose the cheese accordingly and pack it all beautifully in a sturdy cardboard box.

Rococo (020 8761 8456/www.rococochocolates.com) has been much copied but never bettered for its witty and wonderful chocolates, from Artisan bars flavoured with cardamom, chilli and lavender to chocolates shaped like pebbles, coffee beans and asparagus to wafer-thin discs that make the perfect dinner-party or weekend-away gift.

For suppliers of good bread and cakes see p.178.

strong and large enough to be useful but can still fold away small enough to fit into an average handbag. Others can be kept in the car or bike basket.

The range from Onya (05602 696001/www.onyabags.co.uk) is my favourite as the bags are made from parachute fabric which is strong, folds up small and can be dyed beautiful bright colours. Unlike many of the hemp and canvas bags around, they are also large enough to be really useful – some with gussets, others styled like rucksacks with back straps to leave your hands free – while still folding up small enough to be pushed into a keyring-sized pouch.

Turtle Bags (01299 827092/www.turtlebags.co.uk) are string bags made from organic cotton that fold up small and expand with the amount of shopping you put in them to take quite a sizeable load. They come dyed in a variety of colours with a choice of long or short handles.

Carry-a-bag (www.carry-a-bag.com) makes full-size canvas shopping bags in naval stripes or jaunty florals, some with a message printed on the side. These are sturdier and can be stood on the ground, but are more expensive and don't pack away so small.

You'll find cheap shopping trolleys in hardware and luggage shops – even, these days, in plain black or navy rather than the tartan and fake leather of yesteryear. But those wishing to be truly stylish should check out the designs available from Orla Kiely (020 7720 1117/www.orlakiely.com), Verko (020 8201 9444/www.verko.co.uk) and Habitat (0844 499 1111/www. habitat.co.uk).

☺ *Clothes Shopping* ☺

When I was a teenager, it was a much anticipated treat to rush straight from my Saturday morning job in the record library to spend my hard-earned wages, often saved up in a jar beneath the bed for weeks, at Miss Selfridge just over the road. These days, though my love of clothes remains undimmed, I do far less clothes shopping. I'd like to credit this change to growing eco-consciousness and concern over children in Third World sweatshops, but have to admit that a reluctance to bare my post-baby body in a smelly communal changing room is probably equally – if not more – to blame. If you enjoy clothes shopping, then far be it for me to dent that bliss. Shop on. But if, as for me, its pleasures for you have palled, then consider the following alternatives.

✱ Don't. I did this one year as a New Year's resolution – no new clothes or shoes for an entire year – and really enjoyed it. The success of the operation may have been partly due to the fact that accessories were not included in the ban, meaning that a substantial stash of silk scarves, soft leather gloves and cashmere 'wrist warmers' made its way into my wardrobe but, hey, there's nothing like accessorizing to glam up an old coat or dress.

✱ Go second-hand. Fashion queens such as Sarah Jessica Parker and *Vogue* stylist Bay Garnett have been doing this for years, only calling it 'vintage' rather than 'Oxfam' makes it sound smart rather than seedy. Top-of-the-range sources include 'nearly new' designer shops in well-heeled areas where fashionistas are given hard cash for handing in stuff that is sometimes just a single season old. Then there are lovely vintage shops or stalls in markets such as London's Portobello, the Lanes in Brighton and Glasgow's Barras that are always fun to rootle through. (See also the section on antiques fairs, p.275). Even the most unprepossessing junk store may have the odd rail of clothes at the back. Lured by a fine array of old gardening tools on the pavement, I once stopped the car in a village street to find a 1930s gold lace dress and an Anita Pallenberg-style velvet embroidered jacket tucked away in just such a place for a fraction of what they would have been worth to a London dealer.

Next on the list are charity shops: these can be a great source provided you have the patience to trawl through rails of crushed velvet and pink crimplene and the nose for the sometimes unsavoury smell. Shops in well-to-do areas are often a good bet, particularly (though it seems somewhat tasteless to admit it) those with a disproportionately large elderly population. The method favoured by real thrift-shop queens of my acquaintance is to have three or four favoured shops on their 'radar' and pop in frequently to check the stock. If the staff like you, they may even keep stuff back for you that they know you'll like. Or, better still, get first dibs yourself while doing a bit of voluntary work on the side (see pp.69–70). Last but not least, there are car boot sales and even skips, but the treasure-to-tat ratio tends to be a lot lower here.

* Trade with family or friends. When a friend was moving house recently, she turned out her wardrobes and invited ten or so of us along to see if there was anything we wanted. A few people, excited by the challenge, brought a clothes rail along and set up a corner of their own. Before we knew it we had a good old-

fashioned swap shop going on, the fun fuelled by plenty of wine and the odd hilarious trying-on session. I ended up the proud possessor of a classic Armani jacket, and got rid of a few items that had lingered unworn in my wardrobe far too long. It was what you might call a 'win-win' situation and hugely enjoyable into the bargain.

✱ Keep a fashion stash. This is totally contrary to the advice on 'clearing out the clutter' that is doled out by feng shui consultants and programmes such as *The Life Laundry* (www.thelife laundry.com), but many are the times when I've resurrected an item of clothing, sometimes unworn for years, and given it a new lease of life – either via some new item I've since bought which looks particularly good with it, or simply by virtue of the fickle wheel of fashion having turned enough times for short cropped jackets/Oxford bags/leather clogs to be back in vogue. There's no point, of course, in keeping clothes that you really don't like. But there are times when a shape, a colour, a cut of jacket or length of skirt seems more 'right' than at others. And sometimes it's our own shape that changes. Again, the accepted wisdom is never to keep clothes that are too small in the hope that one day you'll fit in to them once more, but I like the motivation of that pair of Liz Hurley white jeans on the top shelf that next summer I really *shall* be slipping into. And when I finally got back to my pre-baby weight two years after the birth of my daughter, I fell upon the clothes I'd missed like long-lost friends. The real proof of the pudding is when friends say, 'That's nice – is it new?'

✱ Buy well-made classics. This sounds incredibly middle-aged and middle-class, I know, but money spent on good jackets, shoes and other basics is never wasted as they keep on looking good long after the cheaper versions have lost their buttons or gone baggy at the seams. Classic clothes – think trench coats, white shirts, well-cut trousers and cashmere polo necks – never go out of fashion, and can easily be jazzed up to the minute with scarves and more ephemerally fashionable items from Topshop and the like. It's a different mind-set, I know, from the one in which you buy a new set of clothes for each season and then get rid of them. But throwaway fashion just isn't sustainable any more. I've never felt easy about the rock-bottom prices at stores like Primark, as in the back of my mind someone must be missing out, but then I heard that charity shops are actually refusing Primark goods as they last so poorly and are so cheap they have no second-hand value. Their short lifespan only adds to their undesirability – wasteful and ethically questionable to produce, they are then only fit for landfill in the space of a few months.

✽ Make-do and mend. If you intend keeping your clothes for longer, you'll have to look after them. This means washing and cleaning carefully and only when necessary, repairing holes and tears before they get out of hand, and protecting wool, particularly cashmere, from marauding moths (see p.167). Good clothes deserve good care. A couple of generations ago, good suits and coats would be kept for an entire lifetime, packed away in tissue paper (with the inevitable smell of mothballs, to be sure) or conserved in special covers. As consumer culture fades, I find myself fantasizing that patches in pretty or contrasting colours will actually become fashionable. Bring Back the Patch, I say!

✽ Reinvent and customize. Old clothes can be reinvented simply by changing the buttons or sewing in a new lining of contrasting silk or tartan. If the latter, which involves cutting out the existing lining and using it as a pattern to make a new one, seems too complicated, take it to a good tailor's or dry cleaner's that offers alterations.

◉ *Home Improvement Alternatives* ◉

Though I worked for many years on *World of Interiors*, which is probably the most beautiful homes magazine ever, I must confess I have an ambivalent attitude to interior decoration and DIY. Don't get me wrong, I love beautiful houses and do my best to make my own look good. But – rather like the good classic jacket with cheap accessories notion outlined above – I would far rather ring the changes within my home using smaller items such as curtains, cushions, throws, even pictures and flowers and so on, than by constant large-scale redecorating.

One of the biggest wastes of time, money and resources in this country has to be our obsession with putting in brand-new kitchens and bathrooms. Who hasn't seen a neighbour install a cheap new kitchen in their property in order to sell it – only for the new owners to rip it out as soon as they move in to make their own 'mark' on the place? And why this constant need to paint, paper or tile our walls in bright colours? Why not just have plain white walls and wooden floors and let the furnishings in our homes – the books, the fabrics, even the flowers in the vases and the fruit in the bowls – create the character and colour? Then a quick lick of paint every few years and a slick of varnish would be all that was needed to keep things spick and span, and a whole lot of time and energy could be spent on more enjoyable pursuits.

But I digress. The object of the exercise is to prevent every weekend being dominated by DIY and shopping for the home, while still enjoying a stylish and comfortable living space. Here are a few tips.

* Don't. Adopt my husband's attitude – frustrating at times, but not without its advantages. DIY, for him, stands for 'Don't Involve Yourself'. Do as little as possible to get by, and bring in the professionals to do the big stuff. Okay, this is not the cheapest option, but if DIY is neither an enjoyable nor on the whole a particularly successful pursuit in your household, it may be well worth the expense.

* Choose manageable projects rather than month-on-month marathons. Ring the changes in a room by painting or papering just one wall (you can really push the boat out here when it comes to quality as the quantities will be relatively small). Or give the downstairs loo a new look by papering it entirely in maps, old music manuscripts, theatre programmes or newspapers.

* When it comes to large pieces of furniture such as sofas, beds and dining tables, buy to last. Quality shops will have huge reductions in the sales and the investment will pay off in terms of comfort and durability (which means, of course, less shopping in the long run).

* Buy second-hand wherever possible, from auction houses, antique and junk shops, even jumble sales and car boot fairs. This not only saves on money and resources, and will often give you far better quality than the superstores and such like, but also the shopping process itself is far more fun than getting lost in Ikea only to be told at the end of your maze-like meanderings

that the item you want is no longer in stock. See below for further details on specialist fairs and markets and salvage yards.

�./ Commission a one-off piece from a local craftsperson or carpenter. This can be hugely enjoyable and rewarding, and you'll have the added satisfaction of knowing that no one else will have a piece like it. If you don't already have someone in mind, attend the end-of-year shows of your local art and design colleges and see whose style and ideas you like. Chat to the makers about what you want and ask them to come up with a few sketches. Choose well and – who knows? – you could end up with a piece by the next Terence Conran or Marc Newson. Check out websites such as www.craftanddesign.net and www.ukcraftfairs.com.

✦ Go to specialist fairs and markets. One of the most entertaining and cost-effective ways to furnish a house is to frequent one of the fantastic open-air furniture fairs such as those held several times a year at Ardingly in Sussex. Many of these will be for dealers only on the first day but it is usually possible simply to pay the extra fee to get in early on and get first look at everything. Look for good shapes – dodgy finishes can usually be stripped off relatively easily, and a slap of filler and a coat of Farrow & Ball flat oil paint conceal a multitude of sins. The prices tend to be extremely low for larger items – but you have to factor in the cost of transport and delivery. When looking for sofas, chaises longues and the like, however, it tends to be best to choose one whose covering you can either bear to accommodate or can cover with attractive quilts or throws. Upholstery – unless you can do it yourself – is expensive, and if you decide to re-cover you could end up paying more than the piece is worth. Visit www.antiques-atlas.com (0161 613 5714) for listings.

* Look in salvage yards. A visit to a salvage yard can be incredible fun – and good ones can supply everything from reclaimed floor-boards and roll-top baths to unusual light fittings, old church pews, classical columns and so on that can be incorporated into the house or garden. Salvo (01225 422300/www.salvo.co.uk) is an international directory of UK suppliers of architectural salvage, from used timber, bricks, stone and cast iron to smaller items such as garden furniture and pots.

* Finally, if you can't beat them, join them. Making your own stuff for the home – from a simple shelf to walk-in wardrobes – can be immensely satisfying and money-saving, provided you know what you are doing. Consider joining a carpentry evening class or apprenticing yourself for free to a friend or relative in the trade. Get some good tools in. Just try to make sure you don't spend the entire weekend slaving over a hot Black & Decker . . .

Gardening

I love gardening, and my ideal weekend would have to involve at least a morning or an afternoon pottering about outside. Indeed, when I do my big annual spring and autumn clean-ups, I try to organize the weekend's activities around time in the garden, followed by a lovely long bath and an evening out doing something completely different like seeing friends or watching a good film. But I do know that for many, the prospect of having to tame and tend the often unruly patch of nature outside their back door can be daunting, with mowing the lawn and tackling the buddleia among the looming chores that can dominate a weekend. Here are a few tips for making it all less onerous and more fun.

✻ Don't. Rather than rush hither and thither forgetting what you were trying to do in the first place and resenting the fact that you are having to garden at the weekend anyway, take a day out to enjoy your garden in peace. It might seem self-indugent – and indeed, to keen gardeners it might even seem impossible (I'm forever leaping up from my chair to pull a weed or prune a straying branch). But, trust me, it will not only be enjoyable: it will also pay dividends as you get to know your garden properly and will be able to make any future plans from a position of sound knowledge and experience. So if anyone asks what you are doing as you lounge in your deckchair or pace slowly up and down, the response is, 'Important research'. Having a pen and pencil handy will not only make you look more serious to onlookers who may be keen to enlist your services elsewhere, it will also be useful for making a rough plan of the garden, showing large permanent items such as trees, sheds etc., and listing other observations.

Start by just sitting as still as you can and looking and listening. What birds and insects can you see and hear? (You may also need some sort of identification guide.) What are they doing? Do they seem to be favouring any specific plants or bushes? Be aware of the light, and track its movement throughout the day, marking on your plan any particularly warm suntraps (especially those in the mornings and evenings which you'll be able to enjoy on working weekdays too) and any areas that receive no direct sun at all. Shady areas may be good for ferns or a log pile for insects to hide in.

Take your gaze and hearing slightly further afield. How exposed do you feel to neighbours and overlooking windows? Are there any ugly buildings or other features it might be possible to screen out? Might any irksome noises, from passing traffic to chatting neighbours to screams from a nearby playground, be muffled by new sounds you might add to your garden – trickling water, for instance, or the swish of bamboos?

Time to get the creative juices flowing now. So treat yourself to a cup of tea – or perhaps even a glass of wine or beer. Let your mind roam as you fantasize about your ideal garden and how you, your friends and family might like to use it. Do you like to eat outside? At what time of day? Do you like to sit in sun or shade? How and where might you encourage wildlife? Is there room for a pond? Where – out of sight but near enough to be convenient – is the ideal place for a compost heap? Is there also a relatively remote area that could be left untouched for wildlife? By the end of the day you'll have quite a respectable-looking plan and list of future activities to show whomever might be interested. Next, of course, it will be time to do something about them.

✱ Knowledge is power. Books such as Alan Titchmarsh's *How to be a Gardener* are all very well, but nothing can compare with knowledge gleaned first-hand from Those Who Know. Get a friend or relation round for an hour or two – bribe them with a good lunch afterwards, or exchange their know-how with the equivalent time of your own on a different subject – to walk around your garden with you and tell or show you how to prune and propagate each tree, shrub and plant in turn. If you don't have a friend who can do it, it's worth paying a professional gardener to come – but make sure they do the work at the same time as telling you about it! Make notes in a notebook, draw pictures or take snaps on a digital camera, as you will never remember everything.

✱ If your garden has got seriously out of hand, or you have just taken on an overgrown property or allotment, enlist help! Throw a garden-clearing party in which everyone fills a (recyclable) garden waste bag before they can tuck into the free beer. Exchange a few hours' gardening time with a knowledgeable friend for baby-sitting or other duties you feel able to provide. Or pay a professional to come and sort out the basics for you so you feel you have the energy to proceed. (Working alongside them – see opposite – is one of the best ways to learn. Thinking of it as training is a good payoff for the expense.)

✱ Don't bite off more than you can chew. Choose one area you're really going to dote on – it could be a particular bed or border or the terrace near the door – and concentrate your energies there to begin with. Somewhere that is in full view of the house and easily accessible makes good sense. It could even be the front garden or a collection of pots outside the French windows. Keeping on top of one area and seeing it looking good should be ample reward for the labour involved – and might inspire you to take your efforts further.

✱ Rather than make endless lists of garden chores that you know you'll never be able to work through, decide on perhaps three main tasks for the weekend, none of which will take interminably long, but which will make a big difference to the garden's appearance (and thus how you feel about it). Mowing the lawn, if you have one, has to be top of the list, I'm afraid, and will probably need doing every week or two in high summer; try paying or bribing a teenager if you can't face it yourself. Next comes a little light weeding, particularly in the beds and borders nearest to the house, and the removal of any dead, decaying or otherwise unsightly plant matter. Another quite small chore that makes an impact out of all proportion to the effort involved is trimming the edges of the lawn (upright shears are the job here, with a sharp spade or lawn-edger if things have got really out of hand). Like trimming one's hair or nails, or plumping up the cushions on a sofa, this instantly makes a garden look well groomed and cared for, and detracts attention from other less attended-to areas.

✱ Then choose one manageable project which will be fun to do and enhance the rest of your life in at least one other respect: for instance, plant a tree with attractive blossom and edible fruit; create a herb garden (see pp.103–8) which you can use in cooking or to make herbal teas or other remedies; start a small salad or vegetable bed (see pp.95–9 and 124–5); or make a pond that will attract fascinating and beneficial wildlife to your garden (see p.284). See the seasonal sections for more details and further ideas.

◎ *Allotments* ◎

Contrary to what you might think, you don't actually have to love gardening to enjoy an allotment. A friend of mine who didn't have a garden of her own used to do the minimum with her plot to avoid being evicted by the Weed Police (site committee) and just sit in a deckchair reading in the sunshine while her neighbouring plot-holders laboured all around. This approach is taking it to extremes, and now that allotments are fashionable, with long waiting lists in some areas, might not be looked on with such tolerance. But there is more to allotmenteering than growing strictly serried rows of prize carrots and potatoes. These little plots of land, often on the outskirts of cities or on the fringes of parks, golf courses, railways or other areas of open land, can become many things to different people: quiet refuges from the working week; classrooms or laboratories in which to learn and experiment with new skills; symbols of independence, in which raising your own organic food becomes a personal stand against the stranglehold of the supermarkets; nature reserves in which birds and butterflies are encouraged and enjoyed; sociable spaces in which friends and family can work, play, talk and even cook alongside each other.

Taking on an allotment is a huge commitment, however. Most plots that come up on the waiting list do so because they have been ill-tended, so in all likelihood there will be a lot of initial clearing to be done. The plots are large (a traditional allotment is five poles – the antiquated measurement dating back to before the Agricultural Revolution, and around 150 square yards to the layman), which is a lot for one person, or even one couple, to weed and water regularly, especially in high summer. Well cultivated, though, they will raise enough produce for more than one family. What I did – and what I highly recommend – is to share a plot (or two, or three, which is what we eventually ended up with) with other people. That way you share the responsibilities and the fun – not to mention the endless supplies of super-fresh organic fruit and veg. You can also go away for more than a few days without worrying unduly about the watering, or whether the slugs are devouring your lettuces or your baby courgettes are morphing into marrows. Pooling skills and resources is another benefit of joining forces.

My own allotment partners – two gay men – were great at heavy-duty tasks such as making raised beds from old scaffolding planks and digging in mountains of manure, while I was quite happy to take on most of the weeding. And we all had other friends and neighbours who loved to come along and lend a hand from time to time. There were Saturdays where ten or more people would turn up during the course of the day: some with their children to spot newts and dragonflies around the pond, others to pick blackberries to make jam, some bringing plants from their own gardens that needed a new home – and even some, occasionally, to help us work! – all congregating for cold beers and a barbecue as the sun went down behind the trees. If I had to choose the favourite meals in my life, these impromptu gatherings, in which freshly picked salad, tomatoes still warm from the sun and sweetcorn boiled in a billy can were accompanied by a well-earned drink and lots of laughter, would have to figure high.

Other key ways to make having an allotment fun and manageable include:

✳ Only grow the stuff you really like.
✳ Grow produce that is either hard to find or expensive to find as organic produce in the shops: asparagus, for instance, is relatively easy to grow once the bed has been prepared, and having one's own personal supply of this most delectable seasonal treat is an incredible life-enhancer.
✳ Choose crops that really benefit from being used fresh. Many

strawberry and raspberry varieties found in the supermarkets, for example, have been chosen for their ability to store and travel well rather than for flavour. And no shop-bought produce can compare to new potatoes freshly dug from the soil or sweetcorn dropped into a pan of boiling water a few minutes after picking, before the sugars turn to starch.

✸ Make lots of salad leaves a priority. Rocket is almost impossible *not* to grow, as even the slugs don't like it and it obligingly sets its own seed. And when it comes to other leaves, start off with one of the 'cut and come again' mixes containing green and red, frilly and round, hot mustardy and plain leaves – they're a good way of discovering what types you like best and which grow well in your soil. Harvest when the leaves are young, either by cutting the whole plantlet down and waiting for it to re-sprout, or pulling off the outer leaves to let the inner ones rejuvenate the plant. Once you get into the rhythm of sowing a line or two of seed every couple of weeks you'll never want to touch one of those over-priced, chlorine-washed supermarket salad bags ever again. Red leaves, by the way, seem much less popular with slugs and snails, in my experience.

✸ Include some sort of den or shelter. Sheds are ideal – and to me, a rickety shed fashioned from lengths of skip timber is part of the make-do, makeshift aesthetic that makes allotments so special. If, as in my own site, sheds are banned as being contrary to some local by-law, you can still get round it by erecting a temporary tent or tepee (technically you may be obliged to move this every twenty-eight days, but who's counting) or (as we did) creating a lovely living willow bower. As well as providing shade and shelter, there is something about a framed view of a garden that enhances pleasure and inspires contemplation.

✸ Dig a small pond. It is amazing just how quickly a pool of clear water in a plastic liner becomes a beautiful place buzzing with abundant forms of life, many of which are beneficial to crop production. Make sure the sides are shallow enough for creatures such as frogs and toads to hop in and out, and give them plenty of large stones to hide under; they'll pay you back handsomely by eating your slugs. Ponds (with the correct safety precautions, of course) are also great for keeping children happy: watching the wildlife, dipping with nets and jam jars and viewing the contents through magnifying glasses and so on.

✸ If you like having flowers in your house, reserve a bed or two as a cutting garden; there are books on the subject, such as Sarah Raven's *The Cutting Garden* that will tell you what to do, and you can buy seeds, bulbs and plantlets from garden centres or online. Once you've started growing your own organic fruit and vegetables the anomaly of flying in roses and lilies from as far afield as Kenya and Columbia seems more and more absurd, and fresh-picked flowers have a longer life and a sort of glowing aura that florists' flowers just can't compete with.

Make the allotment the centre for all kinds of creative pursuits – not just gardening – particularly if you have kids. Useful items such as scarecrows, plant supports and bird scarers (anything from strings of shiny objects such as unwanted CDs to artificial 'hawks' suspended from trees) can provide the focus for some fun creative projects. And they'll not only cost less than the shop-bought alternatives but look heaps better, too.

✸ Don't neglect your stomach: gardening is hungry and thirsty work. Either bring supplies in a cool box or Thermos or arrange for a friend or partner to pop along bearing lunch at an allotted time. Keep a barbecue safely and securely stored on site for enjoying your produce at its freshest and best. Invite your friends round and enjoy!

☺ *Cleaning and Tidying* ☺

'We can't come out, we've got to clean the house,' must be one of the saddest excuses for not seeing friends on a sunny Saturday. But you hear it a lot – not least because CHAOS (Can't Have Anyone Over Syndrome), or the shame of having friends see the squalor into which your life has descended, can have a similarly detrimental effect on one's social life. I'm not a great fan of cleaning and tidying myself, but here are my tips for keeping on top of it with minimum effort.

* Pay someone else to do it. In my experience this has always been money well spent. If you can't afford a cleaner, enrol some willing children. Tell yourself it is a vital part of their education. I grew up with an elaborate system of rotas for changing beds, washing floors, cleaning ovens and so on at weekends, but these days a whole generation of children of working parents with cleaners is growing up knowing nothing about domestic duties. Bribe them if necessary.

* Set a timer for a ten-minute tidy-up per room. I came across this idea in a book and didn't think much of it till I tried it, but it works extremely well. You can get much more done than you think in the short time, and having the deadline – a ticking alarm if you can bear it – hanging over you prevents you getting

waylaid by reading the magazines you're putting out for recycling and so on.

✹ Have a place for each member of the family – a small drawer, a basket on the stairs, an attractive box or whatever – into which any post or other little items pertaining to them gets put. When the receptacle is full it's time for them to empty it.

✹ Try to keep the entrance to your house welcoming and clear from clutter even if other parts slip from time to time. The first impression on entering should be calm and uplifting – for yourself as well as visitors.

✹ A few times a year – even if you have a cleaner – knuckle down, put on some great music (I find Toots & the Maytals and Dolly Parton particularly effective for some reason) and have a jolly good clean up and clear out. No ineffectual waving of the feather duster here, we're talking humping heavy furniture about, emptying kitchen cupboards, dusting books – the works. There are places where even the most diligent cleaner won't get – and festering corners encourage moths, mice and worse. Some people I know – my own mother being one of them – claim to enjoy a good clean as a cathartic experience. I don't – but I do like the feeling of having done it, and make sure I reward myself with a luxurious bath and a good night out (or in) afterwards.

✹ Having good kit really helps. Call me shallow, but I'm always going to feel more inclined to sweep the kitchen floor with a good old-fashioned wooden broom and sturdy metal dustpan than with an ancient scuffed plastic thing. Labour and Wait (020 7729 6253/www.labourandwait.co.uk) do lovely plain household stuff if you can't find it in regular hardware stores, or you might prefer colourful modern plastics, in which case Lakeland

(015394 88100/www.lakeland.co.uk) is the place. The blissful hardware section in John Lewis (08456 049049/www.john lewis.com) – just walking around it makes me feel domestic and virtuous – even has nifty enamel boxes and buckets labelled 'Housekeeper' if you feel you need to go that far. Whatever gets you behind that broom is worth it, in my book.

❋ If you have children, or live in a shared house, try introducing a Chore Jar. Write enough basic chores on bits of paper to keep everyone going for an hour – plus some random treats and rewards such as 'Have a biscuit', 'Sit down for five minutes' or 'Swap a chore with someone else'. Everyone takes a piece of paper and carries out their chore or treat, taking another when each is done (it might be necessary to keep an eye out for slackers here, or introduce a minimum number of tasks or slips of paper per person).

❋ Have plenty of flowers or potted flowering plants around. And light a lot of candles in the evenings. There's nothing like beauty to distract from a little unruliness about the edges.

❋ Have a de-cluttering session. These days, almost everything can be given away or recycled, which all adds to the worthy glow. See p.109 for more ideas and info.

⊙ *Laundry* ⊙

Again, having good kit and a well-thought-out working layout help immeasurably. I've got a thing against noisy washing machines in kitchens, particularly kitchens that are also dining rooms and sitting rooms, like ours, and so we put our washing machine in the utility room (otherwise known as the 'Futility

Room') in the basement. Good idea, you might think, but as most of the laundry is generated from the top of the house, we're forever carrying bundles of sheets and clothes down three flights of stairs to be washed and back up again. Ever since reading *Domestic Bliss* by Rita Konig, I've coveted her little laundry cupboard where the washing machine, laundry baskets and all accoutrements are tucked away in a cupboard in the hallway of her tiny flat, all noise and mess confined to one hidden spot. Another pet hate is damp laundry hanging up to dry all over the house – trousers draped along radiators, pants suspended from shower rails and so on. This is a tricky one to get around when I've also always had a thing against energy-guzzling tumble-driers (the average model uses 3000W of electricity per hour of drying). Old-fashioned ceiling airers are probably the answer: they have a lot of room on them, and hoist all the washing up high where it is out of the way and likely to dry fastest. Above the bath or at the top of a stairwell are good places to mount them (check where your joists are first), and there are traditional and slightly more modern models available, according to your style. Try large department stores or choose from the range at Eco Washing Lines (0800 280 2236/www.ecowashing lines.co.uk).

I know it's anathema to say it, in these days when washing machine ownership is almost universal and the average usage is a load per family unit per day, but I sometimes yearn for the camaraderie of the launderette of my student days – or for what I imagine was a very efficient and sociable system of the communal laundries in Glasgow tenements. When I lived on my own in a small central London flat, I managed perfectly well without a washing machine, taking good stuff to the dry cleaner's and trundling the rest to the launderette for a service wash, and back again in the evenings, dry, folded and ready to put away. Without a husband and child, both of whom generate huge amounts of washing, I'd go back to that system at the drop of a hat. What definitely helps is that the husband in question does do our laundry. He says he likes it – honest – and operates a system of strict colour segregation (five categories) that would be beyond my time and patience. Apparently he used to help his mother as a boy – another good reason for getting today's children to help with the household chores.

☺ *Exercise* ☺

Doing something active should definitely be part of a healthy weekend. But make it something you enjoy, and in the fresh air if possible. Gyms can be airless, soulless places – unless you like the smell of sweat and the sound of wall-to-wall MTV. They can also cost an awful lot of money, giving the obligation to go an added financial edge. (I know I'm not the only one to have joined a gym and slacked after the first few months so that each swim or weights session, when later calculated against the monthly direct debit, cost me £75.) You may be a member of a wonderful gym that you enjoy frequenting regularly, in which case, well done you. But it's always worth exploring the alternatives. (See Sunday, p.306 for the more leisurely options.)

I used to run, but many years ago, on a work trip to Bali, I remember taking an early morning jog along the beach from my hotel. As I puffed and panted along the sand, clad in sticky black Lycra with sweat running in rivulets down my face, I became aware of the local people watching me as they did gentle stretches on the sand and wandered down to the sea. Whatever their age, without exception they were slim and supple, with clear eyes and skin – and looking at me in a most bemused way. All of a sudden it struck me: these people are beautiful and fit because of their way of life, as a by-product of not over-eating, of avoiding stress and doing gentle (or in the case of some of the men, quite strenuous) physical work in the course of an average day. I vowed then and there to try to follow their example, to see if and how I could maintain a good level of fitness just by keeping healthy habits and fitting physical exercise into each day.

I've done this largely through dog walking (a brisk forty-five minutes to an hour every morning) and by cycling wherever I can. In summer I swim in the sea or in our local London lido whenever I can (see pp.125–8) and play a little table tennis in the garden, which can be surprisingly strenuous if played with gusto. My concession to a set regime is a twenty-minute series of yoga-derived exercises some mornings, and a weekly Pilates session round the corner (which I attend with a friend and follow with a bowl of noodles at the Japanese noodle bar that probably undoes all the good work).

But everyone has different health needs and inclinations. My husband enjoys rowing, and has installed a rowing machine in our basement. I keep threatening to tack up an attractive riverside or beach scene on the back to inspire him, maybe one day, to take his hobby out of doors. But on the whole I am overjoyed to be married to a man who has no particular sporting vice that totally dominates his (and our) weekend.

Other ways of keeping fit while having fun include the following.

* *Cycling*: This is by far my preferred means of transport – on a fine day, at least. Not only are you unaffected by traffic jams, but you can also ride at leisure through parks/bridleways/footpaths that are out of bounds for cars, and get good exercise into the bargain. I favour an ancient Dutch sit-up-and-beg model, which is picturesque but quite heavy-going. I'm told a cross between a tourer and a mountain bike is a very good choice for shortish distances/around town. A big basket on the front and a rack on the back means you can carry quite a bit of shopping; to transport more, including children, provided you're brave enough, look into the fantastic bikes prototyped by the Christiana community in Denmark with a huge sturdy wooden box on the front that can be covered with a tarpaulin in bad weather.

True, cycling in the city can be terrifying at times, and all urban cyclists have their close-shave stories to tell. But it can also be exhilarating. I remember thinking once, as I whizzed around Hyde Park Corner in London with taxis and double-decker buses zooming past only inches away, that this is the nearest most of us get to hunting/being hunted these days, and that there is a certain thrill in having to rely on all your senses just to stay alive. Perhaps we all need a little risk in our lives. As if to prove the point, I stopped cycling when I became pregnant, and three years on, having just got to the stage where the hall is no longer blocked by a buggy, cannot wait to get into the saddle once again.

✳ *Dance classes*: The more strenuous the better – think salsa, lindy hop or tango to name but three quite lively candidates that will tone the muscles and get the calories dropping off. Added to which, if you're single, there are an awful lot of people who have met their future partners through joining dance classes . . .

✳ *Football, rugby, cricket, netball, volleyball*: These need plenty of organization and involve lots of people. Team sports have a terrible tendency to dominate the entire weekend, as many a 'sports widow' or the rather more rare 'sports widower' will confirm.

✳ *Swimming*: In particular, outdoor swimming in the sea, rivers or lidos (see pp.125–8). Don't bother counting the lengths, just set a time limit of half an hour or so on the clock and let your mind wander as you swim – much more fun. All the more so if the baths you frequent have a sauna or steam room in which to reward your efforts afterwards.

✳ *Tennis, squash, badminton*: Having to book a court and keep an appointment with a partner is a good way to ensure exercise features in your weekend. It's sociable, too, and there's always the possibility of rewarding yourselves with lunch or a drink afterwards. If you haven't got a regular playing partner and still fancy a game, check out your local sports centre to see if they have any 'Singles' sessions where you just turn up, sign up and play with whomever else appears. Could be a disaster, could be fun, could be the start of a friendship or more.

✳ *Yoga, Pilates, t'ai chi*: All three have their advocates, and if you find an activity that works for you, weaving a regular class into the course of your weekend can be an enjoyable and sociable way of keeping toned, fit and stress-free. One friend of mine swears by t'ai chi every Saturday morning with a small but devoted group in our local park. I see them moving slowly beneath the trees when I am walking my dog and think it must make a wonderfully peaceful and quietly energizing start to the weekend. Another prefers a yoga class on Sunday evenings to help him wind down and prepare for the week ahead.

Calories Burned by Various Different Types of Exercise

Figures are for an average performance of one hour's exercise.
For a fully comprehensive list see:
http://www.nutristrategy.com/activitylist4.htm

Baseball	352
Cricket	352
Cycling	422 (leisurely)–844 (fast)
Dancing	317–522
Football	493 (casual)–704 (competitive)
Ice skating	493
Riding	281
Roller skating	493
Rugby	704
Running	563–809
Squash	844
Swimming	422 (leisurely)–704 (fast)
Table tennis	281
t'ai chi	281
Tennis	493
Walking	246 (moderate)–281 (brisk)
Yoga	281

8.

Bring Back Sunday

*I*n this open-all-hours age, it is perfectly possible to do almost everything one traditionally did on a Saturday – from shopping for food and clothes to going to the garden centre – on a Sunday, too. But, call me old-fashioned, I like my Sundays to have a markedly different rhythm from the hustle and bustle of the average Saturday. And it seems I'm not alone. Research conducted in 2007 by Keep Sunday Special (www. keepsundayspecial.org.uk), a movement founded in 1985 to campaign against Sunday trading, has found that 46 per cent of British people find that the shops being open on Sundays only adds to weekend stress levels, and that up to 71 per cent of us would be content for the larger shops to close on Sundays as long as smaller local shops were open. An overwhelming 87 per cent of those interviewed felt a common shared day off each week was important for family stability and community life, while 90 per cent of shop workers were against any extension of Sunday opening hours. Personally, I miss the calm and quiet that used to descend on our city centres on Sundays. It was as if, just for that one day a week, the crowded streets could get their breath back – and, indeed, the break in the relentless activity of cars and bustling shoppers did, quite literally, clear the air.

But we can still vote with our feet and keep Sunday a shop-free day. Getting the necessary chores done on Saturday means that Sunday can ideally be a day of rest and recuperation – mental and emotional, as well as physical. For me, the ideal Sunday includes something that feeds my soul – it could be anything from going to church (see pp.312–14) to a yoga or meditation class (see pp.314–15) or solitary walk – and some quality contact with nature. It's also a great day to spend with friends and family, either round a table tucking into a tradition-al Sunday lunch, going on a walk or taking them on a trip down memory lane (pp.308–12).

❀ *Breakfast* ❀

My perfect Sunday would always start with a good breakfast. Some people make breakfast into an art form. The designer Tri-cia Guild, in her book *Think Pink: Mood and Colour for Modern Spaces*, has endless artful shots of trays laid with hand-embroi-dered linen napkins, fresh flowers and little glass pots of jam to go with crusty bread and croissants. Slightly less glamorous but totally fascinating, 'Jen of Brooklyn' has a blog (www.simply breakfast.blogspot.com) consisting entirely of photographs she takes of her breakfast every day, from a mushroom omelette and a cup of tea to stewed berries and yoghurt or cake and a coffee in a café. I'm more than content most of the year round with porridge in winter and a smoothie or Greek yoghurt, oats and fruit in the summer, but at weekends I sometimes push the boat out, especially if we have friends staying.

Breakfast in bed is always a treat and I'd never turn it down, but I'm just as happy pottering about the kitchen and spreading out over the table with the newspapers. It's reassuring to read health reports emphasizing the importance of a good breakfast, and that stocking up early in the day on carbohydrates and low-GI foods is actually a good way to avoid temptation later on. Protein in the mornings is supposed to make for a sharper mind and more effective metabolism during the rest of the day, but I draw the line at one report that said two eggs is the perfect daily breakfast. That's fourteen eggs a week, even without those that might go into cakes or salad Niçoise or egg mayonnaise . . . No thanks.

Here are some of my favourite ideas for breakfast, more than one of which can be combined as brunch, which is a fine week-end institution (see pp.304–5).

* *Blueberry muffins*: A super-light, fluffy and fragrant treat, which will cook while the coffee is brewing. (See recipe on p.304.)

* *The 'Full English' fry-up*: The all-time favourite of my husband, who was brought up on a full cooked breakfast every day of the week. In my more abstemious childhood it was confined to Sunday mornings after swimming and I have continued the tradition. There are, of course, endless combinations and permutations including everything from eggs, bacon and beans to sinful treats like fried bread and 'eggy bread'. My feeling is that free-range organic eggs, good quality bacon (which fries beautifully, not in a watery mess like standard supermarket stuff)

and mushrooms (large field ones, sliced if you like, rather than the small button ones) are essential, with perhaps a sausage or two, baked beans if you're in the mood or even bubble and squeak or pan-fried rosti made from last night's leftover potatoes and cabbage. I've never been a fan of blood pudding (even the name makes me feel faint, let alone first thing in the morning), nor of grilled tomatoes, but perhaps you might be. The trick is to orchestrate it all so that everything is ready at the same time, or else kept piping hot in the interim, as in the best greasy spoon cafés. As someone who has habitually, over the past few years, made cooked breakfasts for a houseful of guests at our seaside house on nothing but a two-ring hotplate, I am something of an old hand at this, using a precarious-looking system of stacked pans and foil-covered plates. For just the three of us, though, I'm a great fan of Jamie Oliver's one-pan breakfast where he slings it all into the same large frying pan – bacon and/or sausage first, followed by mushrooms and then egg. I don't like the idea of eggs and beans in the same pan; however, if you sling beans in once you have browned and cooked your sausages or bacon, they become beautifully infused with the smoky smell and taste of the meat. And you cut down on washing-up to boot. If you have an oven too, hot plates keep your breakfast hot for longer once it's all served up – and don't forget to get those rounds of toast going at the same time . . .

Pancakes and waffles: Waffles are a great treat and surprisingly easy to make. I would never have bought a waffle-maker but we were given one by friends who were visiting from Canada, where waffles are part of every self-respecting weekend brunch, and I've never looked back. Part of the pleasure for me is that, like the washing machine, lawnmower and barbecue, the waffle-maker is an appliance that my husband has seen fit to appropriate as his own, and the mess he makes weighing and whisking and ladling away is well worth the hot, delicately crispy results. We use buckwheat flour, as do those waffle-makers par excellence, the North Americans, and team them with maple syrup, fruit salad and yoghurt – though they are also surprisingly good with smoky bacon.

✳ *Kippers*: I've always liked kippers, but got hooked on them during a holiday in Scotland, where delicious locally smoked kippers for breakfast made a fantastic start to the day. Being smoked, they have a good long shelf life and travel well by post; the arrival of a package of kippers from Ardtaraig Fine Foods in Achiltibuie (01292 521000/www.ardtaraigfinefoods.co.uk) is a welcome link with the Highlands and has me dreaming of our next trip there.

✳ *Fruit salad*: Lovely on its own, or as an accompaniment to muesli, porridge, waffles, pancakes or the like. Sometimes it's just a mélange of whatever fruit we have to hand that needs using up, sometimes a planned and colour-coordinated creation (pink watermelon, orange canteloupe, halved white grapes and blackberries look particularly beautiful) or sometimes just extremely simple – a juicy mango sliced with lemon juice, for instance, or a fragrant ripe papaya spiked with lime. Make it up the night before and douse with a lemon juice and honey dressing to give the flavours a chance to mingle, but save slicing the banana till the morning if you don't want it to go brown. A good dollop of yoghurt on the side is good, with organic Greek sheep's milk the tops.

* *Smoothie*: These are great for a healthy summer breakfast on the go, or as a vitamin-packed hors d'oeuvre if you are going for the Full English later on. Half a banana, a dollop of natural yoghurt and some apple or orange juice make a good base in the blender, with other fruits from mangos to blueberries added as you choose or have to hand. You can also throw in all manner of energy-giving supplements, from powdered vitamins or a health mix such as Spirulina to a sprinkling of wheatgerm or linseed. The easiest way to mix it all up is with a hand-held blender and its tall plastic container, pouring into a more decorative glass if you choose. Don't be tempted to make a smoothie in advance as the mixture may separate and the vitamin content plummets.

* *Porridge*: There are all sorts of fancy variants on the basic recipe for porridge, but I've never managed to better 1 part rolled organic oats to 2½ parts plain water – no sugar, no salt and certainly no milk. Quick porridge oats are not necessary, but leaving the oats in water to soak overnight saves a few minutes. Grated apple, maple syrup and/or natural yoghurt are all good accompaniments, as are a sprinkling of mixed nuts, seeds and raisins – a sort of flapjack in a bowl. This is one of the most healthy and filling breakfasts you can have. I swear by it all winter, and love to see my daughter downing a good bowlful too, even if liberally laced with brown sugar.

✳ *Boiled eggs and soldiers*: The old nursery standby is still a favourite with me, especially if the eggs are newly laid from my sister's hens. Three and a half minutes precisely after boiling starts gives a firm white and soft yolk *just* going hard around the edges. Given my capacity for distraction when cooking, this used to be largely a matter of luck until my sister gave me a brilliant new egg-timer for Christmas. A plastic, egg-shaped device called Egg-Perfect, it sits in the pan, changes colour to tell you when the egg is done to your liking, and is clever enough to take the number of eggs, and starting temperature and quantity of the water into the calculation; get one from Head Cook (01603 722120/www.headcook.co.uk).

'Soldiers' are one of the few things for which I would specify white bread – either sliced from a packet or a squashy bloomer with the crusts cut off – generously spread with unsalted butter and (controversial for some) a smear of Marmite.

I'm sure you have your own favourites. I know people who swear by baklava and Greek yoghurt, a big slice of fruit cake, or even last night's cold leftover takeaway pizza.

For more ideas see the section on Brunch v Lunch on pp.304–5.

BLUEBERRY MUFFINS

140g plain flour
140g wholemeal flour
1 teaspoon baking soda
2 teaspoons baking powder
50g butter
2 tablespoons honey
75g fresh blueberries – or blackberries
1 egg, beaten
275g natural yoghurt

Preheat the oven to 180°C/350°F/gas mark 4. Sift the flours and baking powders together in a large bowl, making a well in the centre. (The mixture can be left like this to speed up the process the next day.) Melt the butter and honey over a low heat, pour into the well with the fruit, egg and yoghurt and very gently fold in the flour. Don't worry if the mixture remains slightly lumpy – over-mixing makes heavy muffins. Spoon into muffin tins lined with muffin cases and bake for 20 minutes till brown on top.

❀ *Sunday Brunch v Lunch* ❀

Some lazy Sundays you may want to plan the perfect breakfast in bed – for you and/or a loved one on a special occasion such as their birthday or the first day of the school holidays (see pp.298–303 for ideas). But I have also begun favouring brunch as an option on a Sunday. I love the notion of only cooking or eating twice a day at weekends; a brunch followed by early supper can be great for freeing up time, plus allowing one to pig out at each meal without feeling too guilty. Inviting friends for Sunday brunch, complete with Bloody Marys or Buck's Fizz and all the newspapers, can be a relaxed and low-key way of seeing people – and it's a great way to mull over/gossip about the events of a big party or wedding the day before. Brunch also works well when you have guests staying: if you have a long walk planned for later, for instance, it means you can all leave in good time on a full stomach and can finish off with a well-earned cream tea or drinks and snacks in a pub as the sun goes down.

The Perfect Bloody Mary

Purists say the perfect Bloody Mary should be custom-made in an individual glass, and the vital proportions are certainly easier to get right in this way, but a large jug on the brunch table is always a cheering sight. Keep any ice separate, however, as not everyone wants it, and it will dilute and separate the mix in an unappealing way. The vodka bottle can also be left alongside, for those who want an extra kick. The following quantities are per glass/portion.

2 parts good vodka
7 parts tomato juice
1 part freshly squeezed lemon juice
4 good few sloshes Lea & Perrins Worcestershire Sauce
6 drops Tabasco
generous grind of black pepper
pinch of salt
½ teaspoon horseradish sauce (not creamed)
1 tablespoon sherry

Stir – never shake – the above together and serve in straight tall glasses or tumblers with a maximum of 1 ice cube and, if you like, a slice of lemon on the edge of the glass.

There's no substitute, however, for the Great Sunday Lunch at least once or twice a month. This is a wonderful institution, whether a good old-fashioned roast with all the trimmings for your extended family at your home, dim sum and other treats with a few friends in Chinatown or a pub lunch or picnic in the country. If you're cooking at home, don't panic about catering for large numbers: cooking for ten need not be any more diffi-cult or stressful than cooking for four, provided you have big pans, choose the right recipe and don't over-reach yourself. A large vat of spaghetti bolognese goes down well in winter, and can be prepared well beforehand, or how about a simple glazed ham with boiled potatoes or just a hot or cold soup with a huge and colourful mixed salad. See the section on Having Friends to Stay (p.218) for other suggestions, including barbecues. My key to survival is to have one course in its entirety bought from a shop – charcuterie and olives from a deli, for instance, or a beautiful cake or tart – a practice that is deemed perfectly smart on the Continent, where no one would dream of slaving away over both a starter and a pudding.

❀ *A Sunday Afternoon Walk* ❀

In order to counterbalance the calorific intake of the above, I'd then follow it with some form of physical activity (see pp.289–93 in A New Approach to Chores). Some might favour tennis, squash or the gym, and though swimming in the sea, lakes or rivers takes pride of place for me in high summer (see pp.125–8), an important component of my Perfect Sunday is a good walk. While city walks can be fascinating, I yearn for open vistas at the weekend – a park large enough for the surrounding traffic to be neither visible nor audible, or ideally open country-side. The choice will depend on where you live, or are prepared to travel, or simply where you have had the lunch that you want to walk off, but it might include a wander around a botanic garden (great in winter, see pp.208–9), a stroll along a beach, a bracing climb up a hill or mountain to admire the view or a gentle meander through beautiful countryside. Stock up on good books of walks in your area for ideas. Make sure to wear suitable footwear and equip yourself with Ordnance Survey maps, a pair of binoculars (for looking at buildings as well as birds) and, perhaps, a Thermos of tea and some transportable cakes such as flapjacks (see p.30). I have never regretted the latter the few times I've been organized enough. A dog will only add to the fun, where they are allowed (borrow a friend's, pp.24–7), but make sure you keep it controlled when on other people's land.

A Sunday walk can also provide fuel and focus for other projects: see sections on wild food foraging (pp.83–6), photography (p.39–44) and reinstating the nature table (pp.154–5). Bringing something back with which to document your walk, be it a fallen twig with blossom on it, a pretty feather or just a printed-out photograph, will help lodge it in your memory for the week – particularly important if you are office-bound or live in a town without a garden or park nearby.

❈ *Find Out About Your Family* ❈

It's amazing how little many of us know about our families, beyond even our parents' generation. You can trace your family tree via the National Archives: their website www.national archives.gov.uk/familyhistory (020 8876 3444) will direct you to official documents such as birth, death and marriage certificates and the ten-yearly census reports. But far more fun is to visit the older members of your family, or invite them over to lunch, and get them talking. Ask them to bring any photograph albums if they can, as it's amazing how just an image or a suddenly remembered place can summon back the memories. Enquire about everything: their homes, their food, their schools, their holidays, early courtship, first job and so on. Make meticulous notes – or a recording if they don't mind – as you're bound to forget those all-important details. Try to construct a rough family tree as you go and fill in other details as you visit other people. If it's possible to borrow their albums, why not get some of the pictures scanned, or entire pages reproduced as a facsimile copy that you can pass on through your own family line? While you're at it, get key figures, or particularly fine faces or fab outfits copied and enlarged, either in sepia or black and white, and place in frames. Why not install an 'ancestors' corner' somewhere in the house – on the stairs or landing or in a downstairs loo? It's a good way of reminding ourselves where we came from, and it can be interesting to trace the resemblances that may have been handed down the generations.

❧ *Go Down Memory Lane* ❧

These next activities may or may not stem from, or be encouraged by, the above. We're always being told that when we are adults we put away childish things: well, get them out again!

Immerse yourself in your childhood, or in the good bits of it, at least. Start by getting out family albums and looking at old photographs – with a sibling or family member if you like. Talk about the old times and the places you used to live or frequent. The next step might be to plan a trip there. Depending on where you live now this might be an afternoon's drive or an expedition abroad. Walking down the road you used to live in and seeing your old school from the outside may well be enough, but if you want to dig deeper, try writing to the new inhabitants of the house, or the headmistress/master of the school to state your intentions. The house-owners may be all too happy to have you to tea, particularly if you can fill them in on the house's previous history; similarly, the school may like you to speak to today's pupils about your memories in return for a quick tour. Bring some photographs, if you can, and a camera to record this return visit. It would be a nice thought to take copies of relevant photos to leave with people you visit on this trip, and to send them one or two of the new ones later. After all, you are adding another layer of memory to all your lives.

Again, it may be more fun if you can take someone from that previous life with you; however interested in your past they are, your current partner and family will experience it differently, and you may appreciate the support and company of a brother, sister or friend who can remember it all as you do. If your parents are around, they may want to come, too. And – who knows? – the trip might even inspire another one, to the homes and haunts of *their* childhoods. Whoever you take, be prepared for the fact that it might all look very different from the places in your imagination. In a worst-case scenario the house may not even be there. It will probably look smaller than you remember. And don't underestimate the emotional impact such a trip may have – a big handkerchief in the pocket is not a bad idea, along with a Thermos of tea (or something stronger!) and biscuits. The local park or woods may also be fruitful ground: did you ever make dens or have picnics there?

You could even book a holiday in a place you used to go to as a child. My husband and I once spent a fascinating few days in Wales, revisiting beaches and hunting down holiday cottages we remembered from our childhoods. On one occasion, I couldn't remember the route to take (as a child one is never driving, so roads are not embedded in our minds in the same way) but was drawn to the right place by the memory of the mountain peaks on the skyline; we used to camp in a field every summer and that line of peaks, which I remember sketching incessantly, was the first thing I'd see on opening the tent every morning. (Needless to say, the field looked tiny compared to the endless expanse of my imagination, and the neighbouring church hall more of a Scout hut, but the stream where we used to wash every morning, make dams and watch damsel flies was exactly as I remembered it, and a real delight to find.)

You can revisit your childhood in other ways too. If you kept any toys, get them out and look at them – even live with them for a few days. Play games such as Monopoly, Cluedo, Mouse-trap and Risk that you remember from yesteryear (reorder from Hamleys (0844 855 2424/www.hamleys.com) or old-fashioned toy companies such as the lovely Bramble Corner in Sussex (01342 826465/www.bramblecorner.com), which is well worth a visit). If you have children of your own, they may well be very interested in this bit. Reread old books (see p.313); even if you can no longer lay your hands on the original copies, many of your old favourites will have been reissued, or if out of print may be available from libraries or through Amazon (www.amazon.co.uk), AbeBooks (www.AbeBooks.co.uk) or eBay (www.ebay.co.uk). Similarly, there are lots of children's television programmes available on DVD for the 'new nostalgia' market. Don't stop at *Bill and Ben* and *The Woodentops*, however: revisit the sitcoms and Sunday night dramas of your teens. Companies such as Razamataz (0844 557 5316/ www.erazamataz.co.uk) have a huge stock of past favourites, from *Tintin* and *Top Cat* to classic series such as *The Forsyte Saga* and *The Onedin Line* to boxed sets of vintage comedy such as *Dad's Army*, *Man About the House* and *Are You Being Served?* Re-watching these can be a comforting, cosy pastime for winter's evenings. You may be surprised by how much you remember – and forget.

Revisiting childhood hobbies and activities can also be great fun. Did you love ponies, but haven't been on a horse since you were ten? Then book yourself a riding lesson. Loved ballet, tap or tennis? Do likewise. Take your own children – or godchildren or friends' kids – rock-pooling, crab-catching, dam-making, pond-dipping or looking at flowers and insects with a magnifying glass (see pp.149–50). Perhaps most importantly, try to revisit that sense of wonder in the world we all had as children, and keep some of it with you in your adult life. Rachel Carson, author of the 1960s classic *Silent Spring*, and one of my all-time heroines, wrote evocatively about this in her little known posthumous title, *The Sense of Wonder*:

A child's world is fresh and new and beautiful, full of wonder and excitement. It is our misfortune that for most of us that clear-eyed vision, that true instinct for what is beautiful and awe-inspiring, has been dimmed and even lost before we reach adulthood. If I had influence with the good fairy who is supposed to preside over the christening of all children, I would ask that her gift to each child in the world be a sense of wonder so indestructible that it would last throughout life, as an unfailing antidote against the boredom and disenchantments of later years, the sterile preoccupations with things that are artificial, the alienation from the sources of our strength.

❀ *Religious Services* ❀

You don't have to be committed to a particular religion to get something out of attending a religious service or meeting. Places of worship are fascinating places anyway, and spending time in a religious building – from the soaring majesty of Salisbury Cathedral or the Hindu temple in Neasden, north London (020 8965 2651/www.mandir.org) to the more intimate architecture of a smaller rural parish church – can be enriching in itself, and a good way to get your bearings and find out about attending services should you be interested. Used regularly as places of worship and contemplation, sometimes over many centuries, such buildings do tend to have a very special atmosphere, whether the style is ancient or modern.

If you're tempted to try a service, don't just head automatically for the mid-morning mass or service, though this is where you're most likely to remain anonymous if that's your wish. Early morning services (matins in the Church of England) can make a

Children's Classics to Reread

The Chronicles of Narnia by C.S. Lewis: Be warned, these may in parts be less magical than you remembered. I certainly used to skip all the preaching and polemic that pervade some of the later titles. Don't forget *The Magician's Nephew*, which officially precedes them all.

Little House on the Prairie and all the Laura Ingalls Wilder books: Life-enhancing, and a timeless lesson in living joyfully and richly on really very little.

Little Women by Louisa May Alcott: I defy you to get past Beth's deathbed (whether in the book or the classic film) without crying buckets.

The Railway Children, *Five Children and It* and other stories by E. Nesbit: Timeless classics from a real storyteller; and the film of *The Railway Children* is quite rightly a classic too.

The Secret Garden by Frances Hodgson Burnett: A personal all-time favourite which I still find magical and uplifting in its message about nature's power to heal.

Swallows and Amazons series by Arthur Ransome: I never got on with these, but others swear by them, especially sailing types, and they're equally popular with boys and girls.

The Wind in the Willows by Kenneth Grahame: My father used to read this to me in bed and I am looking forward to doing the same with my own daughter. The writing is magical; the mysterious mystic chapter 'The Piper at the Gates of Dawn' may come as a surprise.

Winnie-the-Pooh, *The House at Pooh Corner* and so on by A.A. Milne: Be sure to get the original versions, not hopeless new ones from which all the wit and whimsy has inexplicably been erased.

The Velveteen Rabbit by Margery Williams, illustrated by William Nicholson: Touching, timeless 1922 classic about how toys become 'real' through the love of their owners.

peaceful and inspiring start to the day, particularly if conducted
in the poetic cadences of the old 1666 version (the Te Deum
never fails to send shivers down my spine). For many years I used
to like slipping in to the early service at Southwark Cathedral
(where Chaucer is buried) on my way to Columbia Road Flower
Market or the junk stalls of Brick Lane, and I still sometimes like
to steal out at this hour on a summer weekend in the country,
especially if the local church is pretty. Evensong, usually around
5.30 p.m., can also be magical, with its plea to 'Lighten our darkness, we beseech thee', and choral evensong in a place famous for
its choir, such as King's College, Cambridge, is an experience not
to be missed. The UK has far more to offer than just the Church
of England, however: why not investigate Afro-Caribbean spiri-
tualist churches, Gospel choirs, High Catholic mass, Quaker
meetings, or the haunting singing of the Greek or Russian
Orthodox traditions? You could even check out whether it is
possible to attend your local Jewish synagogue, or Muslim
mosque. Wherever you are, sit quietly towards the back, try to
observe and respect the traditions of the people whose worship
you are sharing, and you will in all likelihood be made most
welcome.

❀ *Quiet Time* ❀

Even if none of the above appeals, I would still make a case for
Sunday to include a short spell of quiet contemplation. Modern life is increasingly hectic and busy, and scientists and
doctors alike now acknowledge the mental, emotional and
physical benefits to be gained from meditation. There are many

different styles of meditation, from Buddhist to Transcendental (TM) and you can learn it from books (William Bloom is a personal favourite, see p.317) or by attending groups or courses; ask around, look in local magazines or health food shop windows, or contact your local church or Buddhist centre for recommendations. Learning how to let the mind lie still can be a difficult and sometimes frustrating process, and takes time to master, but simply sitting still in a chair or cross-legged on a cushion for twenty minutes and noticing to which places and people your mind *does* wander can, in itself, be interesting, revealing and ultimately healing. After all, you can't call your mind and soul back if you don't know where they've gone. Solitary meditation can be good – if possible as a daily practice – but the experience of meditating in a group once every week or so is unquestionably more powerful, and may be supportive of your daily practice. If you can't find a group to join, why not start your own? I bet you anything you'll find many more friends will be interested than you'd think. Ideally one or more of you will know a little about meditation and be able to lead the group, but others could participate by bringing short readings to begin the session, and share in a short group discussion afterwards.

Or feed the spiritual side of your life by spending time looking at beautiful books on art, spirituality or nature, or by reading contemplative poetry (see pp.317–18). Sometimes, a simple walk on your own in nature is what is required to still the mind and replenish the spirits. No texting or chatting on the mobile phone while you are doing it, though – don't even take it with you on a walk. Which brings me to the following idea.

❧ *Go on an E-mail/Mobile Detox* ❧

Sunday evening is one of my favourite times for catching up with friends and family on the phone or by letter (see pp.133–7) but for the remainder of the day I try to refrain from other means of electronic communication. We're tied to the mobile and e-mail for much of the rest of the week and those intermittent pings and ring-tones are more intrusive and distracting than we acknowledge. No matter how much we may protest that we need these instant forms of communication, we got by perfectly well without them a few years ago. I'm old enough to remember when walking about 'looking for people' at music festivals such as Glastonbury was the only way to find your friends. Nowadays, I find myself anxious if I have left my mobile phone at home, if only for a few hours. Turning your back on instant contact with others can be surprisingly difficult to begin with, but I now love my weekly detoxes and am contemplating extending them into Saturday . . .

❧ *Stay In Bed All Day* ❧

Whether planned and anticipated, or something you slip into almost unawares, an entire day in bed can be one of life's most glorious luxuries – and it costs nothing! Remaining in your pyjamas or whatever is also a good way of ensuring you don't get tempted to nip out to the shops or get involved in anything you really don't want to do.

To ensure the exercise is glamorous and luxurious, rather than tinged with studenty seediness, it's worth putting in a

Contemplative Sunday Reading

The Cloud of Unknowing: Classic and poetic mysticism by an anonymous British fourteenth-century monk, but still relevant today.

Cultivating Sacred Space by Elizabeth Murray: Inspiring American book on 'gardening for the soul' with illustrated examples.

Handbook for the Soul ed. by Richard Carlson and Benjamin Shield: Collection of more than thirty original essays by some of the most celebrated spiritual writers of our time, including Thomas Moore on 'Embracing the Everyday' and Elisabeth Kübler-Ross on 'Soul Gifts in Disguise'.

Meditation in a Changing World by William Bloom: A friendly, encouraging and practical introduction to basic meditation techniques.

A Path of Hope or any writings by Brother Roger of Taizé: His plea for a 'kind-heartedness that is constantly renewed' is inspiring.

Peace Is Every Step by Thich Nhat Hanh: Practical spirituality from one of the wisest people on the planet.

The Power of Now by Eckhart Tolle: Advice on attaining lasting happiness – through learning to connect with the present moment – that actually works.

The Sense of Wonder by Rachel Carson: Heartfelt advice and lyrical musings on sharing a love of nature with children.

The Tibetan Book of Living and Dying by Sogyal Rinpoche: Mystic and practical reflections on death and how we care for the dying that can end up transforming the way we live.

Wild Geese by Mary Oliver: Wonderfully perceptive and uplifting poetry, much of it based on her tender and meticulous observation of the natural world.

Zen and the Art of Motorcycle Maintenance by Robert Pirsig: The seventies classic is the most popular philosophy book ever written and still relevant and entertaining today.

little groundwork beforehand. Make sure the bedroom is tidy, the sheets and pillowcases fresh and clean, and that you have something loose and lovely to wear (see pp.23 and 319–20 for suggestions on all of the above). Have some beautiful flowers where you can see them from the bed, and some light yet tasty snack food (see p.20) in the fridge. Ordering pizza or a good Chinese takeaway (I recommend a half crispy Peking duck with the little pancakes, spring onions and hoisin sauce to wrap it in) is by all means allowed, however, if that is what you feel like, as this is a day about indulgence. Drinking is also fine, and can contribute to the day's decadent charm. I have a single friend who treats herself to a bottle of good champagne every Sunday

which she sips, in a beautiful cut-crystal glass, from about 11 a.m. onwards, making it last (by putting a silver teaspoon in the top of the open bottle in the fridge) until her bedtime. She says she doesn't get drunk, as the timespan is so long, interspersed with meals and snacks – and anyway the odd visitor usually helps by joining her in a glass or two. Anyhow, what I am recommending is the luxury of it, not the quantity. Fresh juice or smoothies, your favourite brand of sparkling water or coffee from

The Perfect Bed

Take inspiration from good hotels and go for the largest bed, best mattress and most luxurious bed-linen your budget can afford. (The sales are useful here – about the one reason I'd recommend braving them.) Scrimping on the place where you spend so much of your time (even without the odd Saturday or Sunday lounging and lolling around) is a false economy. Similarly, natural materials are desirable: who wants to lie in close proximity to a cocktail of chemicals for eight or nine hours, seven nights a week?

Beds: A 6-foot bed may seem expensive to start with, but it's a good investment in marital harmony, particularly if you have children or grandchildren who like to hop in with you in the mornings. I like a high bed with storage underneath to free up the rest of the bedroom space, but others swear by open ventilated space beneath.

Mattresses: Similarly, a good mattress is an investment you won't regret, particularly if you are prone to back problems. Vi-Spring is the classic pocket-sprung mattress with natural fillings (01752 366311/www.vispring.co.uk for stockists). Norris Bedding (020 8311 8625/www.norrisbedding.co.uk), an old family firm based in south London, is rightly famous for its hand-made traditional mattresses which can be custom-made to fit antique or unusually sized beds. Greenfibres (0845 330 3440/www.greenfibres.com) stocks a wide selection of mattresses and futons using entirely natural and organic ingredients that have not been treated with fire retardants or other chemicals. Its range of beds, duvets and bed-linen is also fantastic, with a great choice for children who are even more susceptible to the effects of toxins.

Bed-linen: I always find white bed-linen the most relaxing on the eye and the easiest to care for, but am not averse to the odd discreet stripe, strip of lace or panel of pretty embroidery. John Lewis (08456 049049/www.johnlewis.com) can't be beaten on quality

and price, and its own make, Jonelle, is great for classic yet stylish basics. Designers Guild (020 7893 7400/www.designers guild.com) always has a good selection, including lovely appliqué and hand-embroidered quilt covers and pillow cases. Toast (0844 557 5200/ www.toast.co.uk) has fresh Scandinavian-looking ticking stripes as well as embroidered and ribbon-trimmed designs in organic cotton and Irish linen. Also some attractive quilts and traditional Welsh blankets. The White Company (0870 900 9555/ www.thewhitecompany.com) has beautiful textured and embroidered bed-linen, in all sizes up to emperor as well as classic whites in cotton and linen, along with a wide range of duvets and mattresses. Feather & Black (01243 380600/ www.featherandblack.com) is a good source if you like tastefully patterned bed-linen, with some lovely floral and damask-type designs.

Second-hand shops and antique fairs (see p.275) are also a good source of quality bed-linen, though, sadly, old beds did not come in king and super-king sizes.

For ideas on what to wear in your perfect bed, see p.23.

freshly milled beans are also great treats – even a Thermos of tea kept by the bed so you don't have to get up and boil the kettle. I love the idea of having as much as possible to hand at the bedside.

Then it's up to you what you do all day. You can keep the telephone nearby to keep in touch with friends, or hide it where you can't even hear it ring, depending on how connected with the outside world you want to feel. Watch TV or leaf through a pile of books or magazines; stick photos in albums or go through old diaries; slap on a face-pack and paint your toenails; write letters or a journal; or simply sit and look out at the view if you are lucky enough to have one. The day is yours, like a lovely empty notebook or a blank sheet of paper spread out before you. Enjoy it!

❀ *Sunday Evening* ❀

The main prerogative here is to beat Sunday Evening Syndrome – those blues that set in around 4 or 5 p.m. and are most keenly felt by the office-bound and students. This is not, in my opinion, the time for going to the gym or attempting strenuous DIY or cleaning chores – just a little gentle laundry or ironing in front of the TV at the very most. I like to be easy on myself, having an early and luxurious bath (see the Quiet Night In section on pp.17–19), reading a favourite book or novel or writing a few letters (see pp.33–7 for more on the forgotten art of letter-writing). Doing something positive to record the high points of a great weekend can be an affirming way to end your Sunday: edit photos on your computer, make a slideshow or print out a few shots to make a collage, put in frames or send to friends (see section on photography, p.39, for more ideas). Write in your diary (see p.56) or update an anthology (see p.55) or Gratitude Journal (see pp.70–2). An American psychologist, Robert Emmons, found that people who wrote in a gratitude journal once a week were happier, and enjoyed better health and more energy than others. And, last but not least, begin to look forward to next weekend by making plans and ringing or e-mailing friends to make arrangements – unless, of course, you are participating in the e-mail/mobile detox on p.316. For the best night's sleep and start to the week, avoid e-mail or phone contact for at least an hour before going to bed. Reading matter that is gentle yet uplifting – poetry, pictures of nature, anthologies of sprititual writing and so on – is the best bet for drifting off easily (see p.317). If I ever have trouble getting off to sleep, I follow some or all of the suggestions below. Sleep well!

A good night's sleep

- A few drops of organic lavender oil on the pillow (literally two or three drops or you'll be overpowered) is wonderfully soothing and calming.

- Rather than sleeping pills, which can be addictive and often leave you groggy in the morning, try herbal remedies such as Quiet Life and Nytol (available from chemists). A medical herbalist may be able to prescribe a herbal mixture made up specially for you, as some people find that Valerian, a common component in ready-made remedies, does not agree with them.

- If persistent thoughts – whether worrying ones or not – keep creeping into your mind, try the Bach Flower Remedy White Chestnut which is used specifically to banish unwanted thoughts. You mix a few drops in water and keep a glass near the bed for sipping from time to time. I'm not a great one for flower remedies, except for Rescue Remedy, but have found this quite helpful.

- If, like me, you have a partner whose snoring keeps you awake, might I recommend a device called Sleeppro (01962 761831/www.sleeppro.com)? Unlike many of the other products we have tested in our household, this is neither unsightly nor uncomfortable, and doesn't involve unpleasant-tasting tablets or sprays. A simple exercise outlined on the website confirms whether or not the particular type of snoring you are dealing with is likely to be helped by the device. It is amazing how effectively it works – I have recommended it to so many people we could form a Sleeppro Saved Our Marriage Club!

- Women lacking in iron may have trouble sleeping, so if you suspect this may be the case, get your iron levels checked by a doctor and/or embark on a course of iron pills or a natural alternative such as Floradix, available from chemists and health food shops.

- A dram of good whisky before bedtime is a great way to doze off, but excess alcohol may actually disturb sleep patterns and is much more likely to make you wake up in the early hours. If you think you may have drunk too much, down a pint of water before bed, adding a few drops of milk-thistle (from herbalists) to help the liver along, and keep another large glass beside the bed for when you wake up dehydrated.

- Though eating a heavy meal fewer than two hours before bedtime is not recommended, there is evidence that a little light snack (the old-fashioned 'supper') may help induce sleep. Tryptophan, an amino acid found in milk, turkey and peanuts, helps the brain produce serotonin, a chemical that promotes relaxation. So the traditional warm milk or bowl of cereal – even a slice of toast with peanut butter – may be a good thing. Plus, the warmth of the food may temporarily increase your body temperature and the subsequent drop may hasten sleep.

- Avoid any stimulants such as coffee, tea or nicotine several hours before bed. (I avoid coffee after midday for this reason.) Many over-the-counter and prescription drugs disrupt sleep, as can vitamin C. Take all vitamins before lunchtime, apart from vitamin B,

which can have a soothing effect on the nerves if taken before
bed.

- Regular exercise can be good for sleep, but avoid anything too
strenuous just before bed, as it may stimulate the body and make
falling asleep more difficult. A little yoga with deep breathing, or
a few simple stretching exercises may help, however.

- Make sure your bed is big enough, particularly if you are disturbed by a restless bedmate; switching to king or even super-
king size can make all the difference. Invest in good pillows –
even therapeutic foam ones (see p.319 for more on this).

- Make your bedroom a temple to sleep and relaxation – no TV, no
desk, and certainly no evidence of work! Have calmly scented
candles and restful books only by the bed. Keep the room well
ventilated, and the temperature a few degrees lower than in the
rest of the house (I swear by keeping the window slightly open,
even in winter). There is no surer way to wake up groggy than in
a too-warm bedroom, and radiators gurgling away behind the
headboard are a nightmare. Avoid having unnecessary electronic
equipment in the bedroom and be sure to switch off any you do
have; the fug of combined electronic fields of different appli-
ances is not conducive to sleep.

- Avoid big illuminated digital clocks: not only are they ugly but
they can make you focus unnecessarily on the time during the
night, increasing anxiety about being awake.

- Keep a regular bedtime, even at weekends – then you really get
to enjoy the lie-in! Oversleeping to make up for a poor night's
sleep can reset your body clock if done for even a couple of nights
in succession and make it harder to get to sleep at night.

- Create some enjoyable night-time rituals such as a long luxurious bath with relaxing oils, a massage, listening to soft music, sipping herbal tea.

- Try reading something soothing before sleep, or even listening to a relaxation or guided-imagery CD. Others swear by the BBC World Service or classical music playing softly.

- If you find yourself anxious, jot down any concerns and resolve to think about them tomorrow, not in the middle of the night. A journal or 'to do' list by the bed is helpful for this purpose, as much of the anxiety may be about forgetting the things that you have to do! Finish by writing down three things to be grateful for (see pp.70–2) – this works.

- If you do wake in the night, try a simple relaxation technique such as focusing attention on different parts of the body from the toes up and 'breathing' peace and sleepiness into them. It may also help to focus on soothing words such as 'peace', 'love' and 'beauty' and feel their energy infuse your mind and body.

- If you can't get back off in twenty minutes or so, don't lie in bed awake. Get up and make a cup of hot milk or camomile tea; go outside and look at the stars; or sit in a chair and read or knit or stroke your cat or do something similarly soothing until you feel tired again. Keep the lights as low as possible – bright light cues your brain into thinking it is time to wake up. No matter how tempting it may be, don't watch television, and on no account do anything remotely work-connected!

- If insomnia and interrupted sleep become a troublesome regular occurrence, see your doctor. Keeping a sleep diary of the hours spent in bed, the time you wake and drift off again over a period of a few weeks may be useful information that can help you get the best treatment.

Conclusion

These are just some of the ideas I've had for bringing fun and pleasure back into our weekends, while still putting food in the cupboards, meals on the table and washing on the line. I'm sure you'll have many more of your own. The crucial thing is to try some of them out. Set aside some time – during a weekend away if this makes it any easier – to re-connect to the aspects of life that you feel are most important and which are being buried, at the moment, under other obligations. Using some of the ideas in the A New Approach to Chores chapter, work out a strategy to free up some time for more enjoyable pursuits. Make a list of activities or pastimes you'd like to try, and dive right in. If time still seems in short supply (and this does appear the curse of our age) try bringing two or more tasks or activities together: meet friends for lunch at the farmers' market; combine keeping fit with taking the dog on a long country walk; socialize with friends while at the same time playing tennis, clearing your garden or allotment or swapping unwanted possessions. And don't forget the unadulterated treats: a lovely long bath or lie-in, cream cakes at your favourite teashop, a tall cool cocktail in the garden and so on. Start small – and soon you'll be wondering how we ever let our weekends get eaten up by the unwelcome and unrewarding stuff.

Sometimes it's just a matter of the right mindset and here the old maxim that 'No one on their deathbed ever wishes they'd spent more time in the office' can come in handy. Looking back over the past year's calendar on New Year's Eve it's not the late nights at the office, the children's tidy bedrooms and chores ticked off lists that you remember, it's the time you left work early to take off camping in the mountains, the day you got up to listen to the dawn chorus, the night at the theatre, the walk in the rain, the impromptu picnic in the park that expanded and extended till the stars came out. Likewise, the items you'd want to save if the house were on fire would be the love letters, the home-made toys, the albums of photos and the handwritten recipe book that goes back generations – not the expensive yet soulless knick-knacks that can be replaced on any high street. We are unique individuals. Our lives should reflect and celebrate this, especially during our leisure time. Start right now. This Friday, draw a line under the working week, get out your slippers – or your dancing shoes – and, however you choose to spend it, have a wonderful weekend!

www.elspeththompson.com

Acknowledgements

Many people unknowingly helped me with inspiration for the ideas and arguments behind this book, not least my own family: my father, Alec Thompson, for teaching me about the stars, birds and basic human kindness; my mother, Margaret Thompson, for showing me how to cook and sew and count my blessings; and my sisters Rebecca and Sarah, for sharing parties and picnics, cast-off clothes and kitchen tips over the years. More latterly, of course, I have to thank my husband, Frank Wilson, for love, laughter, music and knowing how to make (and contemplate) the best real fires – he should really be credited as cocktail, ukulele and fire-lighting correspondent for this book. Also my daughter Mary for her unerring instinct for fun, regardless of the context, time and prevailing weather or mood; and my many clever and creative friends whose lives are woven into the pages of this book alongside mine. Many thanks to Jane Turnbull, my agent, whose ideas and enthusiasm have contributed greatly to this book; to Paula Grainger of Lemon-balm for the nettle detox tea recipe and advice on all things herbal; to Rowan Yapp at John Murray, for suggesting and commissioning this project, to Morag Lyall for her skilful editing, Vanessa Aitchison for meticulous fact checking and to

Alice Stevenson, whose spirited illustrations really bring the words alive.

The author and publishers would like to thank the following for permission to reproduce copyright material:

Mary Oliver and Bloodaxe Books for permission to quote from Mary Oliver's 'Wild Geese'; extract from 'Mushrooms' by Sylvia Plath, from *The Colossus*, published by Faber & Faber Ltd.

Index

Website addresses all omit the www. prefix

331